THE C. ....

MEN AND WOMEN

THE CHANGING ROLES
OF MEN AND WOMEN

Edited by

EDMUND DAHLSTRÖM

Translated by Gunilla and Steven Anderman
With a Foreword by Alva Myrdal

with *The Status of Women In Sweden: Report to the United Nations 1968*

Beacon Press   Boston

First published in Swedish as *Kvinnors Liv och Arbete*
© 1962 Studieförbundet Näringsliv och Samhälle

English translation copyright © 1967 Gerald
Duckworth & Co. Ltd.

Library of Congress catalog card number: 77–159846

International Standard Book Number: 0–8070–4170–x (casebound)
0–8070–4171–8 (paperbound)

First published by Beacon Press in 1971 by arrangement
with Gerald Duckworth & Co. Ltd.

Beacon Press books are published under the auspices
of the Unitarian Universalist Association.

Printed in the United States of America.

Grateful acknowledgment is made to the Swedish Institute
for permission to reprint "The Status of Women in Sweden:
Report to the United Nations 1968."

CONTENTS

THE CHANGING ROLES OF
MEN AND WOMEN

FOREWORD

by ALVA MYRDAL

As is suggested by the title of this volume, the character of the debate on problems of the family in Scandinavia, and particularly in Sweden, has taken a new and unusual turn. It is this novel and unique approach that lays claim to the attention of the observant international public.

In Sweden, the debate has progressed beyond the conventional focus of discussions of family problems, i.e. the conflict between women's two roles—family and work. Its scope has been enlarged to encompass the two roles of men. Men are no longer regarded as 'innocents abroad' in family affairs. Instead, it is becoming increasingly recognized even outside sociological circles that their role in the family must be radically enlarged. No longer can they be allowed to confine themselves to the role of 'provider', they must begin more fully to integrate the family into their life plans. (Unless, of course, they choose to avoid family bonds altogether, a choice made by increasingly fewer men.)

This development has not remained confined to the realm of theory. The debate has extended to the practical details of daily existence. A prominent issue has been that of the time budget of the married couple. How equitably are the hours of work in the home and with the family shared? The way in which the dual roles of married men and women are combined has now become an item of apparently inexhaustible interest to the mass media.

In its original Swedish version, published in 1962, this book was one of the first to apply the 'dual role' approach to the problem. Consequently, its revised English language edition must be of special interest to the non-Swedish audience. This is not to say that the above approach is consistently applied in all chapters. Inevitably, the descriptive sections have had to devote greater attention to the adjustment of women to the labour market—and vice versa.

In this foreword, I should like to draw attention to the rapidity with which the problems of the family in a progressive industrial economy and social democracy such as ours can become the concern of individuals, men as well as women, and of society as a whole.

To the newcomer to the continuing debate, the proposals put forward to ensure the survival of the small biological family unit under changing social and psychological conditions must appear radical and perhaps even Utopian. Yet such steps must be seen in the broad perspective of history: all struggle for, and reaction against, female emancipation has been part of a cumulative process. The stage has yet to be reached where the force underlying this process will have been spent. In Sweden, we are now experiencing a new wave. Personally, I am convinced that this is the way of the future, and have expressed this conviction in several earlier works. And today my belief in the viability of a more equitable sharing of family responsibilities is stronger than ever—stronger even, perhaps, than the beliefs articulated in this symposium.

Having suggested that the Swedish debate has moved to a relatively advanced position, it is important to add that ideologies can never exist independently of their social setting. And the latter is never fixed and unchanging. One interesting and hitherto long neglected project for the social historians would be an investigation of the extent to which social change has been a product of the continuing ideological debate and how the debate has been influenced by social change. That there is an interplay between the two factors is a truism. The more difficult question is to what extent does one determine the other? The ideological debate has been intently followed by specialists in the history of ideas. Social change has been minutely recorded by social historians. The twain have rarely, if ever, met to attempt a thorough analysis of the above problem of causation. Research in this latter area has remained stillborn.

During the short century of industrialization which we in Sweden have experienced, the conditions of family life, as well as of working life, have been rapidly and drastically transformed. Wide-reaching social reforms have attempted not only to ameliorate the effects of some of these changes but also, though to a lesser extent, to direct their course. Currently, reforms appear to be directed towards the objective of greater equality and freedom of choice to women—the rear-guard of industrialization—as well as protection for the family. Yet one cannot help wondering about the extent to which such reforms have been rationally evaluated and whether due consideration has been given to contemporaneous changes in the sex roles. To what extent, for example, have the social reforms designed primarily for child welfare served to bind women more tightly to the home rather than facilitate their freedom of movement? This book throws light on the interrelationship between these distinct and occasionally divergent interests, though the light shines more brightly on some interests than on others. It focuses particularly on the current debate on the sex roles, which is largely ideological in character, and on the more recent trends in the occupational distribution of the sexes. The measures of family policy are treated rather more indirectly. And though the question of the interdependence between the ideological debate and social change is not definitively explored, the book provides a useful foundation for further study of this issue.

What remains to be done in this preface is to give a short historical sketch. This might aid in clarifying the interplay between social change and debate as well as in providing a starting point for an international comparison. What factors in the specifically Swedish situation are significant for countries with a hitherto dissimilar rate of growth of female emancipation? Unfortunately, neither social history nor the history of ideas has been sufficiently explored from this standpoint in Scandinavia, though the area presents itself as a particularly fruitful one for research.

So much, however, appears to be clear. The first wave of the feminist debate preceded the onset of industrialization. A remarkable beginning was made in the 1830s, a decade when a population explosion was threatening to impoverish our old, predominantly agrarian, society and few indications of the remedial changes in store could be discerned on the horizon. At this early stage, a compelling precedent was established for the debate to antecede social change. The caustic and quite modern attack on conventional marriage then launched by Almquist, a romantic-realistic-diabolic author, in his novel, *That Will Do*, has, I believe, no close counterpart in any other country. The freedom of the young, self-supporting heroine together with her impressive integrity must have caused more than a few ripples through the shut-in world of the middle class!

The second wave of feminism in Sweden was one more familiar to industrialized countries, a 'traditional' liberal feminist movement coinciding with the early stages of industrialization. The demands of this movement, as formulated by Fredrika Bremer in the 1850s, were essentially those of greater educational and legal equality for women. At that time such ideas appeared radical. But the necessary reforms were shortly to follow. Indeed, some were already under way. To what extent did the ceaseless discussion with its radical orientation result in creating a psychological receptivity to subsequent and more profound changes? At all events, the immediate gains were reforms of practical importance, the right to higher education, the right to manage one's own finances, etc.

But even before the turn of the century, not only Sweden, but much of Scandinavia was assailed by a new and intense debate on the rights of women and their role within the sheltered walls of the family. This was the era of Ibsen, Strindberg and Ellen Key. The outstanding issues were now the double moral standard for men—the essence of respectability within marriage and the sexual merry-go-round without— the bondage of women within the family, and, as a reaction to all this, the demands for the right to 'free love' for both sexes. Psychologically, ideologically, this was a necessary and thorough airing of much that was old and musty in the family, an entity that had become 'holy' even as it had begun to lose the hold it once had in the agrarian society.

It would perhaps not be amiss to mention the parts played by our forefathers in their debate on marriage and the sex roles. Strindberg led the campaign. His starting point was that man was the under-privileged partner. Given the socially approved emotional advantages of women, man had only to gain by pressing for greater equality. In the preface to *Married* (Part 1, published in 1884 and prosecuted for indecency), he proposed a 'Declaration of Women's Rights' including co-education to ensure a more equitable start in life. Girls were to have the right freely to dispose of their leisure time, as did boys, and the right to select their acquaintances. Thus, 'social intercourse between boys and girls', he suggested, 'would become more free.'

More orientated to practical matters were his suggestions for the management of the family economy. Where the husband desired his wife to be only a housewife (and a mother), he should be prepared to pay her a special allowance, fixed in advance. Out of this allowance, she should share in all outside recreational expenditure; the husband as provider would be responsible for the ordinary expenditure of the family. If, on the other hand, a married woman earned an income through outside employment and did *not* perform the household work, she should share equally in the household expenditure. But if she took on the household work in addition to her gainful employment, she should be free to retain her income and her 'work within the household should be regarded as a surplus and not, as now, the obligation of a slave'.

It is perhaps premature to associate the agitated debate that followed in the wake of our early radical critics with the marital law reforms enacted during the First World War. For the breakthrough in female suffrage experienced at the end of that war was a product of more general, international circumstances (the Russian revolution as presumptive historical pioneer of social reforms was surely not without some influence in England as well as in Sweden). At all events, our grim soothsayers were able to create amongst the Swedish intelligentsia a fairly unrepressed view of the problem. And this tradition continuing from Almquist to Strindberg, Ibsen and Ellen Key—so startling to the first generation as it penetrated to every provincial nook and cranny—must be quite a unique phenomenon on the international scene.

Yet, it seems to be true that each generation needs its own gadfly. In our case, this was provided in the 1930s when the burgeoning science of family sociology was mercilessly used to unveil how irrationally the dominant family type tended to perpetuate itself. In a highly industrialized society, it was asserted, the tradition whereby the man remained the sole means of financial support and the woman performed only the role of housewife could no longer be considered adequate; at most, this could be the pattern of a family type in transition from an agrarian to a highly industrialized society. For those of us who participated actively in this debate it is somewhat disheartening to observe how long it has taken for such ideas to gain acceptance as popular ideology. As early as the 1930s, we had succeeded in convincing Royal Commissions to accept the idea that a career for married women should be viewed as 'normal'. (This is perhaps interesting considering the prevailing high level of male unemployment and Hitler's ascendency within the borders of our Southern neighbour.) This was the time when the family role of women first came to be regarded as an ancillary though highly important part of her life-plan. The official formulation of the demand was not the 'right of married women to work' but rather the 'right of working women to marriage and motherhood'. This particular demand was almost completely satisfied in subsequent legislative reforms: the prohibition against the discharge of women on the grounds of marriage or pregnancy. However, in general, even if such reforms were remarkable for the 1930s, they were never as far-reaching as the programme proposed at that time in the lively debate on the 'new family policy'. That programme included such plans as a reduction in men's working days to allow fathers an opportunity to participate more actively in family life, with its mixture of practical male and creative togetherness and 'creative leisure pursuits for the enjoyment of the family'. In the end, the reduction in hours of work occurred along different lines: a shorter standard work week and longer vacations.

It cannot be denied that great strides have been made in evolving a social welfare policy that has helped the family. In particular, there have been many economic reforms that have tended to shift the distribution of income towards families with children and hence lighten the burden of support for the individual family breadwinner. However, the at least equally important and justifiable reforms designed to 'collectivize' housework services have lagged hopelessly behind. In spite of enormous queues, there has been no concerted effort to build blocks of service flats for families with working mothers. And even worse, few attempts have been made to expand the facilities for child care though this has long bound and continues to bind many mothers to the home, twenty-four hours a day, year in and year out. The various pre-school institutions which could reduce temporarily the almost pathological confinement of mothers—one which brings many thinking young mothers to the brink of revolt—have grown during the past thirty years at a rate so slow as to be almost irrelevant to the need for such institutions and is irrationally moderate compared to the growth rates of child allowances, student grants and overall economic expansion. These truths about how our welfare society has only reluctantly responded to what it has considered 'women's demands' must be entered in the record.

We have still not been able to obtain in Sweden, the welfare state, many of the rational reforms demanded in our earlier programme. Nowhere is this more painfully evident than in the area of tax policy. Today, men who want to divert female potential to care for their personal wants in marriage receive considerable tax subsidies from the state, whether or not there are children in the family. However, during the 1960s we are witnessing the beginnings of a new era. The alert debate has now begun to throw into bold relief the persistence of outmoded traditional attitudes as well as the inconsistencies inherent in many well-meant social reforms. At the level of debate, the role of the man in the family now occupies stage centre while the problem of the role of the women in working life has currently become one of practical implementation, i.e. reforms. The debate on the man's participation in family life has moved beyond the notion of assistance with occasional household chores to consider the issues of more equitable distribution of everyday family responsibilities including those of child care and supervision. At the same time, a certain sharpening can be detected in the tone of the discussion of reforms. Thus, stands have clearly been taken against all 'wifely privileges,' tax advantages, widows' pensions and other social welfare benefits that accrue to a woman solely by virtue of her status as a wife. The protection of the child should not be viewed as the responsibility of one parent alone and welfare benefits should be disbursed to the family as such, even in cases where only one parent has been saddled with sole responsibility.

These then are the new developments in the Swedish debate on the sex roles. They are a valuable continuation of earlier traditions peculiar to Scandinavia, both in the bold realism of their objectives and in the sociological insights contained in their descriptions. We have a great way to go however before research has sufficiently analysed all the problems.

This book should be viewed as a challenge by all who read it. Let people in other countries be prompted to pierce the veil with which conventions and traditions and comfortable conformism conceal our visions of the future, a future which could be more reasonable and profitable for society and more creative and rewarding for the men and women who inhabit it.

Stockholm, 10th April, 1966   ALVA MYRDAL

INTRODUCTION

THE original Swedish book *Kvinnors liv och arbete* ('Women's Life and Work') was published in 1962 by Studieförbundet Näringsliv och Samhälle (S.N.S), an independent research institute financed by Swedish private industry. It appeared as the sex role debate in its modern version had just begun to gather momentum. In many instances the arguments and assertions in the public debate clearly suffered from a lack of overall perspective and inadequate empirical foundation. The aim of the book was to survey and discuss the available data about the position of women and men in the family, the labour market and society as a whole and to introduce new material and ideas to the continuing debate.

The result was a symposium by a group of Scandinavian social scientists examining the sex role question from the vantage points of sociology, psychology, social psychology, industrial sociology and economics. Since few multi-disciplinary attempts have been made to come to grips with the sex role question and since the question is equally relevant to all nations in the sphere of western industrialized culture, S.N.S. has thought it worth while to publish the results for an English language audience.

Certain chapters in the original edition have been reproduced unchanged in the English edition. This is true of 'Sex Roles and Socialization' by Sverre Brun-Gulbrandsen, 'Parental Role Division and the Child's Personality' by Per Olav Tiller and 'Analysis of the Sex Role Debate' by Edmund Dahlström. Other chapters have been extensively revised and brought up to date: 'The Family and Married Women at Work' and 'Employer Attitudes to Female Employees'. Four chapters by the Norwegian sociologist Harriet Holter appearing in the original volume have not been reproduced in the English version, though some of the ideas and problems presented in these chapters are mentioned in the revised chapters of this book. The reason for excluding Holter's contribution is that she is planning to publish a book in English incorporating the essential contents of these chapters.[1]

---

[1] The chapters by Harriet Holter in the original edition were: 'Kjønnsroller og sosial struktur', 'Fra barn til voksen', 'Enslige kvinner i yrkeslivet', and 'Kjønnsforskjeller i yrkesatferd'.

Stina Thyberg assisted Edmund Dahlström with the editing of the Swedish edition. Annika Baude and Siv Thorsell have been responsible for the revisions and preparation of the manuscript for the English edition.

THE FAMILY AND MARRIED
WOMEN AT WORK

by EDMUND DAHLSTRÖM *and* RITA LILJESTRÖM

1. *Introduction: Changes in the Family from Agrarian to Industrial Society*

IN any discussion of changes in the family, it is essential to be clear about what one actually means by 'the family', that is, one's conception of, and where in time one places, the family of the previous period with which one compares the family of today. Of course, both the family of yesterday and the one of today are fictional in the sense that they represent a commonly found family type selected from a rich variety of older and newer co-existing family patterns. This subjectively selected family type provides an essential frame of reference for the discussion. Without it one would run the risk that an argument may be partly inspired by another family type, say, the large agrarian family, or may slide over into comparisons with certain kinds of normative stereotypes of the family. It would also be easier to gloss over age and generation shifts during the latest decades.

The pre-industrial family was essentially an economically integrated and self-sufficient production unit. The work performed by women as well as men required a variety of special skills. Both sexes participated in a work team of family members mutually dependent on the productive efforts of one another. Even elderly, very young and, to some extent, handicapped members were required to contribute to production, each according to his ability.

Industrialization entailed a shift to longer and more specialized production units. The new methods of mass production radically altered work organization and human relations at the place of work. Industrialized working life developed impersonal, utilitarian and 'efficient' relations. New ways of evaluating people were evolved; the monetary value of an individual's capabilities became a key measure of his worth. Work effort became commercialized. The return for labour's services began to be determined largely according to profit-making and contractual principles. Wages were regarded as the most important incentive to maximum effort.

In the agrarian society, the social position of the individual had been determined by family property and tradition. The limits of opportunity for the individual were firmly fixed, allowing a security based on fatalism. The new industrial system introduced a liberal ideology based on the freedom of the individual and social mobility. The competent could create a future for themselves by career advancement and economic success; the individual was no longer bound to his family's station in life. Industrialization broke down certain traditional class barriers and introduced some degree of open competition based on individual ability. But the great gaps between social strata that existed in pre-industrial society did not disappear.

The patriarchalism of the farming family was carried over into industry. In the process, however, authoritarian and hierarchical relations between superior and inferior lost their familial character and became anonymous and bureaucratic. Traditional respect for authority was reinforced and given new meaning in combination with the efficiency and utility criteria of working life and the power position enjoyed by management in the factory system.

The new freedom of the individual in the 'open' society was accompanied by an unravelling of the bonds of solidarity with and duty to one's family. At the outset, this development coincided with a period of mass poverty and deprivation caused by a persistent population surplus and periodic depressions. However, as industrialization progressed to a more advanced stage, and individual workers formed trade union organizations, the state gradually began to assume a major responsibility for the protective family functions formerly discharged by the agrarian family, viz. through pensions, sickness and other social welfare benefits.

1. *The Married Woman becomes Supported*

Industrialization demolished the self-sufficiency of the agrarian working community. Industrial production, influenced by considerations of efficiency, profitability and competition, was based on the employment of labour with economically dependent family members performing unpaid services in the home. The norms at the industrial work place came to dominate society at the expense of the norms of familial relations. In large measure, it fell to men to act and take decisions in the new and growing industrial sector.

From the start, the position of women differed from that of men. The patriarchal legacy, according to which women were considered incapable of managing their own affairs, helped to create a situation whereby women became supported by their husbands. One result of this was that when women did obtain work they were frequently under-paid and precluded from positions of responsibility. Moreover, since employers did not have to consider women as sole sources of family support, female employees were employed or released more readily according to cyclical changes in business activity. In the early stages of industrialization, given the prevailing surplus of labour, the supply of women workers constituted a reserve army of temporary and cheap labour pressing down male wages. Against this background, it was little wonder that the idea gained a firm hold that a woman's place was in the home. Moreover, with the breakdown of the large agrarian family unit, the mother was left alone to care for the household and children. Under the prevailing labour market conditions, there was little incentive to rationalize household work or re-introduce a more collective and widely distributed responsibility for child rearing similar to that which had obtained in the multi-generation agrarian family.

Segregation between the sexes was decisively reinforced by the differences of motivation, values and incentives for work effort inside and outside the home.

If the work responsibility and formal legal status of women both before and after the onset of industrialization are compared, the following can be established:

In the pre-industrial society the woman was essentially a legal 'minor'. She was ideologically and juridically inferior to her husband and she owed him the duty of submission.

As far as inheritance was concerned, the brother was entitled to a share twice as large as that of the sister. The woman's right to education and to independent employment outside the home was narrowly circumscribed; she had access to very few occupations. Political authority was reserved to men. As virtuous wife and fertile mother, the woman assumed a privileged and protected position. In the household, the woman was responsible for important aspects of production. Typically, this was work located closest to the home: house and garden work, wool and flax spinning, milking, care of animals and the farmyard, care of stocks and the preparing of food and making of clothing. As mother of the house, the woman often had an independent, supervisory and influential position.

During the later stages of industrialization women have achieved superficial equality. They have become juridically 'adult' and formally equal to men. They have obtained equal political rights and equal educational rights. Married women at work have become more common and employment has become accepted as a legitimate alternative for childless married women and, to some extent, for women with children of school age. Measures have been introduced to facilitate the careers of women. But the change in Sweden or in other Western European countries has not been a radical one. It remains true today that only a minority of married women permanently combine employment with their role as wife and mother. The woman's most important role is widely considered to be that of caring for the home and children; her work is secondary, something that she can legitimately undertake when the children have become older, when and if it is possible to arrange for the children, if it is necessary to maintain or raise the living standard of the family or as long as the work is temporary. The man's role as the provider and the woman's role as the one supported are regarded as 'natural'. The majority of married women view the house-wife-mother role as most important and pattern their lives accordingly.

For the single woman, industrialization has meant opportunities for self-support. During the agrarian era, when the proportion of single adults in the population was significantly greater than today, a single woman was constrained to stay on as helper in the large family. The married woman enjoyed a relatively higher social status and it was clearly in the interest of all women 'to get married'. Industrialized society presented an opportunity to the single woman to 'live her own life' and pursue a career. In the labour market, however, she was often placed in an inferior position, corresponding in many respects to that which she held in the large agrarian family. And in the process the single women lost their 'roots', their family ties, and the daily and holiday company that the large family had provided.

This outline of the changes in family roles is unsatisfactory in at least one important respect: the development was not the same for all strata of society, nor for all branches of industry. While the wife in the farmer and artisan household was most like a work partner, the upper and middle-class wife tended to supervise servants performing most of these functions.

The advance of industrialization and the increasing absorption of women into the labour force, had widely different effects depending on social class. Women in the lower classes, on the whole, took up employment and contributed to the support of the family or became self-supporting. Amongst the middle and upper classes, however, such a step was less readily taken. It is in this context that one should place the considerable support for female emancipation found amongst the women of the upper classes. For the worker's wife who periodically had to enter into gainful employment or the farmer's wife who performed a productive role in her own household, the cry for the right to work did not have the same compelling force.

2. *The Small Family of Today*

At first glance, it appears somewhat surprising that the participation rates of married women have not been more strongly affected by the fact that industrialization stripped them of their traditional role and transferred essential aspects of the family's previous functions to new social institutions. Industrialization caused most of the productive tasks of the home to be shifted to the industrial work place. In the event, the practice of single relatives living and working in the family home declined and the family became essentially a consumption unit. With the transformation of the organization of society brought about by industrialization a differentiation of the social group structure could be discerned whereby the family became largely responsible for attending to the mental health and emotional adjustment of the individual while the institutions of economic life gave priority to rationality, efficiency and profitability. This change in the social group structure was marked by:

1. A progressive reduction in the size of the family from the multi-generation family to that of one couple and their children.
2. The diminished importance of relatives for companionship, collaboration and support. Social exchange and mutual obligations have been largely reduced to only the closest relatives.
3. The diminished importance of neighbours for companionship, and collaboration. Anonymity amongst neighbours is not uncommon in large cities, particularly in the new residential districts. Even in rural areas, however, there has been a decline in the importance of immediate neighbours as a result of the automobile, mass media, the ecological differentiation in county centres and the progressive de-population of such areas.

Family roles have changed *progressively* and one can distinguish several phases in this development. Some authors have written of two family types. One is *the transitional family*, an example of which is the urban middle and upper class family during the early stages of industrialization. It is characterized by a strong patriarchalism. The man is the family's main guardian and sole means of support, the woman's role is largely confined to the home.

The new family has emerged in recent decades. Typically, both partners have been gainfully employed before marriage and it is often understood that the woman will continue to pursue her career. With the advent of childbirth, the mother leaves her job for a period which may last until the children reach school age. The financial burdens, income, influence and decisional rights are all shared; the man helps with household tasks and both partners enjoy equal opportunity to participate in activities outside the home.

It is interesting to see how views of this development vary according to the attitudes held toward the idea of women working. Conservatives idealize the home and view the participation of women in working life as a deviation from the traditional pattern. The more radical ideology, by contrast, has placed great emphasis on the division of work within and without the home and has perceived continuity in the historical development. Thus, prior to the onset of industrialization, the home was also the workplace for almost all adults, in which men and women worked side by side. During a transitional era, women in an urban environment have tended to stay in the home while men have supported the family by offering their services in the labour market. As production has shifted outside the home women have become 'under-employed'. Today they can work in industry once again side by side with men but this time according to an industrial job division.

The radical interpretation has the virtue of throwing light on essential aspects of the historical development. At the same time, however, it tends to oversimplify and exclude certain other essential elements. The division of labour in the agricultural society took place within the framework of a patriarchal system which was wholly different from the 'democratic' family type recommended in the radical ideology.

II. *Factors Affecting Participation Rates Among Married Women*
1. *Demographic Changes*

The official data on population developments gives evidence of drastic changes in recent years in the life cycle and careers of Swedish women.

The one striking change in demographic trends is the pronounced increase in marital frequency, particularly in the lower age groups. During the early decades of this century, the proportion of unmarried women in the population was remarkably high. Thus, in 1935, 27% of the women in the 35–39 age group were unmarried. By 1960, this proportion had fallen to 10%.

In 1930, 50% of Swedish men waited until they were 30·1 years old before marrying; 50% of Swedish women waited until they were 27·8 years of age. By 1960, the corresponding age for men was 25·9 years and for women 22·9 years.

Marital fertility, calculated as the number of births per thousand married women under 45 years, reached a low point in the middle of the 1930s (1931–35 = 117/1,000) rose towards the middle of the 1940s (1941–45 = 135/1,000) and again fell towards the middle of the 1950s to below the rate during the 1930s (1956–60 = 102/1,000).

One factor of significance for the life cycle of Swedish women has been the *variation in fertility rates in different age groups*. Both marital and extra-marital fertility rates have fallen in the higher age groups (40 years and above), while such rates have remained at a high level or have risen in the lower age groups. The mean age of married women having children dropped from 30·5 in 1930 to 27·6 in 1960 and that of unmarried women having children from 24·8 to 20·6. The dispersion is, however, quite wide. In 1960, the lowest quartile value for married mothers was 23·7 years and the highest quartile value was 32·2 years.

These changes indicate that an increasing number of Swedish families have no minor children. The average family size in Sweden now includes only *one* minor child per marriage (Table 1).

TABLE I

The Number of Children under 16 years in Swedish Families, 1960

Number of children	% of Swedish families
0	46·2
1–2	44·5
3–	9·3

Source: Swedish Census.

Children are born as a rule rather early in Swedish marriages. Premarital conception (i.e. children born during the first seven months of marriage) has risen since the 1930s and occurred in 31% of all marriages entered into in 1960. If we study children born in 1960 and take only marriages entered into in 1950 or subsequently (covering about 87% of the children born in 1960), we find that the mean age for the mother was 24·1 years at the birth of the first child, 26·9 years at the birth of the second child and 29·4 years at the birth of the third child. Hence, the entire family cycle appears to have advanced in time both with respect to parenthood and the burden of financial support. The rearing period occurs earlier and the period of working age after the children have moved out of the parental home has been lengthened.

A contributing factor in this latter trend has been the increased expectation of life of Swedish women. In the 1921–30 period the probable expectation of life for women who had lived to be 15 years was 68 years. By the 1951–55 period this figure had risen to 75 years. As well, there appears to have been a shift in the biological vitality of women: more women are capable of working in higher age groups; and biological maturity occurs at an earlier age than it did several decades ago. These demographic changes—marriages at an earlier age, younger mothers and fewer children—have resulted in a situation when many mothers today have more than half of their working life in front of them by the time that their last child has attained school age [1].

2. *The Economic Significance of the Work of Married Women*

The customary assumption is that the decisive motive for the married woman working is an economic one. There are two types of evidence that tend to support such an assumption. Firstly, women married to men in the lowest income categories have relatively higher participation rates. And, secondly, working married women when questioned frequently indicate that their motive is economic.

Yet perhaps this gives an exaggeratedly rational picture of the motives of married women. For other motives for working may be felt to be less acceptable, say, that the mother views work as a means of self realization, and the economic motive may be used as a convenient cloak for her real motive.

(a) *What is the Significance of the Wife's Income for the Family?*

The increment to the total income of the family earned by the wife can make it possible for it to *satisfy certain indispensable needs*, clothes, housing and medicine. This is particularly true of low income families where the husband does not contribute significantly to family maintenance. In such cases, the employment of the wife will tend to be more permanent.

The wife's income can also contribute to the maintenance of a given external standard. It has been suggested that, in our society, with most of the basic necessities provided for, consumption tends to fulfil a status function. Where couples want to display a particularly high standard in their housing, clothes and leisure habits, the wife may have to work permanently.

The wife's income can help to realize a specific consumption goal. The married couple may want to acquire a larger flat, their own home, an automobile, a television set, travel abroad, etc. Such target-saving tends to play a bigger role at the start of the marriage. That the newly married woman continues with her job until she becomes a mother is today generally accepted in Sweden.

The work of the wife can constitute a form of *security for the future*, a form of insurance against the risk that the husband's income might drop or discontinue; e.g., due to divorce, retirement, long-term illness, disablement or death. The increasing risk of divorce contributes towards a more permanent working life for women.

In certain cases, the wife may have *earned certain benefits* through her earlier work participation or *expects certain benefits*, wage increases, etc., *in the future*. Thus, even though her net increment to the family income does not appear 'to pay' in the short term, it might over the long term.

With her own income, the wife can perhaps attain *a greater measure of influence and respect* relative to her husband. The working wife is not totally dependent upon her husband for her support; she administers a proportion of the family's cash income and she derives the respect accorded to an income earner.

(b) The Rising Standard of Living and Growing Consumption Needs

During the past three decades, there has been a rise in the standard of living as average real income has increased. This development is reflected in the changed pattern of private consumption, i.e. in the considerable increase in the consumption of goods and services by the individual. This increase has occurred in most areas of consumption, food, housing, clothing, furnishing, vacations, travel, recreation, medicine and hygiene. Household services constitute the exception; they have decreased.

In this context, it is worth mentioning the public policies that have led to a redistribution of income between different sectors. Social policies have raised the real income of families with children, students and old age pensioners.

This description, of course, offers no account of the satisfaction derived from a rising level of consumption. For the question of satisfaction involves not only the quantity and the quality of the goods or services consumed but also the 'needs' of the individual, and there is much evidence to suggest that the needs of the individual increase at a faster rate than his or her income.

What significance do these changes in the general real income level and the rise in the income level of special groups have for the work participation of women? Few studies have been attempted of this issue. Any answer therefore must be in the nature of supposition.

A promising approach might be the following. The higher average standard of living, and the rise in the living standard of the family with children reduces the need for the woman to work to raise the family income above a minimum limit. But this does not mean that all incentives for the wife's work participation have been removed; other incentives can emerge. The question of whether a family with children considers a given family income to be sufficient and the wife's incremental income to be necessary will be based on comparisons with the living conditions of other families. An increase in the average income of the family is no guarantee that the gap between 'needs' and income will be narrowed. The needs may have changed their complexion, e.g. from basic necessities to derived wants such as well-styled clothes, holidays, travel, a summer cottage, etc., but these can be equally strong. When one assumes that a higher living standard creates greater security, one tends to underrate the significance of the derived wants for the individual. The risk of losing a given standard and social position can create psychological insecurity as profound as the earlier threat of loss of basic necessities.

(c) The Family Cycle and Consumption Needs

In the foregoing analysis, the whole problem of family-economic motivation has been somewhat oversimplified. For often only the income of the husband or wife has been mentioned with no reference made to the consumption needs of the household.

Consumption needs, using certain accepted standard calculations, can be viewed as a function of the age of the individual. An adult constitutes a complete consumption unit, a child a fraction of a consumption unit that increases with increasing age. The cumulative consumption needs of the household rise with the number of family members and the age of the children.

It is possible to illustrate graphically how the living standard, defined as the average level of consumption per consumption unit, varies for families of different composition and during different phases of the family cycle.

Diagram 1 illustrates how the living standard of the family is affected by the variation in the consumption needs of the family during

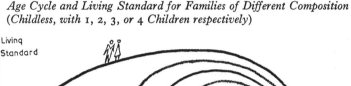

DIAGRAM I

Age Cycle and Living Standard for Families of Different Composition (Childless, with 1, 2, 3, or 4 Children respectively)

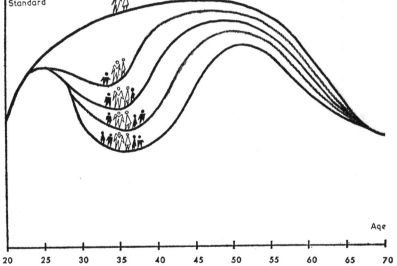

Source: Samhället och barnfamiljerna, SOU, 1955: 29, p. 76.

the course of its existence. The income of the man rises towards the middle of his career and falls as he moves closer to the 60 year mark. The consumption needs of families with children increase with the number and the age of the children. The family of more than one child will therefore have a living standard that decreases and reaches a minimum before the period when the children are ready to leave the home. After this period, the living standard will rise again until the point when the family income begins to drop. The family of more than one child, thus, will reach two income peaks, one at the beginning and one at the end of the family cycle. For the childless family, the living standard will simply follow the variations in family income.

It seems fair to assume that the wife will be more inclined to take up gainful employment when the living standard decreases, i.e., when the burden of financial support increases. However, the burden of financial support is not the only factor that varies directly with the number and age of the children; there is also the work load in the home. The wife's propensity to seek gainful employment tends to increase with a decreasing work load in the home. These factors can best be elucidated by systematically studying their effects through time.

During the *first phase* of the marriage, before the couple have children, the work load in the home will not be great. The burden of financial support will be relatively heavy as much expense will be involved in the process of household formation. Generally, the husband's income will be relatively low at this stage. Such conditions tend to favour the gainful employment of the wife.

During the *second phase* of the marriage, when the couple have children, both the work load in the home and the burden of financial support will increase. The income of the husband will tend to rise. But the vastly increased work load in the home will tend to reduce the propensity of the wife to take up outside employment.

During the *third phase* when the children are at school, the burden of financial support will continue to increase but the work load in the home will diminish. Since the income of the husband rarely rises in scale with the burden of financial support, there will be a greater incentive for the wife to return to work.

During the *fourth phase* when the children begin to support themselves, both the burden of financial support and the work load in the home will decrease. In the event, not only the external obstacles but also the economic incentive for the wife's return to work will be greatly reduced. The latter condition can be a factor contributing to the low participation rates among married women in the higher age groups.

3. *The Extent and Distribution of Housework*

As a rule, the married woman is responsible for the larger share of housework. This applies also to working married women. This work division is largely a product of prevailing family role norms and it is fully justified to describe the mother as carrying out a 'dual job'.

The extent and organization of housework (the type of work in the home, the time it requires, the distribution of housework tasks among the members of the family, the possibility of paid assistance, the mechanical equipment and layout of the residence, the services available and the use of work-saving methods) therefore constitute important factors in the determination of the propensity and capability of the married women to take on outside employment.

Comparisons between homes of full-time housewives, of wives who are part-time employees and those of wives who are full-time employees indicate in part that the total number of hours of work devoted to housework is significantly less in the case of full-time working wives, but also that domestics, the husband and others take on a correspondingly larger share of housework when the wife becomes gainfully employed.

A comparison of the time devoted to various forms of housework by full-time housewives and full-time working wives is offered in the following table.

TABLE 2

Time Devoted to Housework by Wives In Relation to their Number of Hours of Outside Employment (mean values)

Hours of outside employment in hours per week

	None	11–20	21–35	36–	All
Total Household Work	6·25	6·5	4·5	4·25	⩽6·0
Cleaning	1·0	1·25	0·75	0·5	1·0
Cooking	1·75	1·5	1·5	0·5	1·75
Washing Dishes	1·0	0·75	0·5	0·5	0·75
Number of Women	333	43	66	50	492

Source: SOU 1965: 65.

Studies of how housewives and working wives organize housework indicate little difference between the habits of these two groups; the similarities in most instances outweigh the differences. The reduction in housework that accompanies the wife's gainful employment affects all types of work in the home but appears to take its toll most heavily among the more enjoyable pursuits, viz. sewing and needlework. In the homes of working married women, there is some alteration in the pattern of consumption. There is a tendency to rely more heavily on

collective services, e.g. laundries and dry cleaners, restaurants, prepared foods, etc. [2].

A Swedish study found no more negative attitudes towards housework among working Swedish married women than among full-time
housewives [3].

A housewife's ability to simplify and rationalize housework can
affect her approach to employment in different ways. On the one hand,
her skill can make housework easier and therefore so attractive that
it compares favourably with gainful employment. On the other hand,
however, she can employ her skills to reduce the hours of housework
and thereby facilitate outside employment. In any case, a certain
degree of skill in housework would appear to be a pre-condition to a
successful combination of outside work, housework and motherhood.

Comparisons Between Housework and Gainful Employment

The work performed in the home is quite different from that in most
other occupations in several respects. What are some of the features
of this work that make it unusual?

The methods of recruitment are greatly varied. The work force
is, to say the least, heterogeneous. Marriage, the arrival of children,
and the traditional family role division, in effect, are the recruiting
agents. And ability and training appear to be almost irrelevant to
selection.

There are no recognized training courses. The majority of housewives learn the technical aspects of housework in their own home after
they obtain the 'position'.

Housewives are not organized and do not feel part of an occupational
group in the traditional sense. Occupational traditions, occupational
consciousness and occupational solidarity are all lacking.

Housework is unpaid. True, there is formal recognition of the right
of housewives to a share of their husbands' income, but the size of
the share is not determined by contract. The amount the wife is
entitled to receive is not dependent on her work output but rather
on her husband's income. In general, the wife's work output is not
evaluated, her share of her husband's income is not taxed as earned
income, and there is no basis for reckoning her social welfare benefits.
There are no set criteria for efficiency. In large measure, the housewife
simply follows custom and practice in her dealings.

Housework takes place entirely within the family—primary group,
as opposed to most other occupations which occur in a secondary

group situation. Relationships and forms of association are therefore almost totally different. Housework is 'sheltered' from outside competition.

Housework involves great freedom. The housewife decides for herself the schedule of a fairly diversified type of work. It entails responsibility, particularly in the long term as far as the rearing of children is concerned.

III. *Normative Patterns for the Internal and External Role Division Among Family Members*

1. *Role differentiation in the Family According to Small Group Theory*

When one examines sociological studies of family roles, one cannot help being struck by the extent to which this social science has accepted basic assumptions which are so heavily influenced by 'conventional wisdom'. Alice Rossi has written that,

'Sociologists studying the family have borrowed heavily from selective findings in social anthropology and from psychoanalytic theory and have pronounced sex to be a universally necessary basis for role differentiation in the family. By extension, in the large society women are seen as predominately fulfilling nurturant, expressive functions and men the instrumental, active functions. When this viewpoint is applied to American society, intellectually aggressive women or tender expressive men are seen as deviants showing signs of "role conflict", "role confusion" or neurotic disturbance. They are not seen as a promising indication of a desirable departure from traditional sex role definitions. In a similar way the female sphere, the family, is viewed by social theorists as a passive pawnlike institution, adapting to the requirements of the occupational, political or cultural segments of the social structure, seldom playing an active role either in affecting the nature of other institutions or determining the nature of social change.' [4]

The application of small group theory to the family nucleus has become an accepted method of approach on the basis of observations of role differentiation in small experimental groups; it has been found that all such groups must make provision for two distinct group interests. On the one hand, the internal relations of the group must be conducted in such a way that group solidarity is maintained. On the other hand, the group must adjust to, and attempt to realize its goals in, an external environment. Sociologists have found that the leadership functions of the small group can be divided in a manner quite similar to that of the current division of sex roles in the family, and this has been true whatever the sexual composition of the group.

C *Changing Roles*

Originally, it was thought that leadership qualities in problems of 'expertise' and those of 'morale' were two complementary traits that could not readily be found in one person. Later investigations, however, found that such traits are independent of one another. The same member of the group can be capable of maintaining internal solidarity and facilitating the adjustment of the group to the external environment [5].

By analogy to the behaviour of small groups, the father's major function in the family of today has been described as a 'link' between the family and society at large. In his occupational role and as the means of financial support, he devotes himself to long term economic and social goals for the family's *external* adjustment. The mother, in her turn, has been described as a 'link' between the father and the children. Her functions are to express the feelings of the family, to interpret for the father the needs and reactions of the children, to mediate conflicts and to safeguard the internal solidarity of the family [6].

That the expressive role in the family has been allocated to the woman has been explained by the fact that she is the one that cares for the child in its earliest years. In addition to this 'natural' explanation with its implicit reliance on 'maternal dispositions', however, there are at least two other interpretations that are worth considering.

  1. The influence of the external environment on the role division within the family.

It is reasonable to assume that family roles today, in large measure, represent the response of family members to the current structure of society, and the nature of current social policies (i.e. labour market, urban and residential planning, tax and wage policies). In other words, familial role division is influenced by the institutional framework within which the family members act.

  2. The comparative qualifications of husband and wife to discharge 'instrumental' and expressive functions.

This is to assume that the partner with the highest level of education, income and social position tends to discharge the essential 'instrumental' functions. Currently, men are more often the means of financial support for and the status-giver to the family than women. The expressive role of the woman can be viewed as a consequence of the mother's and the children's economic and social dependence upon the man as the provider. This makes it necessary for the woman to articulate and explain the child's needs to the father as well as to take the initiative in mediating and smoothing over internal family proceedings.

In spite of the fact that prevailing family role norms allocate to the woman the task of caring for and preserving the internal solidarity and to the man the function of securing the family's external position, one finds in practice that role division in the family varies greatly according to the inherent abilities and vocational qualifications of its individual members. A Finnish study [7] illustrates the importance of the relative qualifications of husband and wife for 'instrumental' tasks. Comparisons were made of the role divisions in three types of families; those in which the wife had, respectively, a lower, a roughly equivalent, and a higher level of education, than the husband. The results indicated that the higher the wife's level of education relative to the husband, the more inclined she was to unite motherhood with gainful employment. However, the 'absolute' educational level of the wife gave no linear relation to her desire to work.

In families in which the wife contributed to the support of the family, there was a pronounced tendency to balance instrumental and expressive functions more evenly between husband and wife. This was true with respect to the taking of decisions as well as child rearing and participation in household work. The role differentiation in the 450 Helsinki families with children in primary school indicated that the relative level of competence of husband and wife and the wife's pursuit of an occupation can be decisive factors in creating considerable role equality in the family.

2. *Family Relations of Significance for the Work Participation of Married Women*

Since the family is one of many institutions in society the opportunities of family members to develop their own internal work division will inevitably be affected by and conform to the structure of other institutions. When examining the findings of studies of individual and psychological problems related to working married women, it is essential to keep in mind the probable influences of the external social framework.

(a) *Family-Ideal and Role Norms*

Since the married woman is a member of a family, her decision to work or refrain from working cannot be taken in isolation. It is dependent on the views and the needs of the other family members and presupposes a series of practical adjustments, some degree of co-operation and support for the role ideal by the other family members.

Looking at the problem from the vantage point of the married woman, one can discern two sets of relevant factors. On the one hand, there are the questions of (a) what she feels is correct as far as the role of the housewife is concerned (internalized role norms); and (b) how she perceives the ideals and interests of persons in close proximity, their approval or disapproval of the prospect of her taking a job. On the other hand, there are the issues of (a) the opportunity for alternative roles and role ideas in her environment (transmitted role ideals); and (b) the direct requirements and obstacles created by persons in close proximity (transmitted role expectations).

These often varying role expectations of the 'correct' and 'appropriate' work division in the home, the 'ideal' relation between husband and wife and the delineation of the boundaries within which the married woman's (man's) career, personality, needs, ambitions, responsibilities and rights in marriage should be contained can clearly overlap or be mutually exclusive. Cumulatively, the attitudes and influences of family members, relatives, neighbours and the mass media represent a formidable social pressure upon the individual.

Some of the wifely norms that the married woman perceives in her environment can conceivably be projections of her own internalized role ideal. We shall have occasion to return to this point in Chapter IV.

It appears that the attitude of the husband is often of decisive importance in the wife's decision whether or not to work. An American study suggests that the husband's attitude is the factor that co-varies most closely with the work participation of the wife [8]. The negative attitude of men can be attributed, in part, to their general family ideology and opinion of social prestige. It can also be due to the fact that they feel that they can obtain better service from their wives as long as they remain full-time housewives; or that they resent having to share some of the housework. In any case, there is a serious risk of conflict and tension in the marriage, particularly where the wife's employment creates a change in earlier habits. The unwillingness of the man to share housework and his consequent opposition to the wife's attempts to seek employment is a decisive and common reason for the wife refraining from taking a job.

(b) Ideology and Practice in Child Rearing

The reason most often given for the decision by the wife not to take up employment is that of consideration for the infant and the child in its pre-school years. As a rule, maternal presence is perceived as a duty particularly while the child is young. According to the generally accepted family role norms, it is the wife and not the husband who is responsible for the care of children.

The amount of time required for the *direct* care of children diminishes greatly as the child grows older. By school age, the mother's role has become less that of administering direct care and more one of helping with homework, giving guidance and company, perhaps simply being present and available to meet the needs of the child.

It is also possible to point to the more conscious influences stressing the need for the wife to remain at home and care for the children. Psychologists, psychiatrists and pediatricians have frequently asserted that the sound development of the child requires the mother to devote herself unstintingly to the child and give it as much love and care as possible. It has been suggested by proponents of the extreme con-servative view that maternal employment can lead to neurosis and socially deviant behaviour on the part of children. The radical view decries the conservatives' attempts to create a myth of motherhood that would invest in the mother's role in rearing a thoroughly dis-proportionate share of the duties and the blame, and would exclude much of the father's contribution.

Per Olav Tiller points out in Chapter III that the existing studies of mother absence do not support the view that the work of the mother is necessarily detrimental to the child's development. The studies suggest that the mother's absence due to work does not alone affect the child's adjustment but that a number of other environmental factors are equally influential. Tiller concludes that the decisive factor is probably the quality of the contact between parents and children rather than the quantity. He feels that there is a distinct risk in over-emphasizing the traditional role of the mother. The excessive idealization of the mother's role in articles and stories in the women's weeklies and popular non-fiction as well as the mass media in general can lead ultimately to over-protected and over-dependent children who have difficulty in adjusting to an adult role. Tiller's own investigation also indicates the importance of the father in the child's development, a figure often ignored in the media.

(c) *Marital Cohesion*

The existing studies that attempt to elucidate the effect of the wife's work participation on the husband-wife relationship and marital cohesion succeed only in presenting us with a confusing and controversial array of data and assumptions.

A number of investigations of cohesiveness in the marriages of working women offer no conclusive evidence of an association between wifely work participation and a higher divorce rate. One American study indicated a weak tendency of this sort [9]. However, a Danish study found a weak tendency in the opposite direction: the divorce rate was somewhat higher in the families of full-time housewives and somewhat lower in the families of women working full-time [10]. A German study found no significant difference in the divorce rates in families of housewives and working women [11]. According to yet another study, full-time housewives were found to be more often satisfied with their marriage than working women; the latter group had more often contemplated divorce [12]. In a number of cases in this study, it clearly appeared that the wife's work participation was a direct consequence of the marital mis-alliance. It seems reasonable to assume that the interest of married women in working will be greater, the weaker is the cohesiveness of their marriage. Confronted by the risk of divorce, the wife will look to employment as a means of economic security. It is quite probable that her decision to achieve a greater measure of economic security through work, in turn, creates new tensions and aggravates old role conflicts in the marriage.

At a certain level of generalization, it is possible to distinguish here between two rival assumptions: the first is that the institution of marriage rests upon a pronounced role differentiation, i.e. that the need of husband and wife for one another and their mutual satisfaction can be assured most readily by a differentiation of functions, a complementarity, within the family. The second is that role equality within the family creates the pre-conditions for a wider area of common interests for husband and wife. According to this latter view, the work participation of the wife can actually redound to the benefit of the marriage. Relations between spouses will become marked by a greater degree of equality as they are increasingly able to participate jointly in different activities.

The findings of a Finnish study of family companionship and cohesion gave some support to this latter view [13].

'In the study, whose material was collected in a series of interviews made with 454 married women in Helsinki, a view is taken of the companionship of spouses—defined as a joint participation—in housekeeping, in directing the socialization of their children, and in the use of leisure. The examination shows that companionship is cumulative in these fields: if it appears in one field, it will appear in others as well. Similarly cumulative is lack of companionship. It came out too, that in families with a wife engaged in wage-earning work, companionship was altogether more extensive than in families where the wife stayed at home. Joint participation in activities for safeguarding the family's financial situation proves to be functional, as regards its consequences to the family, at least in so far that the companionship obtaining between spouses who behave thus will grow stronger too in their other fields of activity.'

In the Swedish debate, the argument has been put forward that excessive role differentiation can constitute a threat to family cohesion [14].

'The most serious weakness of the tradition is, however, that when it places almost exclusively upon the woman the responsibility for the care and supervision of the child, it creates an alienation, a gap between the husband and wife in marriage. For the woman is then forced to live in a special world: she has sole rights to intimate contact with the children; she becomes financially supported by the man, she becomes generally isolated from vocational and social life. And the man in turn is relegated to his special world: he becomes and often feels as if he is a "supporting machine"; his relations with the children become superficial; he is stimulated to even greater efforts than before in his vocational and social life outside the home.

'In this way, the tradition creates the groundwork for tensions and conflicts within marriage, particularly where one or the other spouse attempts to introduce egalitarian reforms. Conflicts can more readily be resolved by compromise in a marriage characterized by a greater degree of equality, but this is seldom true of marriage of the traditional type. . . . Both the man as well as the woman are damaged by the alienations and separation and the child is often caught sitting in between.'

3. *The Effect of the Married Woman's Work Participation on the Influence and Social Prestige of Husband and Wife*

(a) *Influence and Decisions Within and Without the Home*

The discussion of the relative influence of husband and wife in the family touches upon many different areas of decision. In many such areas, it is difficult to determine who has the most say. According to fairly widespread norms, certain areas are viewed as the wife's special field of competence (rearing, purchasing food, etc.), while in others the husband is expected to exercise the greater influence (banking, the family economy in general, etc.). According to a number of American studies, the wife has acquired greater influence within the home than the man, extending in part to 'instrumental' leadership. This power take-over by the wife in the home has been explained by the extensive absence of the father. Rossi has observed that:

'The traditional woman's self-esteem would be seriously threatened if her husband were to play a role equal to her own in the lives and affections of her children or in the creative or managerial aspect of home management, precisely because her major sphere in which to acquire the sense of personal worth is her home and children. The lesson is surely not lost on her daughter, who learns that at home father does not know best, though outside the home men are the bosses over women, as she can see only too well in the nurse-doctor, secretary-boss, sales-clerk-store manager, space Jane–space John relationships that she has an opportunity to observe.' [15]

With a job, the married woman runs the risk of an increase in her husband's control of and participation in the rearing process, household planning and the purchasing of food and goods. Is it likely that the work participation of the wife will lead to a situation where more family decisional areas will be shared? In other words, is the working married woman prepared to relinquish some of the real power that she has attained through the father's regular absence from the home? At a more theoretical level, to what extent does greater equality between husband and wife involve a complementary and balanced leadership based on *specialization in different decisional areas*? And, given this, can specialization be related to the individual qualifications and interests of the partners independently of the traditional discriminatory family sex role norms? Or, will greater equality between husband and wife lead to the development of wider joint areas of decision within and without the home?

The democratic view of the family can be said to be officially accepted, corresponding most closely to the spirit and the letter of the laws relating to the family.

A greater equality between the sexes is apparent in rearing and training practices, in the patterns of association among children and young people in organizations, at workplaces and in the social exchange of adults. Certain of the traditional sex role norms have been expunged. The view of the woman as the weaker sex and the one requiring protection has been greatly modified.

Relations between husband and wife have changed. Sociologists have described the development as one from institutionalized patriarchalism to equality and companionship. Marriage, according to the

currently dominant view, is a product of mutual affection and assent;
both partners are thought to play an active role in preliminary love
play, with both having an equal right to satisfaction and happiness
in marriage. Both have the right to consideration and influence in
resolving family crises and both are assumed to play an active role in
the marriage within the framework of a pattern of role differentiation,
which is today in the process of transformation.

There are also influences, such as the mass media, that idealize the
man as 'the one who decides', He is the one that takes the initiative
(not only sexually) but in all major contexts. Given the prevailing sex
role norms and socialization practices, there are many factors that tend
to 'predestine' men to a superior and women to an inferior position.
These tend to predispose women to pass on to the man the responsibility for taking decisions, solving problems, etc., and assume a passive
and helpless position to protect their femininity.

The administration of income and expenditure is a key function
in the balance of power in the family, a function generally discharged
by the husband who takes care of the family accounts [16]. In some
countries, e.g. in Scandinavia, the housewife has a legal right to
economic equality. Her effort in the home is considered to be equivalent
to that of her husband on the job and to entitle her to a share of the
family income sufficiently large to cover both her own and the household's needs. There seems to be evidence, however, that the woman's
right to a share is more formal than real: neither men nor women seem
aware of its existence and wives have difficulty in asserting their rights
under it.

It has been suggested that the married woman's dependence on
the husband for economic support, standard of living status, social
company, and style of life, affects her self-esteem and produces ambivalent feelings towards men. From the husband's vantage point, again,
the economic dependence of the wife entails increased insecurity
and tension for him in his working life. If the man is not capable of
meeting his obligations to his wife, he may experience feelings of guilt
which could create enmity toward her. A marriage in which the entire
burden of financial support falls upon one person, the man, creates
pressures upon him to advance in his career, to take on extra work, etc.

IV. *Sex Roles and Socialization in the Family*

The sex role norms of today are a legacy of the role division principles
of a pre-industrial society. All social systems are confronted by the

need to solve the problems of division of work. In less highly differentiated and technically specialized societies, tasks can be distributed according to principles that ignore individual endowments. It is questionable however whether in a highly differentiated and specialized society such as our own, sex can continue to be a decisive factor for the division of work.

Sex differences are not considered to be merely biological differences related to the fertilization function. They have become a social distinction of the highest rank in the estimation of an individual. The sex of an individual goes beyond inherent biological qualifications; it determines what aptitudes and inclinations shall be developed and what motives and aspirations shall be awakened. Sex has become a social screening device separating human needs into feminine or masculine needs, directing boys and girls into different careers, cultivating different interests, clothing them in different colours and calling them different names. Appearance and actions have come to be dealt with differently depending on whether they are manifestations from a girl or a boy. That which society has defined as 'masculine' has become a lack or a deviant feature in a girl. And a 'feminine' trait is subjected to unrelenting ridicule when displayed by a man.

1. The 'Standardization' of Relations

The separation of production from family life that resulted from industrialization was an important factor in the preservation of wide differences in sex role norms despite the growth of equality and democracy in society generally.

For boys, the goal of the rearing process is preparation for rational and effective dealings with people. For occupational life is marked not only by standardized production patterns but also standardized relations among people: rules, formal instructions, bureaucratic authority and treatment based on formal qualifications and evaluations.

Girls, in contrast, are reared to preserve the family: to deal with people attentively, with consideration and care and with understanding for exceptions, the occasional breach, the irrelevant, and extenuating circumstances.

2. Intimacy—Anonymity in Personal Relations

The first roles the individual learns are exceedingly diffuse, namely, relations with his parents and within the family. As the number of contacts increases experience is gained in playing separate and distinct roles. Relations become more segmented and impersonal.

It has often been maintained that girls live in a more confined environment. They are bound more tightly to the home, they are more strictly controlled and more dependent on the parents.

Books for girls concentrate on the home, the boarding school and love relationships, while books for boys deal with tales of conquest and experiences in a world of adventure. Girls are assumed to prefer company in pairs, with a best girl friend or boy friend, while boys form gangs and groups of friends. Girls, thus, are reared largely for intimate relations while boys are reared to deal with a larger number of interactions.

It should be observed that one's position along the diffuseness-specificity continuum can be determined both by the amplitude of the attention devoted to different social and psychological qualities in another person and the extent to which one gives of one's own personality in the interaction, i.e. how confidential, spontaneous, and candid one is with another person.

If one focuses on the differences in the sentiments that constitute respectively the diffuse and specific orientations, it is evident that the diffuse approach takes as its values, loyalty and permanency. Such relations, moreover, develop a strong mutual dependence and place a premium on consideration. Specific relations, in contrast, are fleeting, they emphasize personal freedom and independence.

Both men and women in their early childhood learn largely common and overlapping personality traits and values, but sex role differentiation ensures that the *order of precedence* should differ for the two sexes. Consequently, an analysis of the sex roles can concentrate on shifts in order of priority for the different norms.

Both men and women should express feelings and be objective. But women are expected to be more expressive and less objective than men. The result of the prevailing differences of degree and priorities are respectively 'femininity' and 'masculinity' in our culture.

3. Norms for Control and Differentiation of Feelings

That women are more emotionally expressive and men more objective has now become part of today's 'conventional wisdom'. The assertion appears to be a truism until one begins to analyse the more far-reaching consequences of an affective role differentiation.

If one traces sexual differences in emotionality back to the socialization process, one finds there discrepancies both with respect to the *norms for the control of affective expression*, i.e. rules relating to the spontaneous expression or control of feelings, and with respect to the *norms for the affective differentiation*, i.e. rules that attribute particular feelings to different sex roles.

Harriet Holter [17] has suggested that girls are to a great extent encouraged to express feelings openly while boys are trained to control their feelings. At first glance, such a hypothesis appears to be reasonable, but it suffers from its disregard of the norms governing the differentiation of feelings. These latter norms reserve aggressiveness and dominance for boys; expression within this affective sector is far more acceptable for boys than for girls. The norms for sensitivity, viz., tenderness, fear, tears, seeking protection, and compassion, in contrast, are prescribed for women. Holter's hypothesis should be modified to assert that *girls and boys are socialized to spontaneous expression of different affects. The acceptable range of affects for girls is wider than that for boys.*

The specialization of girls in sensitivity probably results in a greater consideration for the feelings of others, while the learning of dominance produces a self-assertiveness and create the pre-conditions for a lack of consideration for others' feelings. An unfamiliarity with sensitivity breeds independence in boys and lessens the influence of evanescent sentiments.

A sentimental orientation entails not only emotional expressiveness but also receptiveness to sentimental communication and an ability to manipulate others through feelings, i.e. to exploit emotions instrumentally in order to attain certain objectives.

If girls are socialized to maintain an extensive affective range, they should after all tend to be aware of emotions and observe others' moods. They learn to adjust their own behaviour in accordance with the 'emotional' climate as well as to utilize emotions as a means of influence over other people.

If boys profit less by emotions as a means of social communication, the perception of emotions tends to be less relevant for them. They do not learn to detect what others feel and think in all situations. Their relations become less emotionally complicated, more concrete and direct. Their behaviour is directed more by rules and instrumental signals in the environment.

In other words, it is quite likely that the female sex role is based on the learning of attentiveness to an affective signal system (cues) which diverts the attention of women away from the more technical and structural aspects in the environment. Girls are socialized to be specialists in feelings. They learn to adjust their behaviour according to their own and others' feelings. This is not parallel with imitation but entails recognition that success and failure are linked to understanding and the observation of what others think and feel rather than more objective and concrete environmental signals.

Social learning is based largely on imitation of behaviour that is successful. But the significant question is whether *imitation is a guide in the learning process enabling one to direct one's attention to the relevant signals in the environment* or *whether it is an obstacle to independent problem-solving because dependence on stereotype diverts the individual's attention away from such signals.*

As a rule, it is easier to adjust one's behaviour to signals from others' conduct than to discern on one's own account the relevant signals in a complicated environment. Miller and Dollard [18] illustrate this point with the following examples.

A child in a strange room is confronted by four closed doors. Which one is the proper exit? Three mistakes are possible if the child attempts to experiment by itself. However, if it follows someone's example, it can discover the exit quite quickly.

It is easier to drive behind the vehicle of a friend to find the right way in a strange city than to fend for oneself even with the aid of maps. A child can learn to avoid snakes, dogs, pieces of glass, sharp edges and dirty objects (five different signals) or to avoid the same objects as its parents avoid. The imitation of the parents' avoidance is based on one signal, namely, observation of negative affective reactions by the parents.

If the pre-conditions for successful imitation are present as a result of previous learning, the process of learning independent behaviour by further imitation is obviously facilitated.

The following reflections appear apposite to the problem of sex roles:

Since it is more profitable in many situations to imitate rather than experiment oneself, stricter role norms are required to offset the imitation tendency and prescribe initiative, intrepidity, independence, risk-taking and activity. Boys conspicuously more often than girls are subjected to imitation-inhibiting norms. One can point to sex differences, in part during childhood and adolescence and in part the later role distribution in sexual relations, where men have learned an initiating and women an object-role [19].

Conceivably, an affective orientation will tend to fetter the individual in personal relations that emit affective signals (cues). There is the risk that the individual will become somewhat dependent on the thoughts and feelings of other persons, adjusting his or her behaviour to theirs, rather than take into account that which is the object of their behavioural adjustment. In the event, the ability to tackle problems independently will be weakened and intellectual receptivity fostered rather than innovation. Confinement to 'models' or 'signal senders' can also favour the development of an authoritarian relationship.

If the individual learns to adjust to different situations and choose between alternative courses of action by observing and being receptive to the thoughts of others, it is reasonable to assume that he or she will develop a need to have reality interpreted, corroborated and evaluated.

Accompanying an affective orientation, therefore, will often be a desire for open and confidential personal relations, a need to be socially accepted and to function in a secure social context.

For the diffuse and affective personality, all social problems are reduced to questions of individuals and psychology. No social structural factors dictate political decisions; the distribution of resources and power are merely questions of ethics. All forms of satisfaction and explanation are sought in personal relationships. Feelings are a guide to action and a regular source of concern or self-satisfaction.

4. *Ascribed and Achieved Roles* (*External attributes-efforts*)

The distinction between the terms ascribed and achieved was drawn originally with respect to two different principles of role division. Sex roles as such are examples of ascribed roles. The individual has neither the possibility of choice nor the opportunity to qualify for the role. An occupational role is an example of a role that is achieved through effort and qualifications. The rearing of boys and girls is marked by an ascribed biological distinction, sex, but after the sex bound socialization of childhood, one encounters the distribution of roles based largely on achievement. In much of modern society, e.g., in the educational system, the labour market and decision-making organs, the individual's position is determined largely by his or her personal competence and capability.

The existence of established sex roles entails, however, that along-side the evaluation of individuals according to merit there is a second measure which places a premium on qualities ascribed to the sex of the individual. This has its compensations; prestige is given to a pleasing appearance, youth, style and charm. In the debate on the sex roles, it has been maintained that the existence of double standards, one for performance, the other for attractiveness, is calamitous for women.

There is a clear conflict between 'ascribed femininity' and the requirements in industrial life for job qualifications and effective performance. In contrast the male sex role coincides with such essential occupational role norms. The successful occupational role is based on performance: effectiveness, qualifications, information, activity, independence and initiative. Sex role success for the woman consists in being beautiful, pleasant, soft, impulsive, harmonious and adaptable. Along these lines men and women develop their respective 'I-ideal'. They strengthen their self-esteem by different means, means that correspond to the expectations created by the division of work in society.

If the traditional female ideology has to some extent lost its force, the same cannot be said of its romantic variant, the role ideals that dominate the mass media: Weekly magazines, advertising and the cinema. There, the young woman is essentially a sexual partner (or marital partner), and great weight is given to beauty, sex appeal, beautiful clothes, charm, sensuality, devotion, passivity, acquiescence, and the housewife-mother role at the expense of the vocational role. The glamour role undermines the young woman's preparation for a career by elevating the married woman's glamour to a status symbol. A new middle class criterion for a good wife is the ability to be an attractive and pleasing hostess, capable of performing a public relations function for the husband in social life.

5. *The Social Prestige of the Married Woman*

How does the working married woman's role compare to the housewife's role from the standpoint of social prestige? According to some authors, the honours go to the mother and housewife; the woman can win status through her position in the home. According to other authors, however, the married woman perceives the role of supported housewife as rather low in prestige; and tends to view a job as the only means of attaining prestige equivalent to that enjoyed by men. There have been few extensive studies in this area. A Swedish investigation of how mothers perceived their role as full-time housewives gave no evidence of a tendency to deprecate its worth [20].

It has been suggested that the respect that a married woman can gain through her work is dependent on the following factors: the prestige of the job; the prestige accorded to the housewife role; the income and status of the husband; and the living standard of the family [21]. A woman with incomplete vocational training married to a wealthy man, thus, would rarely chose to work, while women with good vocational qualifications married to men with low income should often be gainfully employed. The prestige factor and the family economic factor should thus work hand in hand.

How does the married man perceive the effects on his status of a working wife? It has been said that the wife's work participation can create a potential status problem. Married men can feel threatened by the fact that they are no longer solely responsible for the support of their families, that their wives are no longer economically dependent upon them. On the other hand, they could conceivably achieve increased respect for their progressive attitudes or for their marriage to a successful wife. An additional problem is the effect of working wives on the mutual regard of husband and wife. Do they experience greater respect, companionship, rivalry or increased distance between them? No direct study has yet been undertaken in Sweden to answer these questions. One can only point to the increase in the 'collegiate' marriage, i.e. marriage between partners of equivalent education and training.

6. *Primary group Technique for Family Relations—Secondary Group Techniques for Relations in the Labour Market*[1]

One thing that emerges with striking clarity from the foregoing analysis of the sex roles is that two different types of social techniques are called into play, one designed for intimate primary group relations, the other for more anonymous secondary group relations. In other words, boys are prepared for an occupational role, girls for a family role.

The typical modern occupational roles consist of impersonal secondary group relations in contrast to primary group relations which are based on feelings of affinity and personal contact.

Primary relations direct themselves to a person as a whole. They are open and intimate. They embrace all possible qualities in the person and features of the situation. The display of feelings is acceptable; indeed the norms prescribe feelings in a love relationship, a friendship and within the family.

---

[1] This section is derived from the contributions of Harriet Holter to *Kvinnors liv och arbete*, Chapters 2 and 9. The initiated reader will no doubt recognize the debt owed by the role analysis to Parsons' pattern variables.

The evaluation of others is based on personal and subjective grounds, i.e., much depends on the relationship and the circumstances of the occasion. The emphasis is placed on ascribed qualities, external attributes: beautiful, young, daughter of the Managing Director. There is less concern with merit and qualifications.

The *secondary relation* restricts itself to consideration of the particularly relevant sides of the person's character. Feelings are to be omitted. Restraint, objectivity and discipline are necessary conditions for smooth collaboration between persons who have little in common save the job itself.

Treatment and evaluation are standardized and are based on formal grounds. One lives according to generally applicable rules and regulations. Emphasis is placed on achieved qualities, capabilities, competence and skill.

The ideal for the occupational role is one of delimited personal contact, emotional self-discipline, generally applicable rules, and evaluation based on performance.

Throughout childhood and adolescence, marriage and the family are presented as the most important, sometimes the only life objectives for girls. Consequently, women in vocational life conduct themselves more according to the rules of family life than those of the labour market.

That the sex role is a handicap for women in working life has been illustrated by industrial sociological studies in Norway [22], Sweden [23] and England [24], of the attitudes of male co-workers and supervisors.

The attitudes found can be summarized as follows: Women lack stability in working life. They do not feel identified with their job. They are unconcerned with the difficulties such an attitude creates for co-workers and supervisors. They lack deep interest in their job and in training. They seldom enquire about promotion possibilities. They are not well suited to foremen or other supervisory positions. They are too nervous and cannot be objective. Were they to be placed in supervisory positions, they would display favouritism based on personal grounds.

Women lack the disposition for promotion. They underestimate themselves and lack self-confidence. They are satisfied to be menials and assistants to men; they even accept lower wages.

No man would prefer female supervisors, but many women declare that they prefer receiving orders from men. Women display antipathy towards members of their own sex.

Unlike that among men, solidarity among women is weak; their relations are marked by intrigue and envy. Women have no concept of the rules of the game at the workplace. Men follow determined rules and understand unwritten practices where reasonable. Women are well suited to subordinate positions. They are submissive. They protest less often than men. They go on until they are asked questions and do not raise questions themselves. They are compliant, self-conscious, and willing to work. They tend to be found in routine work; they are quick, handy and patient.

The conflicts and tensions of women at the work place are generally related not so much to the job as to relations in their private life. They involve themselves emotionally in human relations and tend to introduce irrelevant details such as conditions in their home. They worry about the morals of employees, implicitly their sexual morals. They comment on appearance and dress.

Women are innately conservative. They resist change on the job and cling to the familiar.

There appears to be a fairly general feeling that women have little conception of what is reasonable and accepted in working life. Women, it is thought, do not go by the prevailing rules of the game. They vacillate between primary and secondary positions.

However, it is possible to turn the problem around. Are the rules of the game played fairly with female employees? A woman can seldom be certain of the yardstick with which she is being evaluated—i.e. whether she is being evaluated according to her face, her feminine qualities, her work performance, her understanding or her solidarity. When she stresses competence, she is accused of being unfeminine. When she stresses her femininity, she is accused of being incompetent. This naturally creates a double standard for women in working life.

Passivity, insufficient initiative, insecurity, inadequate vocational ambitions and dependence can all be regarded in a new light when viewed as symptoms of the conflicts women experience between primary and secondary group values as well as their response to the contradictory reactions they are confronted with in their environment. This is also a possible explanation of 'sex differences' at the workplace. The woman's 'innate conservatism', anxiety and resistance to change are quite possibly the consequences of role conflict and the miscalculation that often accompanies an unsettled position.

The link between the family roles and the personality is an important one. Even were the external conditions improved to allow married women to pursue permanent careers more easily, it is not at all certain that male and female attitudes could be readily altered. For here, as in many other contexts, one must allow for a time lag during the course of which the attitudes obtained in childhood and youth continue to be passed on from generation to generation. There is a sluggishness in the system that prevents family role norms from being easily changed by influences which are essentially only external, e.g., changes in the legal position of women, changes in employer practices, propaganda for new patterns in family life.

V. Changes in the Family and its Environment Affecting Working Married Women

1. Demographic Trends

One the one hand, the greater frequency of marriage has increased its likelihood for young women and hence has tended to reduce their ambitions to master an occupation and support themselves.

On the other hand, the rising divorce rates have increased the risk that women might be single, a factor intensifying the motivation to obtain training and a position for the sake of security. This latter tendency, however, is offset somewhat by the higher re-marriage rates.

The low fertility rates in the higher age groups and the low average number of children per family together with the longer expectation of life allow a longer period of employment for the married woman after active motherhood.

However, the lower marriage age, the higher fertility in the lower age groups and the lower mean age of motherhood, tend to militate against the acquisition of vocational experience and training by women while young, a factor creating obstacles to women attempting to enter economic life in early middle age.

Upon closer scrutiny, thus, the net effect of these demographic changes appears to be strongly negative as far as female work participation is concerned. In case after case, young women are either unable to complete their education or training. In addition, thoughts of early marriage and family formation tend to lead many young women to lower their vocational ambitions and apply for shorter and simpler courses of training than are commensurate with their abilities [25].

For women who marry at an early age the years of exploration and vocational preparation coincide with those of early motherhood. The problems of vocational adjustment thus often become entwined with

those of active child rearing. This is particularly true for women in
occupations demanding much extra effort in the form of overtime or
further training in the early stages. Many clerical and administrative
positions are of this sort. One plausible explanation for the discrepant
distribution between men and women in white collar positions—with
83% of the women in the lowest levels as opposed to 24% of the
men [26]—is offered by the absence of women from work at the start
of their careers.

The young woman as well as the young family tend to give little
thought to the consequences of inadequate vocational preparation and
early family formation for the wife's attempts to become economically
active after the children are no longer infants. The wife, by acting in a
certain way at the start of her life and family career—e.g. by failing to
obtain adequate education and training, by quitting her job, by organiz-
ing her home so that she is indispensable to its management, by
rearing her children in such a way that they become strongly dependent
upon her—*could conceivably create the conditions reducing her own
degree of choice*. Causality in this area has, as yet, not been sufficiently
studied to allow any conclusions to be drawn.

Those mothers desiring to continue to work and to take only short
leaves of absence during their children's infancy, however, are confronted by almost insuperable obstacles due to the shortage of day
nurseries and other forms of organized child supervision. For all
intensive purposes, society today does not allow the young mother
real freedom of choice; in practice she is excluded from economic
life [27]. She has little opportunity to maintain contact with the labour
market or gain vocational experience.

2. *Division of Work and Work Requirements in the Home*

The shift of consumption to more finished and processed goods, the
better planning of homes and the increase in labour-saving devices
have all reduced the quantum of work in the home.

New social benefits such as free school lunches, home services
for the elderly, shorter hours of work, and the reduction of the work
week to five days, both of which have increased the man's availability
to participate in housework and child supervision, are all factors
increasing the opportunity for married women to work.

On the other hand, the higher living standard, manifested in larger
sized homes, better furnishings, more leisure consumption and improved health have tended to expand work in the home. Services for

the maintenance of the home have become more expensive and the availability of new materials has transformed maintenance work into a leisure activity for the family.

The higher economic standard has decreased the need for mothers to work to meet the basic needs of the family. Greater social security has had the same effect. On the other hand, derived consumption needs increasing faster than consumption resources have tended to create an economic incentive for the wife to work.

3. A Milder Social Climate

A culture can create different ideological climates for relationships between the family and other institutions depending upon, *inter alia*, the degree to which their norm systems have been integrated. Industrialization involved a spatial separation of home and production and a harsher working environment which together generated a greater need for consensus and emotional support within the family.

With the 'democratization' of society and the growth of the welfare state, there has been a pronounced change in the social climate. Focusing directly on industrial relations we can observe the following:

1. The distance between supervisor and subordinate has narrowed. Authority based on fear has been supplanted by greater frequency of contact and equality in forms of address (language), tone of association and external appearance.
2. The methods used by supervision to influence and control employees have become marked by the influence of human relations concepts. Punishment and the threat of punishment have been replaced by more positive disciplinary methods.
3. Communication between management and employees has been improved and has begun to flow in both directions. Participation by employees in decision-taking at the work place has become a recognized ideal.
4. Flexibility, the ability to inspire co-operation and sensitivity to the needs and desire of employees have emerged as desirable supervisory traits.

Along with the greater democratization of industrial supervision, there has been a general 'humanization' of familial and institutional treatment of children, the ill, criminals and deviant individuals of different types. The spread of psychological, medical and biological research has created the foundation for greater insight into and tolerance

and understanding of the varying needs of the individual. This movement to a milder social atmosphere can be described as the 'feminization of society'.

Quite clearly, this development has not been uniform in coverage
or extent. There are also symptoms of a 'brutalization' of the social
climate: the new weapons of mass destruction in international relations; the faster pace and increased competition in working life. As
well, the institutional treatment of human beings is increasingly
becoming something in the nature of a profession, requiring special
training on the part of persons discharging such a function. In the
event, there is a grave risk that the role relationship formerly characterized by some degree of mutuality may be replaced by the neutral,
authoritarian relationship of expert to client.

The greater attention given by companies to the morale and satisfaction of their employees is evidence of the integration of family
norms with other social norms. However, at the same time, there are
signs of an increasing tendency on the part of the individual family to
identify with large collective groups and wider social interests.

4. *Changes in Sex Role Norms and Family Patterns*

The legislation removing many external and formal obstacles to married
women attempting to work has probably contributed to the development of housewife role norms that are more compatible with their
participation in economic life. However, there are still strong norms
against working married women that derive their strength from the
persistence of an older family ideal and older role models. Their
perseverance in the face of changed conditions is due largely to their
continued influence in early socialization.

The privilege and ideal of the early middle class, i.e. having a full-
time housewife, has come within the reach of almost all families. Given
that most of the occupations available to married women seeking
employment are among the worst paid and least attractive in the
labour market, it is little wonder that the ideal has become a widespread
reality today.

The housewife ideal of earlier times obtained sustenance from the
notion of a 'feminine mystique' propagated by much of the mass
media. This metaphysical emphasis on feminine qualities and conduct
implicitly contains an attitude unfavourable to working married women.

Modern child psychologists have indicated the deep significance of
emotional contact for the harmonious development of the child. It

has devolved mainly on the mother to satisfy this need in the child. The importance of a *qualitatively* rather than merely a quantitatively satisfying relationship between both parents and the child is currently given greater stress by many psychologists and at the same time there is a marked tendency to abandon the concept that the child needs *one person* to care for it most of the day [28].

A factor that has helped to promote female work participation has been greater equality between girls and boys in the schools. Accompanying the basic reformation of the Swedish school system [29], has been a considerable expansion of education facilities. This should have far-reaching consequences for the future evolution of relations between the sexes.

5. *The Isolation of the Family*

Sociologists have commonly interpreted the increasing frequency of marriage as an indication of its growing significance as a primary group in a society that lacks alternative institutions of co-habitation in durable, loyal and supportive collectives. For, apart from the family and to some extent the work group, the relation of the individual to others is largely characterized by membership in secondary groups: mass movements, organizations, temporary acquaintanceships and anonymous gatherings. Indeed, the sociological literature on the family contains warnings of the undue influence over its members exercised by the little, relatively isolated and in a technical economic sense, irrationally organized family group.

In an analysis of the primary group functions discharged by the family, it is useful to distinguish between two separate problem areas: 'internal' and 'external' family relationships.

In the first category, there is the issue of whether or not the married couple has become chiefly responsible, perhaps even totally responsible for the satisfaction of the psychological needs of family members, viz. sympathy, personal understanding, encouragement and support.

Certain commentators have registered scepticism about the extent to which the family is capable of giving realistic guidance and constructive support to its members. They suggest that the almost total 'acceptance' of the individual by the family can tend to promote resignation and stifle productive dissatisfaction, sometimes a prerequisite to personal attempts to overcome difficulties. It has occasionally been asserted that the process of psychological need-satisfaction by the family, based as it often is on sentimentality, fictitious self-assertion, and the disarming of suspicions, can result in a flaccid adjustment to prevailing social conditions.

One thread in the research on the family has been the quest for criteria for mental health, i.e. for the sort of qualities that the family should promote among its members. One study has suggested the following six qualities of 'human fitness': physical health, intelligence, the ability to relate to and work with people, independence and self-esteem. To the extent that the family strengthens and develops these traits on the part of its members, it can be viewed as fulfilling a positive primary group function [30]. This can be described as a 'therapeutic view' of the family.

In the second category of problems, i.e. those of external family relationships, there appears to be a tendency for the therapeutic view of the family to be based on an implicitly negative evaluation of society outside the private circle. To the family are ascribed new curative functions in an essentially hard world of large, anonymous social units with which the individual finds it difficult, if not impossible, to relate meaningfully.

Sociologists have vented their misgivings about the weakness of the links—personal contact and activities—between the family and other social institutions. It has been suggested that owing to the weakening and dissolution of the ties of kinship and to other generations, the individual has lost the awareness of an organic social context. Under such circumstances, it is asserted, the family in an unfriendly society is not merely a means of guaranteeing emotional satisfaction to the individual; family solidarity and its preservation have become ends in themselves. According to this view, the capitalist industrialized society has become characterized not so much by individual and class egoism, but by family-egoism; a family-egoism that entails, among other things, a rejection of much social obligation, a relative indifference to social and political problems, and a preoccupation with the problems of assuring a place in the sun for its own members [31].

If we recall that in our society married women are expected to be primarily responsible for the therapeutic functions in the family, it becomes strikingly clear that adherence to the therapeutic view of the family, with its latent mistrust of public and social relations, as well as adherence to family-egoistic criticism of the desirability of bridging over the gap between the family and social institutions by drawing the former into many different areas of political, social and productive activity, creates a foundation for certain distinct value judgements about and role ideals for the family.

The therapeutic view of the family places the role of the housewife-mother in the centre of a group separated from society at large, while criticism of the excessive egocentricism of the family would naturally lead to more 'outward directed' interests and ambitions, a greater trust of collective services, co-operation with neighbours and the social institutions of the municipality, and possibly a stronger involvement with political issues.

If women continue to be oriented towards family-primary group life, if they continue to refrain from pursuing an occupation and career for a considerable time while their children are young, and if the discrepancy between the primary group life in the home and secondary group life in economic life remains as great or increases, then the difficulties confronted by women attempting to return to economic life after a period of active motherhood will continue to be almost insuperable.

However, one factor, the changed group structure can help to create a greater incentive for the married woman to take up employment. By breaking up her vocational career, the woman often loses contact with the work group and other secondary group relations; she thus runs the risk of inhibiting her development at an age that is generally highly 'fruitful' for most human beings. The question is whether the married woman will accept the socially isolated position entailed in the role of housewife, an isolation that is particularly pronounced in modern urban and suburban society.

REFERENCES

1. Myrdal, A. and Klein, V., *Women's Two Roles*, London 1956. They found that the average age of mothers with two children was about 34–35 years and that of mothers with three children about 40 years when the youngest child began school.

2. Holm, L., *Hem, arbete och grannar*, National Institute for Consumer Information Papers 1958: 4.

3. Dahlström, E., *op. cit.*, Sections 5.1 and 5.3.

4. Rossi, Alice S., *Equality between the Sexes: An Immodest Proposal*, Daedalus, Spring 1964.

5. Eskola, *Some Factors Influencing the Differentiation of the Roles of Spouses*, Helsinki, 1960.

6. Grönseth, E., *Familie, individ og samfund*, p. 98.

7. Eskola, *op. cit.*, p. 85.

8. Weil, M. W., *An Analysis of the Factors Influencing Married Women's Actual or Planned Work Participation*, American Sociological Review, 1961: 1, p. 91 *et seq.*

9. Goode, W. J., *After Divorce*, Glencoe, Ill. 1956.

10. Dahlsgård, I, *Udearbejdets problematik*, in Familien og samfundet, Copenhagen, 1958.

11. See Pfeil, E., *op. cit.*, p. 384.

12. Dahlström, E., *Mödrar i hem och förvärvsarbete*, Section 6.4, Gothenburg, 1959.

13. Heinilä, K., *Family Companionship and Family Cohesion*, Helsinki, Yearbook of Population Research in Finland, 1961–62.

14. Rådslag 65., *Familjen i morgondagens samhälle*, p. 34.

15. Rossi, *op. cit.*, p. 642.

16. Wolfe, D. H., *Power and Authority in the Family*, in Cartwright, Studies in Social Power, Michigan, 1959.

17. Holter, H., *Kjonnsforskjeller i yrkesatferd*, Kvinnors liv och arbete, Stockholm, 1962, p. 342.

18. Miller & Dollard, *Social Learning and Imitation*.

19. See e.g. Chapter II.

20. Dahlström, E., *Mödrar i hem och förvärvsarbete*, Sections 5.3 and 6.4. Swedish Broadcasting Corporation, Gothenberg, 1959 (unpublished stencil).

21. Boalt, G., *Familjesociologi*, p. 106 *et seq.*, Stockholm, 1959.

22. Holter, H., *Kvinnors liv och arbete*, Stockholm, 1962, p. 329 *et seq.*

23. Thyberg, S., *Kvinnors liv och arbete*, Stockholm, 1962, p. 377 (A summary of this investigation is presented in Chapter V in this book.)

24. Zweig, F., *Women's Life and Labour*, London 1952.

25. Compare Chapter IV, where it is shown that the participation rates of women in the age groups 20–24 years are equal to those of women in the higher age groups, while men in the 20–24 age group have significantly lower participation rates than men in the higher age groups.

26. See Chapter IV, Diagram 3.

27. For a more detailed discussion on the freedom of women to choose between home and work, see Chapter VI.

28. See Chapter III.

29. See Chapter IV.

30. Foote-Cottrell, *Identity and Interpersonal Competence*, Chicago, 1955.

31. Grönseth, *op. cit.*, p. 101. The author refers to Schelsky, T., and *German Studies* from after the second world war.

SEX ROLES AND THE
SOCIALIZATION PROCESS

by SVERRE BRUN-GULBRANDSEN

What is the Socialization Process?

FEW creatures come upon this earth as helpless as a human being and none has to endure such a long and complicated learning process. An individual is required to learn a large 'lesson in humanity' before being accepted as a full member of society. This is not simply a question of formal education; it is primarily one of acquiring behaviour and attitude patterns, learning habits and values which allow an individual to live in a complex society without being drawn into too many or too deep conflicts. The child must be gradually introduced into social life—it must undergo a process of socialization.

Parents are usually the most important intermediaries in the socialization process. More or less consciously and according to plan they attempt to guide the child's development in certain directions. They try to teach the child elementary and gradually more complicated behaviour which is appropriate. They also subject their children to a number of unconscious influences which are quite as important as those which were conscious and planned.

But parents are not alone in rearing the child. Children come into contact with their peers, with adult neighbours, with school teachers and others who, on the whole, subject them to more or less telling influences.

In addition to direct personal contacts with individuals other than their parents, children are influenced by their physical environment and by the mass media to which they are exposed: radio, television, comic series, books, etc.

Most of the influences to which children are subject in their daily life are random and therefore without any clearly noticeable effect. However, many of these influences are systematic, for many socializing intermediaries share a common view of how children ought to behave.

These intermediaries subject children to influences which are quite uniform, systematic and more or less goal-conscious.

Children, too, are prey to systematic influences working in different directions. Parents may have certain opinions while teachers or friends may hold the very opposite view on the same subject. There is no one universally accepted aim in child rearing or in the socialization process. Of course, in any society there is unanimity over the broad objectives. But the details often provoke widely varying views and consequently the various socializing intermediaries do not necessarily reinforce one another in the process of influencing children.

Parents are not entirely free to determine the make-up of their child. They are confronted by certain limitations. In the first place, there are constraints imposed by the child's inborn characteristics. Inherited physical and mental differences predispose children to react differently to different types of influences. However, though our inherited 'equipment' imposes certain limitations these limitations are usually rather wide.

On the other hand, all differences among people or among groups of people cannot be traced exclusively to biological differences. They also spring from the perennial, systematic influences created by differing values and ideals among rearers. The aim in child rearing is not the same in the Congo as in Scandinavia: nor is it the same in Stockholm as in Lofoten, or in the Olsen household as it is in that of the Hansens. For Olsen is strongly religious and abstains from drinking alcohol. He carefully watches his expenditure and is politically conservative. Hansen is an atheist and a political radical. He is fond of a drink now and again and does not accumulate worldly goods. Seen through ordinary Scandinavian eyes, the children in these households appear to be growing up in completely different environments. Yet, were we to view the entire situation from a distance and observe how the parents treat their children in concrete situations, we would probably be struck by the similarities in most cases rather than the differences. And were we to observe the results of the socializing process, we would find as a rule that the children of Olsen as well as those of Hansen have become accepted citizens of the same society: they have all remained comfortably within the limited area of variation upon which society affixes its approval.

Even if the goal of rearing is the same among a group of parents, there is apt to be great disagreement over the best methods to obtain this objective. There are no immutable laws governing child rearing. Some maintain that parental firmness and severity will produce kind and obedient children. Others claim that this goal can best be attained by affectionate and understanding treatment. We shall not attempt at this point to determine which position is most tenable, for the question is exceedingly complicated and warrants lengthy treatment. We merely wish to offer this as an example of how differences in rearing methods may be a reason why the socialization process leads to differing results.

The results of parents' efforts rarely correspond to their expectations. With the best of motivations, and the strongest beliefs, parents often guide their children in totally different directions from those they really intended. They find the undesirable and unexpected results of rearing confusing as well as disappointing and are often inclined to look elsewhere for the explanation. Bad friends, bad comics, 'the times we live in' and inherited characteristics are the rationalizations most often used to account for these results. Such explanations may be true but they can also be an attempt to shun responsibility. Generally speaking, we must accept the fact that child rearing is such a complicated process that there will be a great many unanticipated and unplanned results some of which may strike us as unfortunate.

In this chapter we shall examine environmental influences upon the child primarily from one particular viewpoint, as an expression of social pressures. As mentioned in the introductory paragraphs, society 'requires' that children learn many behaviour norms. Children must learn to behave in certain ways in certain situations. They learn these norms through innumerable environmental influences but particularly from their rearers as these 'norm-senders' encourage certain forms of behaviour on the part of the 'norm-receivers'. Behaviour conforming to these norms is rewarded; behaviour deviating from these norms is punished.

In other words, rearers use positive and negative sanctions systematically. These sanctions can vary from slight, barely perceptible facial expressions to strong praise or rebuke. Positive social sanctions typically take the form of smiles, approving remarks, displays of pleasure, embraces and selection for responsible jobs in the family group. The forms commonly assumed by negative social sanctions are an 'eloquent silence', derogatory remarks, reprimands, sullen looks, rejection of friendship, exclusion from the group and corporal punishment. Some of these measures are used primarily in the family while others are used mainly in the school or in their groups.

Under these continuous social pressures, most individuals learn to adjust their behaviour to avoid negative social sanctions and earn positive social sanctions. In other words, they learn to conform to the norms of parents or group. When new norms or norm systems must be learned, some violations must be expected. Many social norms are not clearly formulated and they must be learned largely through 'trial and error' with the process guided by negative and positive sanctions. But in many cases the feeling of being subjected to external pressure ceases and the individual accepts the norms to such an extent that his behaviour would remain unchanged even were these external pressures removed. In such cases, the norm has been 'internalized' and the sanctions come from the individual himself in the form of satisfaction when he lives up to the norm and dissatisfaction (or 'bad conscience') when he violates the norm.

Sex as the basis of Variations in the Socializing Process

In the foregoing paragraphs, we have discussed the socializing process undergone by children in general terms and listed several reasons why this process produces varying results. The description has been far from exhaustive but has brought out certain points which provide the necessary background for an examination of whether the child's sex has a decisive effect on the manner of its rearing and in turn what effects this has on typical behaviour and attitude patterns.

Psychological differences between the sexes always imply the possibility that they may stem from biological differences, i.e. that they may be genetically sex-linked. But this is extremely difficult to prove. A better approach to our problem would therefore be to study the extent to which actual differences in behaviour and attitudes between the sexes can be traced to environmental influences. This will be the approach taken in this investigation. We do not exclude the possibility that biological differences can be significant in the cases we study; we merely focus our attention on environmental variations.

Of course this path is also fraught with difficulty. By emphasizing environmental variations we encounter the problem that environmental influences vary greatly among different cultures, societies and social classes. To surmount this obstacle in our study of sex differences we must work with groups which are as homogeneous as possible. One glaring weakness in our present knowledge of sex differences is that a disproportionately large part is based on investigations among the Western European or American urban middle class. We know very little about variations within individual cultures or differences between widely differing cultures.

A special difficulty confronting us is that it has become fashionable in our modern society to adhere to a particular ideology, the 'ideology of equality', when discussing differences between the sexes. Among large sectors of the population, it is fully accepted at the verbal level that men and women are equal and ought to have equal rights and that boys and girls ought to be treated as similarly as possible. Yet this widespread verbal acceptance does not accurately reflect ingrained feelings and attitudes or actual behaviour. Such discrepancies create certain difficulties for the researcher seeking to differentiate between expressions of a surface ideology and expressions of a more basic condition. This can be illustrated by the following example.

In one investigation we interviewed 75 randomly chosen mothers, living in Oslo, with children in the second or fifth forms of the primary school [1]. Among other questions we put the following: 'Do you think that boys and girls should be brought up in as similar a manner as possible?' More than 95% of the mothers answered yes to this question.

Now the formulation of this question can be criticized. It is clearly suggestive in the sense that it is 'easier' to answer yes than no. But in our view, it offers a good example of how easy it is to get people to declare verbally their adherence to the idea of sex equality.

When we undertook the investigation we had a corollary hypothesis. We thought that the results would be less unanimous were we to pose more concrete and specific questions relating to the treatment of the child in certain areas. This turned out to be not far from the mark. Among the answers to the question, 'Do you think that boys and girls ought to assist equally with work in the house?', there was considerably less unanimity: 77% answered yes without reservation while 23% had certain reservations or unreservedly answered no. In the same enquiry another question was posed: 'Do you think that parents ought to place great emphasis on teaching girls housework because this will be useful to them if they become housewives?' There was near unanimity among the answers that parents should do just this. In response to a question, about 80% of the mothers felt that boys should have instruction in domestic science at school but most mothers felt that boys should receive less instruction than girls. Moreover, the mothers were not in favour of girls receiving instruction in carpentry at school. A bare 8% thought that girls should receive as much carpentry instruction as that given to boys.

It has long been the practice in Oslo primary schools to offer fewer hours of theoretical subjects to girls than to boys and make up the difference with classes in cooking and sewing. (That girls did as well as boys in the theoretical subjects was irrelevant.) We asked the mothers if they thought that this practice was right or if they wanted girls to have the same amount of instruction in theoretical subjects as that given to boys. Almost 60% thought that the prevailing practice was right, while only 30% disagreed with it. The remainder were uncertain.

Finally, we posed this question, 'Who do you think ought to receive a better education, boys or girls?' Approximately half of the mothers thought that both should receive the same education, while the rest thought that boys should be favoured—were it necessary to make a choice. Not one expressed the view that girls should be so favoured.

Without delving further into the questions, we can interpret the answers already given to indicate quite clearly that the unanimity among the mothers when the question is posed in general terms breaks down and becomes functionally differentiated in line with traditional views when the questions are more specific.

Now, of course, objections can be raised that most of the questions in the investigation were related to the school and that the mothers possibly didn't associate these with rearing issues in the narrow meaning of the term. This is certainly true, but on the other hand it is equally true that the school supervises an essential part of the socializing process undergone by children.

This enquiry among Oslo mothers is rather limited and too much importance should not be ascribed to its findings in detail. There is good reason to believe, however, that its major findings do reflect a typical conflict between the prevailing ideology of equality between the sexes and an unwillingness to accept the full consequences of this ideology. We should also note that this study has been conducted purely on the verbal level. We would probably find even greater variance from the logical derivations of this ideology were we to look at actual behaviour as the basis of comparison.

A small but interesting example of discrepancies between rearing ideology and actual parental behaviour is offered by the results of an investigation by Eva Eckhoff and Jakob Gauslaa [2]. This study covered eighteen families and followed the course of development of their children over many years with frequent interviews and other investigations. Before the children were born, the expectant parents were asked how they intended to bring up their child. After birth, the answers from the parents of boys were compared with those of the parents of girls. No significant differences were found in the rearing ideologies. At a much later stage, however, quite large differences in rearing treatment could be observed. For example, it appeared that girls were breast fed on an average for only three months after birth while boys averaged six months. This difference is so great that it is improbable that it was due to coincidence, despite the fact that the number of subjects was small.

The parents were also interviewed when the children were six years old. On the basis of these interviews, the authors found evidence of remarkable differences between the treatment accorded to boys and that to girls. They found that the mothers treated boys with more emotional 'warmth', gave in to them more easily and punished them less severely than girls. They found expressions of the same tendencies in their interviews with the fathers, though these were less clear. The fathers too appeared to treat the boys with more warmth, gave greater consideration to their wishes and controlled them less than the girls. The authors based these findings on the parents' description of their actual treatment of the children in concrete rearing situations. In this way, the possibility that the 'official' rearing ideology might colour the data was kept to a minimum.

Since the number of subjects in this investigation was small, the authors drew upon material in Eva Nordland's thesis on 'The Relation between Social Behaviour and Child Rearing' [3]. This thesis was much wider in scope but produced roughly the same findings: boys are treated with greater patience, care and attention than girls. However, while girls are not punished more severely than boys, neither is the reverse true.

The results of the Eckhoff and Gauslaa study are most interesting and quite unreconcilable with popular opinion. We have now encountered the first indication that the sex of the child determines the manner of its upbringing and that differentiated treatment starts at a very early stage even though parents may not be entirely aware of the process. Yet differences in treatment can readily be found in many other stages and situations. On the whole, boys are rewarded for behaviour which conforms to the pattern thought suitable for boys by the parents and punished for behaviour deviating from this pattern. The same is true for girls.

This process creates at a fairly early stage a rather clear and somewhat stereotyped image in the minds of individuals of both sexes of what boys and girls are, how they behave and how they ought to behave. In other words, boys as well as girls learn very early in life the basic pattern of social sex roles and the differences between these sex roles. These images may become clearer and more elaborate at a later stage, but their pattern appears to be assimilated as early as in the primary school ages.

This is brought out in an investigation among 120 Oslo school children aged eight and eleven [4]. We related a simple story to these children about two twins, Per and Kari, 'who are as old as you are'. The story line followed the twins from the time they awoke in the morning (and only one made the bed. Was it Per or Kari?) to the time they went to sleep (and only one said a prayer. Was it Per or Kari?). During the course of the day they encountered a number of ordinary situations as well as several more dramatic incidents which called for such qualities as courage, cunning and willingness to sacrifice. Nothing was mentioned in the story about which of the twins did a particular thing and the children were to indicate whether it was the boy or the girl. All together, 36 questions were put to the children.

It appeared from the answers that the boys as well as the girls were largely in agreement. For instance, 94% of the children thought it was Kari that made the bed and 97% thought she was the one who said the prayer. Some of the actions were such that we ourselves had no clear idea of whether they were typical of one sex or the other and on these questions attempts at identification produced great disagreement among the children.

It also appeared that there was slightly more agreement among the 11 year olds than among the 8 year olds. Apparently, the younger children were still able to play a little with functional distribution in an imaginary story. They could amuse themselves by allowing the male to engage in typically female activities and the reverse. However, there was scarcely any evidence of this among the 11 year olds. The pattern of sex roles seemed to be so well established and so fixed a reality that they could not conceive of violating the norms even in an imaginary story. Indeed, we are prompted to suggest—even though our empirical evidence is not complete—that opinion about sex roles is clearer and more absolute among this age group than among any other, even though certain areas are obviously unknown to the members of this group. To them, the rules of the sex roles have become basic laws which may never be violated. The norms are in the main well internalized. This is true both for boys and girls. And it is worth mentioning that all these children were reared by mothers claiming that boys and girls should be brought up in as similar a manner as possible.

In addition to the story of Per and Kari we put several other questions to the children. 'Who do you think help more in the home, boys or girls?' 'Who do you think are more polite to grown-ups, boys or girls?' These questions were designed to find out partly who they thought most often performed certain activities and partly who to the greatest extent possessed certain traits. These were largely similar in purpose to the questions asked about the twins, Per and Kari.

Here, too, we found a good deal of uniformity amongst the answers. There was a high degree of agreement between the answers of boys and girls as groups, although some variations could be observed in the answers to a few questions. We found no greater agreement among the 11 year olds than among the 8 year olds. This may indicate that the younger age group also has a rather clear notion of sex differences in behaviour and personal traits or rather of the stereotyped version of these differences. For a number of questions were such that it was impossible to believe that 8 year old children could have based their answers on personal observation and yet there was broad agreement amongst them as to whether the activity or quality in question was faminine or masculine. These answers suggest that the children were probably expressing many of the stereotyped ideas with which they were indoctrinated at a very young age. Clearly, small children can have only a limited view of life in all its multiplicity but in situations within the scope of their experience, the main threads in the pattern of differentiated sex roles appear to be amazingly clear.

And let us repeat that most of these children have been brought up by mothers who profess verbally to believe in equality and similarity in child-rearing. Yet it is difficult to believe that the children have not learnt a considerable part of their knowledge of adult and child sex differences in their home and from their parents. There has certainly been a significant difference between experience and teaching. Because the parents have so completely internalized their views of social sex roles they are unaware that they clearly and systematically influence their sons and daughters through numerous negative and positive sanctions to accept different behaviour patterns.

In another investigation [5], we selected a group of 80 boys and 80 girls 14–15 years of age and during two school hours asked them to answer a number of questionnaires. One of these questionnaires contained the question, 'Which is a suitable activity for boys and which for girls?' This was followed by a list of 64 different activities, for example: 'Helping with the washing up at home', 'Going to romantic films', 'Not bothering much about torn clothing', 'Coming late for school'. The young people were given five possible answers from which to choose: (1) Suited only to girls; (2) Best suited to girls; (3) Suited equally well (equally poorly) to boys and girls; (4) Best suited to boys; (5) Suited only to boys.

Naturally there was some variation among the answers, but on the whole this was amazingly slight. The answers of both boys and girls were quite consistently similar, irrespective of whether the activity in question was typically masculine or feminine. Among the girls, however, there was some tendency to give answers which were less extreme and to maintain that activities were suited as well (or as poorly) to both sexes. This may indicate that the earlier mentioned ideology of equality awakened a greater response among girls than among boys. But in general it appears that boys as well as girls have practically identical images of the sex roles; they describe them largely in the same way.

We also compared these answers with those of young people in different sections of the country. Again we found that the variation was very slight. The same basic pattern recurred among rural and urban young people and among young people living in the Eastern as well as the Western parts of the country.

We then went a step further. We listed the same activities on another questionnaire but this time posed the question, 'How much do you enjoy engaging in this activity?', 'How much do you enjoy washing up?', 'How much do you enjoy seeing romantic films?', 'How much do you enjoy chopping wood?'. Here too the young people were offered five answers from which to choose, varying from 'very much' to 'very little'. We found an expression of what we can term the 'average interest' of boys and girls in each particular activity. There were great differences between the answers depending upon the sex of the subject. Comparing these differences with the results of the earlier study of how youths view certain activities as typically masculine or feminine, we found, as we expected, certain clear relationships. These can be illustrated by a few examples.

The young people thought it far more suitable for boys to see films abour war and crime and the boys indicated that they greatly enjoyed seeing these types of films while there was no such expression of interest among the girls. Also all claimed that romantic films were particularly well suited to girls and the girls indicated that they greatly enjoyed such films, while the boys expressed no such inclination. Books about travel were equally well suited to both sexes so the young people thought and there was little difference in their stated interest in this activity.

This is not to say that the boys consistently stated that they enjoyed all activities that were typically masculine and that the girls indicated that they enjoyed all typically feminine activities. For instance, the boys did not particularly enjoy chopping wood, despite the fact that this was one of those activities recognized by the group as most typically masculine. But the girls indicated that they enjoyed this activity even less than the boys. Similarly, washing up after a meal, darning socks or mending clothes, enjoyed little popularity among the girls but even less among the boys.

Throughout the study, however, differences in the likes and dislikes of boys and girls for certain activities seemed to be closely related to their stereotyped view of sex roles. Generally speaking, the more an activity was clearly recognised as typically masculine or typically feminine, the larger was the difference in preferences for that activity between the sexes; members of the sex to which a given activity is allocated according to the popular notion of sex roles showed a more positive or less negative attitude towards the activity than members of the other sex.

Here we encounter a crucial feature of the entire socialization process and particularly the way in which the stereotyped view of sex roles is assimilated. Children are not led to accept the sex role pattern by force or violence, but usually by more subtle means. Boys are encouraged to engaged in typically masculine activity and rewarded for doing so. As a consequence, such activity becomes more enjoyable for them and they develop greater interest in or a more positive attitude to it. They tend to continue to engage in such activity and in the event meet with further reward, reinforcing their positive attitude and encouraging them to continue such behaviour. In contrast, girls who attempt to engage in typically masculine activity will often be 'punished' for not behaving in accordance with their established sex role. Their immediate pleasure in the activity will gradually lessen as they receive clear indications from their environment that such activity on the part of a girl is frowned upon. They will become increasingly more reluctant to undertake such activity and eventually find it uninteresting. During the same period they are encouraged to engage in typically female activities, which in turn are taboo to boys; the latter are 'punished' if they attempt to engage in such activities.

We must keep in mind that this differentiated rearing of boys and girls starts very early and lasts throughout life. From early childhood on, children receive almost innumerable small 'pushes' in systematically different directions. As we saw with the 8 year olds, the major threads in the established pattern of sex roles are swiftly assimilated. And children gradually develop different attitude patterns and preferences which are appropriate to their particular sex role. They learn to enjoy what they are supposed to enjoy according to the views prevalent in their environment and on the whole they become satisfied with their sex role. We shall have occasion to return to this point subsequently.

As the sex role pattern becomes assimilated and this is followed by relatively positive attitudes to the accepted roles, certain behavioural inclinations are created within each sex. This is a process which makes people view certain sex differences as inherent. It becomes 'natural' for a woman to behave in a manner which she has learnt to be typically feminine and a man to behave in a manner which he has learnt to be typically masculine. This feeling gradually becomes so strong that it is difficult to change it. This confronts those who hope to obtain greater equality between the sexes with one of their major obstacles. Many people interpret an attempt to introduce greater similarity to sex roles as an attempt to change human nature. Developments thus far have disproved many of the assertions and predictions of opponents to female emancipation in the past century. And the future will probably prove that many differences which are now viewed as 'natural' are in reality a product of early indoctrination.

In our material on the conventional views of sex roles there was some interesting information about asocial or delinquent behaviour. We intend to examine this more closely but first let us see what the children have to say themselves.

The story of the two twins Per and Kari, included behaviour that was improper in many of the situations. For example, one of the twins did not do homework, was late for school, often fought, was troublesome in class, cheated and stole money from the mother. Who behaved in such a way? The children had no doubt, 'It was Per'. The overwhelming majority of boys and girls immediately ascribed all disapproved behaviour to Per. The 8 year olds were almost 90% in agreement that Per was the malefactor while the corresponding percentage among the 11 year olds was an average 97%.

We find the same tendency almost as clearly expressed in the answers to direct questions about who carries out practical jokes, who teases more, who is more disobedient to parents, etc.: 13 out of 14 types of behaviour which are largely asocial were clearly ascribed to the boys. The one exception was, 'to tell tales on others', which most agreed was more typical of girls.

In the study of the 14 and 15 year olds, the subjects were asked to indicate the extent to which certain types of behaviour was suitable for boys or girls. The questionnaire contained about 20 more or less asocial or delinquent types of behaviour ranging from 'To be careless with one's homework', to 'To break and enter and steal'. The majority of the young people thought that all such behaviour was better suited to (or rather less poorly suited to) boys than to girls and the more delinquent the behaviour, the greater agreement there was that it was more typically masculine.

These results suggest that asocial and delinquent behaviour is clearly associated with the concept of masculinity assimilated by children at an early age. They seem to feel that almost all behaviour that is negative and improper falls within the male province. Girls by contrast possess many good and positive qualities. They are generally kind. This they themselves maintain and the boys agree.

One may wonder whether it is possible for an ordinary 8 year old to have such a clear image of asociality in male nature. Of course, the image does not have to be correct in the sense that it accurately depicts actual differences in the behaviour of the sexes, but it seems as if the picture was quite clear. The stereotypes are 'internalized'. This may partly be due to the tendency to generalize from personal experience at school or at play, but such an explanation is far from complete. Throughout much of the socializing process, children are continually subjected to the notion that males possess certain socially undesirable traits manifesting themselves in asocial behaviour. As a result, even when totally unfamiliar behaviour is described to an 8 year old, as long as he senses that it is asocial, he will tend to view it as typically masculine.

Interestingly enough, because asocial or delinquent behaviour is largely ascribed to the male role, the environment tends to react less strongly to a boy than to a girl committing the same delinquent act. In the former case, expectations act to soften the reaction. Indeed, if the act is not too serious, it is often viewed as a confirmation of the boy's 'masculinity'. Boys shouldn't be too nice, too 'soft' or over-conformist. In contrast, a girl engaging in asocial behaviour awakens a strong sense of outrage. For not only has she committed a delinquent act; she has also violated a social norm of her sex role.

We asked the children what their reaction would be to male and female friends engaging in certain types of socially undesirable behaviour. There were five possible answers to choose from, ranging from admiration to strong disapproval. In all cases of asocial behaviour, the children judged the girls more severely than the boys. In another investigation among Danish school children[6], Elsa Øyen obtained strikingly similar results. Our children were asked to select a fitting punishment for men and women who had broken the law in various ways. The girls as well as the boys wanted to punish women more severely than men for committing the same illegal act. Of course this feeling is not carried over into criminal law, where if anything punishment is mitigated for women. But it is, nevertheless, a distinct feature of social relations.

In the preceding material, we have examined certain aspects of the role distribution between the sexes. Sex roles are still clearly defined even if the differences are somewhat less clear than those prevailing in our grandparents' time. But why is it that certain forms of behaviour are ascribed to the male role and others to the female role? This interesting problem has yet to be solved and it is too large to be treated in detail in this chapter. Some insight can be gained by taking up a new distinction, namely that between the masculine and feminine ideals. In contrast to sex roles, which are marked by certain forms of behaviour attributed to one sex more than the other, sex ideals are characterized by certain positively-valued traits ascribed to each of the sexes. The existence of a trait can be demonstrated by certain forms of external behaviour, but there are other means as well. Behaviour that best demonstrates possession of a trait included in the sex ideal is the sort that is most strongly ascribed to the sex role.

Yet, as we have said, there are means other than behaviour to demonstrate possession of certain traits. For example, it is evident that a certain degree of physical strength is a quality included in the male ideal, yet it is not necessary for a man to be a blacksmith or a ditchdigger—both typically masculine activities—in order to demonstrate this quality. Participation in athletic activities can achieve the same purpose. In other words, negatively valued behaviour, say boxing, can be used to demonstrate positively valued traits.

Among the traits most closely associated with the male rather than the female ideal are independence, daring, courage, wisdom, physical strength and practical and technical knowledge and skill. Those qualities most frequently attributed to the female ideal are kindness, meekness, helpfulness, sentimentality and good nature. The lists are far from exhaustive but serve nevertheless to illustrate important differences. For a man to demonstrate his masculinity, he is forced to engage in behaviour requiring great effort, in some cases greater effort than is desirable. Depending on the capabilities of the man, this effort will take a respectable form and result in fame, wealth and high status or in deviant behaviour. In contrast, a woman can demonstrate her femininity by relatively less demanding efforts. The external rewards may not be as great but neither will be the effort and consequently the possible failure.

It can hardly be denied that men have played and will continue to play the most important role in a number of fields which are highly valued in our society. Men dominate such fields as technology and science, invention and discovery, art and cultural life in the widest sense, the executive, legislative and judicial branches of government, and industry and trade. However, men are also predominant among the population in our prisons and alcoholic institutions and in our suicide statistics. There are many more men than women who die in accidents[7]. This trend begins in childhood and increases steadily up to about the age of 30. At that point, the rate of deaths by accident in Norway among men is fifteen times as great as that among women. There is a relatively high premature death rate among men. Many more men than women die at a fairly young age from illnesses which can partly be blamed on overloading the human organism, such as ulcers and heart disease.

Thus, while the male may enjoy certain advantages under the prevailing pattern of sex roles, he also suffers distinct disadvantages: asociality, illness and premature death. We think that there is a connection here and that the causes can be traced to the upbringing we give our children. Boys notice quite early that the symbols of masculinity are rewarded and they work hard to achieve such rewards. This leads not only to great successes but also to defeats. The athlete who collapses in the attempt to win a gilded medal offers a tragic example of far more common events in life where men try to demonstrate that they possess the qualities which since early childhood have been held up as part of the 'masculine' ideal.

But since the male role entails so many drawbacks and so much discomfort, should one not expect greater objection to it and more refusals to carry it out? Wouldn't a 'male movement' be more likely than the 'female movement' we all know? What do the men say themselves?

Are they pleased with their sex role? Are the women as dissatisfied as is suggested in the public debate? We put some simple questions to all the children in our two studies on just this point. We asked them, 'who do you think has a nicer and easier time of it, boys or girls?'. Only 24% thought that the boys were better off while 57% thought this was true for the girls. 20% thought that there was no difference. There was little difference between the answers of the 11 year olds and the 8 year olds. But the answers of the boys and girls were different in certain respects. Approximately the same number of girls and boys thought that girls were better off, i.e. 55% of the girls and 58% of the boys. But only 14% of the boys as compared to 35% of the girls thought that boys were better off. On the other hand 29% of the boys, as compared to 10% of the girls thought that there was no difference. Generally speaking our data indicates that the children of both sexes felt that the girls had the greatest advantages, though the girls become aware of the advantages of the boys' role at an earlier stage.

More than 70 of the mothers of these children were also interviewed and asked the same question. The answers differed considerably from those of their children. 46% of the mothers felt that the boys had the better time of it while only 13% thought that the girls were better off. The rest thought that there was no difference.

Before we look at these results more closely let us first observe the reactions to a few other questions. We asked the children, 'who do you think will be better off when they grow up, boys or girls?'. Of those asked, 71% thought that the girls would be better off. Only 15% thought that the boys would be better off and 14% said that there would be no difference. There were no distinct differences between the answers of the two sexes or the two age groups, though there was a slight tendency for the older children to think that the boys would be better off. The mothers, however, had a completely different opinion than the children. As many as 57% thought that there was no difference, 28% of the mothers thought that the boys would be better off while 15% thought that the girls would be better off.

Much has been written about the camaraderie of boys and their pleasant imaginative play and the rivalry and disharmony among girls as well as their quiet and uninteresting forms of play. The children were asked, 'who do you think enjoy themselves better together, boys or girls?'. Here the answers were also in the girls' favour. 56% answered 'girls', 23% 'boys' and 21% 'no difference'. The boys were more inclined than the girls to answer 'boys', a tendency which was true to a lesser degree among the 11 year olds than among the 8 year olds.

Again the reaction of the mothers differed. 47% thought that there was no difference. 36% thought that the boys enjoyed themselves more while only 18% that the girls did.

The children's answers to the preceding questions give no indication that they considered the boys to be privileged. On the whole, the girls seem to be rather more satisfied with their sex role than the boys. This is quite contrary to the view popularly held. And in any event, it is contrary to the views of the mothers who might be expected to be most qualified to answer the question—second only to the children themselves. But there is reason to believe that the mothers' answers are projections of their own opinions and reflect the more stereotyped ideas of the sex roles held by adults. But while from the adult viewpoint the role of the male appears to be more favourable, men having greater opportunity to attain higher status and the more highly salaried positions, the 'apprenticeship' appears to be an exceedingly arduous one to the boys. For in their youth they are required to develop the qualities and skills that will later allow them to win in a competitive society.

There was yet another question put to the children: 'Would you rather be a girl or a boy if you could choose freely, or would you be uncertain of your choice?' Most of the children indicated that they would rather be what they were, although 13% deviated from this pattern, most of whom were uncertain of their choice. A breakdown of this average by sex reveals that 12% of the girls and 15% of the boys were unwilling to choose their own sex. This difference is very slight but it is significant that we find no stronger tendency among the girls to want to change their sex, a tendency which is quite common among adult female subjects.

Among the 8 year olds, only 7% gave answers deviating from the majority while among the 11 year olds as much as 20% (17% for girls and 23% for boys) fell into this category. This may suggest that boys as well as girls between the ages of 8 and 11 obtain a more subtly differentiated picture of the related advantages and disadvantages of the sex roles, with the result that more begin to wonder whether they were lucky in the draw. In any event there were no clear differences between the answers of the two age groups grouped according to sex.

From the earlier mentioned results, one could reasonably anticipate that boys would want to 'opt out' of their sex more often than girls. But we found only weak tendencies in this direction.

We also asked the 14 and 15 year olds which sex they would rather be and their answers were quite different. Only 71% of the girls indicated that they wanted to be female, while 29% either were uncertain or wanted to be male. Among the boys, 84% wanted to be male and most of the others were uncertain. The tendency to choose one's own sex is significantly greater among boys than girls. In another and smaller sample, we found the even stronger tendencies along the same lines. The shift probably reflects the fact that the young people have begun to acquire greater insight into the value system of society. They have discovered gradually that the male role is valued more highly. Prior to this point, both boys and girls had not noticed this difference. Indeed they had considered the girls to be privileged. However, after a rather free and secure childhood, about the time of puberty girls are guided into the sex role of an adult woman. Then they discover not only several restrictions and obstacles that they were not aware of but also that their role is not highly valued. At the same time, they become aware that even if there is great pressure on them to behave in a feminine manner, there are very small expectations that they can participate in a competitive society. They discover, too, the advantages of the female role; that an academic degree or occupation are not necessarily basic to their success and that appearance and internal qualities can often be more important criteria. Not surprisingly, we found that filmstars and 'kind hearted people', especially those making some kind of humanitarian contribution, become the ideals of girls in their adolescence.

For the boys, the transition to the adult male role is a totally different experience. Youth to them meant great freedom. Now admiration is seriously awakened for masculine, i.e. active, forward and aggressive behaviour. Their ideals are war heroes, explorers, athletes, and supermasculine film stars. They feel under pressure to demonstrate that they too possess the traits of these ideals. Basking in the admiration of masculinity prevalent in their surroundings, they walk out into the world with the feeling that there is no alternative to making an active effort in a competitive society. They recognize that it can often lead to failure and they fear possible failure.

From the standpoint of society, the aim of the socializing process is to find individuals able and willing to fill the roles and positions with which society is constructed. It is not sufficient to differentiate education in schools and practical apprenticeships. Different personality types are required for different jobs and society is interested to ensure that at any time there is an adequate supply of different personality types[8]. Society is still such that some must become officers in the army while others must attend to the sick. Some must swing the hammer while others must type. The question of who is to end up in which occupation is by no means a trivial one. In the organization of a differentiated socialization process, it is theoretically possible to use many different criteria as the basis for selecting individuals for different types of socializing. In our society the choice as a rule has largely been based on one very clear criterion, i.e. the sex of the individual. This choice was of course no accident. In earlier days, the relatively greater muscular strength of the man and the fact that women are child-bearing were probably decisive factors. Yet upon this foundation has been erected a system which has greater implications than that the men perform the heaviest work and the women look after the children.

Today, in our modern society, there is even less objective foundation for the choice of sex as an important criterion in differentiating the socialization process. The traditional system, however, has gained such a firm hold that almost by itself the process continues; parents consciously or unconsciously rear their children largely in the same way as they were reared: change is introduced, but slowly and over a span of generations.

We may ask whether attempts should be made to increase the pace of change? One cannot give a scientific answer to this question, but it does seem only fair to allow women gradually to obtain their share of accidents, ulcers and heart failure as well as criminality, alcoholism and suicide and receive in compensation more managing directorships.

REFERENCES

1. Brun-Gulbrandsen, S., *Kjønnsrolle og asosialitet*, Oslo, 1958. Stens.

2. Eckhoff, E. and Gauslaa, J., *Kjaerlighet og trygghet i oppdragelen av gutter og piker*. Tidskrift for samfunnsforskning, nr 4, 1960.

3. Oslo, Universitetsforlaget, 1955.

4. Brun-Gulbrandsen, S., *op. cit.*

5. Brun-Gulbrandsen, S., *Kjønnsrolle og ungdomskriminalitet*. Universitetsforlaget, Oslo, 1958.

6. Øyen, E., *Retssystemet i unge øjne*. Oslo, 1960. Unpublished disser-
tation.

7. Brun-Gulbrandsen, S. and Ås, B., *Kjønnsroller og ulykker*. Tidskrift for samfunnsforksning, nr 2, 1960.

8. Skårdal, O., *Towards a Theory of Occupational Orientation*. Särtryck
från Meldinger fra Norges Landbrukshøskole, nr 6, 1960.

PARENTAL ROLE DIVISION AND THE CHILD'S PERSONALITY DEVELOPMENT

by PER OLAV TILLER

IN the preceding chapter, mention was made of the growing acceptance of the ideology of equality in child rearing. Sverre Brun-Gul-brandsen found that more than 95% of a group of mothers answered 'yes' to the question whether they thought that boys and girls ought to be brought up in as similar a manner as possible. Since many parents are guided by this egalitarian ideology in the treatment of their children in concrete situations, they are often genuinely surprised to discover that their boys and girls have developed complementary personality traits. To find an explanation for such discrepancies we must look to the many unconscious attitudes, expectations and reactions directed by the parents to their children; for ultimately these prove to be as decisive in the development of the children as their parents' professed ideals.

The view that the conscious goals of child rearing—the ideals and expectations that are verbally expressed and figure prominently in the indoctrination of the child—are the most decisive factors in the child's upbringing is widely held. This accounts for the frequent expressions of disappointment when child rearers discover that the child is not living up to the ideals inculcated in it. It also explains why undesirable forms of behaviour in a child are frequently attributed to its 'nature', a 'nature', moreover, that is considered to be different for each sex.

It is therefore essential to recognize that many factors influence social learning along with the conscious parental goals in child rearing. Social development always occurs in an emotional context and in a group upon which the individual is dependent for his existence such as the family. Socializing proceeds on the basis of dynamic emotional ties which exist within this structure. To understand the workings of the socializing process, therefore, it is important to avoid an undue emphasis on conditional mechanisms—such as positive and negative sanctions—and examine the total emotional situation in which the child finds itself and how this situation is perceived by the child.

Early Phases of Development

The most important and profound influences on the formation of the individual are those introduced in the earlier stages of its development. For, as the child becomes progressively more enmeshed in already learned reaction patterns, it becomes less malleable and hence less susceptible to outside influences. This process has perceptive as well as affective aspects. As perception develops there is increasing consistency in the interpretation of sensory impressions or stimuli. These eventually both perform signal functions and serve as symbols. In the event, the child's memory begins to function and it becomes capable of reacting according to its own concepts. Viewed from the motivational standpoint, we can see that the child possesses a large armoury of potential reaction forms and learns to select some while inhibiting others. The selected reactions are combined and further integrated into a steadily more complex behaviour pattern.

This learning process occurs throughout in an emotional context and on the basis of needs or states of tension of a biological or physiological kind. These states of tension will be reduced or eliminated depending on certain reactions in the child or changes in its environment. They will remain or intensify if these reactions or changes are not forthcoming or if new reactions appear. The newly born child is almost entirely without experience and only modestly equipped to reduce tension through instinctive automatic reactions; it is helpless and almost totally dependent on other people.

From the start, then, the sources of tension reduction are not found in the child itself. The child will begin quite early to perceive another human being, usually the mother, as such a source. In the beginning the mother probably represents the very absence of tension. As long as the child is not separated from the mother, that is, before birth, no special states of tension are experienced, or if they are experienced they cause no anxiety because there is an automatic process of need-reduction.

However, when the child experiences a need and its demands for reduction or satisfaction are not met or remain unanswered, two new elements enter the picture. First, the child experiences anxiety and the feeling of helplessness. Secondly, it becomes aware of the fact that another human being, the mother, controls the means to satisfy its needs. Control is exercised in the sense that satisfaction can be given or withheld. Consequently, in our society—as in most cultures we know of—the child will primarily view the mother as the means to reduce its needs.

From the start, the mother, consciously or unconsciously, makes use of this control in the rearing process. Satisfaction can be bestowed as a reward for certain types of behaviour on the part of the child. Or— possibly a better way of viewing it—satisfaction can be withheld as a sanction or penalty for undesirable behaviour on the child's part. The simplest and most familiar example of this is the mother's attempt to teach the child regularity in the satisfaction of its needs. Feeding must take place at certain times; the child is to go to sleep at certain times etc. This method of child rearing is not universal. There are societies where the timing of satisfaction is determined almost wholly by the child's physiological 'rhythm' and there are many individuals amongst us who would subscribe to this type of 'self-regulation'. However, even under such conditions, the form of satisfaction, as well as the degree of tension reduction, will remain essentially dependent on the mother's disposition. When irritated with the child's behaviour, she will tend to make the process of need-satisfaction less enjoyable for the child.

Consequently, it becomes vital to the child to reach and be accepted by the mother, to gain her love. After 'I' has become separated from 'you', subject and object, the child continually seeks a reunion. This presupposes also that the child is capable of perceiving itself, ego, as object, as the object of the alter's attitudes, feelings and impulses. This step represents a very important phase in the development of the ego. The desire to reunite with the alter and the need to be accepted and loved by the mother, provide a very effective foundation for learning the mother's views, for learning the concepts of good and evil.

If the mother and her attendant tension reduction are not forth-coming the child will experience anxiety and despair. It will attempt with the means at its disposal to retrieve the mother; it will resort to a symbolic representative for its need-satisfaction or tension reduction. Along with the separation of 'I' from 'you', subject and object, the mother is present in the child's imagination and the latter attempts to combine this image with external indications of the mother's presence. One way of achieving this is for the child itself to represent the mother; by imitation, to reproduce her voice and movements. In a sense, the child attempts to play the mother's role. Eventually the child will perceive that role playing can bring with it need-satisfaction, for instance by singing to itself and then falling asleep, the sleep being conditional upon the song.

In similar ways, the child will gradually become capable of feeding itself, seeking warmth etc. If we view this process as an imitation of the behaviour of the mother, the child is not only object but also subject in this situation. In this way both separation is overcome and anxiety is dispelled by the child in its imagination becoming the mother feeding the child as well as the child being fed by the mother. This represents an early form of identification, perhaps the most effective mechanism in social learning, that is, the learning of roles.

To ascertain the importance of this process in the socializing of the child, it is necessary to examine in greater detail certain characteristic features of the structure of the family. We have already observed that the mother usually cares for the need-satisfaction of the child. This is true for almost all cultures of which we are aware and has a biological basis: the physiological equipment of the mother. Yet there is considerable variation in the extent to which other members of the family participate in child care.

Industrialization and the transition from an agrarian to an urban household has had the consequence that men perform their vocation or function outside the family premises. In an earlier period, the family was to a much larger extent a cohesive working unit. Today, the essential role of the man, the father, is to provide the family with the material necessities of life by earning the medium of exchange, money. Thus, for a start, the man's *direct* functional relationship with the child has been weakened.

At the same time, the mother's role in the primary group—the family—has correspondingly altered; her most important tasks have become those largely related to child care. In the event, she has acquired a decidedly more central position in the rearing process than the father and possibly one even more central than she held in earlier times.

Clearly, these changes may have had important effects on the pattern of contact relations between parents and children and hence on the character of the socializing process. With the spread of an egalitarian ideology, we might perhaps expect to find less differentiation of adult sex roles in the socializing process. Yet though the child rearers may consciously entertain the goal of equality of treatment, the experience of the children themselves will nevertheless differ in at least one essential respect; each will enjoy a different degree of contact with the parent of the same sex. Let us examine more closely the significance of this difference.

We have already indicated that all children will at first identify with the mother. In the earliest stages of development, the mother is usually the most important sources of need-satisfaction for boys as well as girls. We can therefore reasonably expect that children of *both* sexes will initially tend to identify with the mother.

However, it must be emphasized that the child's development of social relationships with the mother and father occurs in phases. At the start, there is no real *social* contact between mother and child. A child can hardly be considered a social individual before it has begun to discriminate between itself and other persons. It must first have begun to perceive itself as an individual, separate from others. In other words, it must experience a certain degree of ego development. The child's ability to discriminate, however, occurs at a very early stage and is associated with a gradual severance of the primary connexion to the mother, a separation that is followed by feelings of tension and anxiety.

The process of separation is encouraged not only by the rearer, but also by a tendency to liberate itself on the part of the child during the course of its growth and maturation. If we observe the development of the child in the first year, we will see an individual who is gradually becoming more independent and exercising greater freedom of move- ment: first from the embryonic state within the womb, then from the dependence upon one human being as a source of food and then from the protection and control of the family. This readily discernible trend in the child's development must be kept in mind when we discuss the possible effects of parental or maternal absence on the child.

Later Phases of Development

We have already indicated that the adult family roles, those of the mother and father, in our society are relatively complementary. The differentiated rearing of boys and girls can be viewed as the lynch-pin in socialization to these complementary adult roles. In socialization, identification with one or the other parent is an effective foundation for learning one or the other sex role.

For almost all children the earliest primary object of identification is the mother. Yet, this need not be decisive as far as the sex role is concerned. For, in the infant state the child is hardly capable of dis- criminating between the sexes. Such perceptual discrimination does not occur until a later stage; it is particularly noticeable between the ages of three and five. It is considered fairly normal for children during these years to identify with the parent of the same sex. The mechanism involved in this process of identification is a highly complicated one and cannot be examined more closely here. The important point to note is that the process of sex-determined identification is highly dependent on the prevailing structure of the family. There is reason to suggest that such identification may be relatively easier for the girl, largely because she is in a position to build directly upon an already developed identification with the mother.

Compensatory Masculinity

Another reason why it may be easier for the girl to identify with the mother than it is for the boy to identify with the father is that the parental role division in our society is such that the girl enjoys the presence of an adult model, to imitate and identify with, so much more often than the boy. The girl daily encounters a human being who demonstrates the type of behaviour associated with her sex role, a role which is both expected and required from her. By contrast, the boy often lacks regular, intimate contact with the father as the latter engages in behaviour typically associated with the male sex role.

Since boys as well as girls are today commonly reared by, and identify with, the mother one may wonder how it is possible for the sex role behaviour of men to continue to appear so complementary to that of women. It almost appears as though boys and girls react in disparate ways to the same rearing experience.

However, it is evident, as has earlier been observed, that irrespective of the sex of the parent exercising decisive authority in the rearing process, boys and girls will be subjected to different treatment as well as different expectations on the part of the rearers. So much is clear. But what needs to be further explored are the different foundations upon which boys and girls learn their respective sex roles. If the sex role is not internalized through the process of identification, how is it adopted by the boy?

Given the circumstances of our modern family type, it seems likely that boys will have an insufficient foundation for masculine identification. In this context, the concept of 'compensation' emerges as an important explanatory factor. Compensation is one type of adjustment mechanism related to the child's need to view himself in a certain way and have others view him in such a way. To the extent that the 'self-image' is unsatisfactory in some respect or deviates too markedly from the idea, the child will attempt in some way to compensate for this deficiency.

This raises the question of the extent to which the concept of 'masculinity' in our culture is essentially a compensatory device, based upon deep feelings within male children that they are inadequate in some respect or deviate too widely from the ideal. Before we discuss in greater detail the content and manifestations of compensatory masculinity, a short survey of certain relevant empirical findings appears warranted [1,2].

Empirical Data on Father Absence due to Work

One method of examining the typical modern urban family is to study an extreme example of this family type, that is, a family or families in which the father is almost completely absent or more or less permanently separated from the rest of the family. One such study has been an investigation of the children of Norwegian sailor families. The following description of this investigation is limited to those aspects of the adjustment of these children which are particularly relevant to the sex role problem.

The sailors' children were compared with children in the same locality, in families in which the father was at home some part of each day. Altogether 80 children were selected. Half were sailors' children, the remaining half were the control group. Each group had an equal number of boys and girls and the children were all about eight to nine years of age. In order to obtain an extreme case of paternal absence, it was stipulated that the father should have been at sea for most of the child's life. As it turned out, this resulted in a group of children whose fathers were all of officer rank. Consequently, the control group was selected from among children of fathers of higher position and in general of the same income level and social status as the ship officers.

Paternal absence in the homes of ship officers lasted on the average for a period of two years with intermittent visits of an average of several months or less. It is reasonable to expect that in such families the mother is the more important rearing authority and that she provides the only adult model, the only object of identification for the children during a considerable part of their development. Were a prediction to be made regarding the development of boys in such a family situation it would probably be that they would tend to identify with the feminine role almost as much as their sisters. It would be interesting to see whether there are compensatory mechanisms that make it possible for these boys to adjust reasonably well to the masculine role even in this family environment. There is little doubt that the mothers in these families quite consciously attempt to rear their sons to adjust to the male role. However, as we have previously observed, conscious rearing efforts may be a less significant factor in the child's development than the dynamic mechanisms and tendencies created within the child by the family situation.

One purpose of the study was to isolate a number of predictable psychylogical differences between the children of ship's officers and the control group, differences perhaps directly attributable to father absence from the homes of the experimental group. One intervening variable that had to be taken into account was the mother's adjustment to the situation. We assumed that the lonely mother would tend to turn to the child to compensate for dissatisfactions due to the father's absence. This assumption appeared to be borne out by the findings. Ship's officers' wives tended to be more isolated and more inclined to rely on their children for company than the mothers in the control group. Moreover, they tended to be considerably more protective in the treatment of their children than the mothers in the control group. This was true of their treatment of their daughters as well as their sons.

This pattern of over-protectiveness explains a great number of the differences between the two groups. We found for instance that the ship's officers' children were in general less mature emotionally and socially and more dependent on their mothers than the children in the control group. We also found that the boys from homes with the father often absent experienced special difficulties in relating to their peers. There were signs that these boys tended to inhibit their aggressions and there was some indication that they preferred to play with girls rather than boys. It appears likely that their handling of aggression problems as well as their excessive dependence created special difficulties in social exchange with other boys. That such difficulties were experienced more frequently by the boys than by the girls from sailor families suggests, too, that father absence has a greater effect on boys than on girls.

This would also follow from our assumptions regarding the potential identification conflict of the sons of absent fathers. We found, as did others in earlier investigations, that the sons of absent fathers tended to idealize their fathers more strongly than the boys in the control group. As well, several findings suggested that the former identified with the feminine role more strongly; in general they displayed more 'feminine' traits than the boys in the control group. We had also hypothesized that the feminine identification in the sons of absent fathers would probably be disguised or masked by compensatory masculine traits. That is to say, we had assumed that the sailors' sons would simultaneously display exaggerated masculine traits along with feminine traits. The results offered much to support the hypothesis of compensatory masculinity in the sons of absent fathers. Moreover, this meant some indirect support for the hypothesis of feminine identification in this group.

There is also much evidence to support the idea that compensatory masculinity is accompanied by a tendency to develop an attitude pattern or ideology characterized by a basically rigid view of masculinity and femininity, of the 'proper' roles of men and women. Perhaps one could tentatively put forward the notion of compensatory ideologies, compensatory in the sense that they avert identification conflict or an identity conflict and defend the man against feelings of inadequacy.

One attendant characteristic of compensatory masculinity is anxiety about deviant behaviour and feelings of inadequacy whenever the individual recognizes feminine traits within himself. This can lead to a limitation of the degree and quality of contact between the two sexes. To have contact with a woman on a level other than purely sexual can be experienced as shameful and deviant. Since men with a compensatory masculine strain running through their personality have little real understanding of masculinity, their attitudes toward the sex role become rigid and oversimplified. This type of man will be on guard against behaviour that does not clearly conform to his version of the sex role. Naturally, this places great constraint on their contacts with other individuals and their actions. This will be particularly true of certain aspects of family life. Thus, compensatory masculinity can lead to a lessening of the degree and the quality of contact between man and wife and father and children.

Ironically enough, the anxiety about certain aspects of family life experienced by men of this type, in conjunction with contempt for and protest against the mother, can result in keeping the man away from the family home and estrange him from wife and children. In this way, such men are likely to develop in turn into 'absent' fathers.

Data on Early Maternal Absence

Previously we have discussed or described a common family situation in our society, though in an extreme form in the case of the sailor's children. Given the frequent incidence of father absence in families, it is possible to study this phenomenon at length. For paternal absence appears to be symptomatic of the family institution in our culture. However, when we turn to attempts to study the development of the child in the absence of the mother we meet with a serious difficulty. It is almost impossible to study this question without limiting one's subjects to children in an institutional situation. In other words, there are hardly any motherless families with children growing up with their father as their sole or predominant parent. It is a commentary on the strength of the traditional family form that if one wants to study the effects of maternal absence, one must confine oneself to the extreme case of the dysfunctioning of the family. This phenomenon has created much misunderstanding about the effects on children of the mother's absence due to work.

Central to this discussion are the well-known data from studies carried out by Rene Spitz and others, which show that children separated from the mother at a very early age and placed in an institution readily develop a syndrome termed 'anaclitic depression' characterized by regression, lack of contact, rejection of other people and retarded development [3,4]. A number of studies of this type provide a rather forbidding picture of the harmful effects of maternal deprivation. Bowlby has gathered much data to support this view [5]. This literature has constantly been cited in discussions about the mother's role, often as support for the argument that the mother should not work outside the home.

There are several reasons why the results of such experiments with institutional children cannot be applied to the case of maternal absence from the family due to work. Firstly, most mothers working outside the home have children who are much older than the subjects of the 'institutional' studies. Secondly, the children in institutions suffer from many other deprivations and frustrations of their need for contact, etc. not least of which is the total lack of contact with the father. It is a testimony to the strength of the traditional pattern of parental role distribution in our society that few if any specialists have interpreted the symptoms of institutional children as stemming from insufficient contact with the father. Yet surely this factor cannot be ignored.

Data Concerning the Children of Employed Women

Far more relevant to our discussion are the studies carried out among the children of employed women. For these offer the clearest parallel to studies of paternal absence due to work. This is not to deprecate the worth of the studies of Spitz and others. They provide a good foundation for our knowledge of early ego development and also throw much light on the basic needs of infants. However, popularizations of their findings, usually in the form of unwarranted generalizations, have been responsible for much unnecessary anxiety and feelings of guilt on the part of many mothers. Little attempt has been made to distinguish carefully between the effects of a broken home in general, the low living standard of the family, and an unfavourable family situation on the one hand, and maternal absence on the other.

It should be noted at the outset that many of the studies of the children of working mothers have often been poorly controlled. They have frequently produced inconsistent results, results which have suggested contradictory theoretical explanations. They have seldom focused on the truly central aspects of the child's personality and have not always used methods or measures which have been sufficiently reliable. Having registered these reservations at the start, we may now turn to some of these studies.

One extensive European study is of particular interest. Ferguson and Cunnison studied a group of boys in Glasgow all of whom had left school at a particular date in 1947 [6]. The family background of the boys was thoroughly investigated including, among other things, the incidence of parental absence. The data on the whole suggested that there was an association between delinquency and bad environmental conditions in general; however there was no correlation between employment on the part of the mother and delinquency in the child. Indeed, the number of boys who committed delinquent acts between the ages of 8 and 17 was if anything lower among the sons of employed mothers. The authors concluded that maternal absence due to work may have undesirable effects on younger children but appear to present no handicap for older children. They observed in this context that the fact that the mother helped to shoulder the financial burden appeared to improve family morale and stimulate sons to contribute more actively in the home.

An experienced social worker also evaluated the atmosphere in the families studied. The atmosphere in the families of employed mothers was often rated as 'good'.

These results point to a possibility that a vocational career for the mother can actually have beneficial effects on the child's development. And indeed a number of studies do tend to substantiate this hypothesis. Nye found that the children of mothers working in part-time employment were generally better adjusted than the children of mothers who were full-time housewives [7]. In another study, he also found more positive attitudes towards parents on the part of children of employed mothers. In the case of children of mothers who were employed full-time the results appeared to suggest an either-or tendency in their attitudes towards parents.

There are relatively few Scandinavian studies in this field. A study by Blume-Westerberg however is worthy of mention because it throws light on the age of the child as an important factor. Blume-Westerberg carried out an investigation among all children in the 1st, 4th and 7th forms in two of Gothenberg's school districts [8]. She focused on three aspects of the child's level of adjustment: absence from school; achievement in school; and the degree of serious behavioural disturbance. The results indicated no appreciable differences between the children of employed mothers and other children as far as absence from school was concerned. However, there were notable differences in school achievement between the two groups. Among the children in the first form, the children of employed mothers produced lower average results at school than the other children. In the seventh form, however, the former group produced higher results, and in the fourth form there was no difference in average results. The incidence of serious behavioural disturbance (as judged by teachers and school nurses) was approximately twice as great among children of employed women in the 1st and 7th forms as among the other children.

These results are not easy to evaluate. Yet the differences observed between children in different age groups command our attention. It is quite conceivable that the children in the 1st form were separated from their mothers at an earlier age than those in the 7th form. This could account for the relatively poorer school results among the 1st formers. However, it is also conceivable that the effects of maternal absence, provided that they are not very serious, can be gradually overcome. According to this view, disturbances are more in the nature of transitory reactions to a change in the family situation.

In a more recent study, Blume-Westerberg gathered statements of teachers and school nurses concerning 4,000 children in the second and sixth forms in schools in Gothenberg, Malmoe and Stockholm [9].

In addition, more than 1,000 mothers were interviewed by the school nurses. 480 of these mothers were employed full-time while 589 were either full-time housewives or employed part-time. All employed mothers of the children were selected for study while the other mothers represented a random sample of the housewife-mothers of children in the classes studied.

As far as school achievement was concerned, little difference could be discovered between the two groups of children either in the 2nd or the 6th forms. Also, a report on behavioural disturbance among the children indicated no difference between the two groups of children in the 6th form. However, at the 2nd form level there was a considerably higher incidence of behavioural disturbance among the children of employed mothers than among the other group. It appeared, moreover, that the differences in the 2nd form were almost exclusively due to disturbance among boys. This is true of the general data as well as the answers of the interviewed mothers.

Blume-Westerberg divided the employed mothers into two groups based upon their reasons for employment; that is, into those working primarily for the financial reward and those who were particularly interested in their job. When she then compared the frequency of behavioural disturbance on the part of the children of the mothers in these two groups, she found that the frequency was much higher in the children of employed mothers in the first category than in the second category.

This difference was statistically significant for the children in the 2nd form. At the 6th form level, however, only a tendency was indicated. The association became clearer when teacher evaluations were combined with the mothers' descriptions. Moreover, there was a similar tendency with respect to school achievement. Children of mothers who considered themselves compelled to work for financial reasons consistently displayed lower results at school than other children. This finding was true for both forms.

These results would appear to provide added support for the earlier mentioned suggestion that it is not the fact, by itself, that the mother is employed that is decisive for the child's adjustment, but rather other circumstances in the child's environment that may or may not be associated with the mother's employment.

With the one exception of Blume-Westerberg, none of the studies mentioned have specifically treated the important problem of sex differences when analysing the effects of maternal employment on the child. As a consequence, they offer little in the way of data to evaluate the significance of maternal employment for the sex-role adjustment of the child.

In another study, Douvan and Adelson examined the problem of adjustment in boys and girls and found that maternal employment was particularly significant for the adjustment of girls [10]. Thus, the daughters of employed mothers showed much stronger tendencies than other girls to idealize their mothers. This was apparent, among other things, in the career plans of the girls. This tendency to idealize their mothers displayed by the daughters of employed women offers an interesting parallel to the tendency of sailors' children to idealize their absent father, even though it is not wise to draw the conclusion that the same mechanism is at work in both cases. If we focus only on the working class girls in this study, we find evidence of neglect on the part of children of working mothers. This manifested itself in greater dependence and striving for security.

One study by Siegel and three co-authors can be interpreted to suggest that maternal employment can have positive effects on boys and girls [11]. Hoffman has observed that a closer analysis of the Siegel data indicates that the boys tend to become more conformist and dependent and the girls tend to become more aggressive, dominating and independent in the families of working women than in other families [12]. This suggests that characteristic sex role differences are evened out somewhat in the homes of working women.

Hoffman has underlined the important effects on the child of the mother's satisfaction with and liking for her job. In her study, she took as a starting point two fairly common theories [13]. The first, which she termed the 'guilt-overprotectiveness theory' asserts that mothers who enjoy their work experience feelings of guilt towards the child because of the satisfaction derived from work outside the home. In the event they tend to compensate for their own guilt feelings and attempt to shield the child from the possible ill-effects of maternal absence through the devices of exaggerated attention, too-ready acquiescence and overprotectiveness. The second theory, which Hoffman termed the 'neglect theory', states that mothers who are not satisfied with their work experience fewer feelings of guilt towards their children. They allow themselves to deviate from the conventional maternal role and display less positive feelings or emotions towards their children. As well, they tend to put pressure on their children to take on some of the tasks in the home, and so lighten their own work load.

Hoffman put forward the hypothesis that the children of these two types of mothers would develop different personality characteristics. The children of the mothers in the first group, i.e. the 'guilt-over-protective' group, would lack self-assertiveness, show few aggressive tendencies and be passive. The offspring of the second group would display opposite tendencies: hostility and self-assertiveness. Hoffman also predicted that both groups of children would deviate from children of mothers who were full-time housewives.

The 176 children selected for study were from complete, white families and were in the third to sixth grade of primary school in Detroit, USA. The mothers of one half of the group of children were employed and 65 of these women enjoyed their jobs while 23 were dissatisfied with them.

The results indicated, firstly, that the children of employed mothers who enjoyed their work described their mothers in more positive terms than the children of dissatisfied working mothers. To be sure, negative descriptions were more frequent among the children of working mothers than among those of housewives, but this was largely owing to the accounts of children of mothers who were dissatisfied with their work.

In general, the mothers in this latter category were less involved with the child and more often used the child's services in the home. On the whole, these children were more self-assertive, protesting and hostile than the children of working mothers satisfied with their job. 'Satisfied' working mothers were more positive in their emotional attitudes towards their children, they resorted to milder forms of discipline, but their children were less capable of performing tasks independently and were less self-assertive.

What emerges from the Hoffman study is the importance of specifying more closely the mothers' attitudes to—and opinions of—their jobs. It seems to be fairly clear that when we combine the two groups of mothers, we obscure certain important relations. Indeed, one may speculate whether similar differences may arise between the children of satisfied and dissatisfied housewives.

It is further worth mentioning that even this well-controlled study does not come to grips with all aspects of the problem. We know very little, for example, about a variable as important as the fathers' adjustment and reactions to the situation. It is also possible that we could get a clear understanding were the mothers' motivation for working and certain other traits in their personalities investigated. Finally, it is important to bear in mind that the particular personality traits of the children investigated were relatively insignificant. It would probably be more worth while to attempt to discover personality differences which indicate more systematic or permanent tendencies which would allow us to predict something about the subsequent development of the child. Moreover, many of the personality traits investigated in the studies referred to above were based on value judgements and were rather unclearly defined. These criticisms are especially true of the variable, 'adjustment'.

Since the above studies in part have produced results that are difficult to interpret, we can assume that certain other variables of importance must be sought. Three variables, in particular, need to be continually borne in mind.

Firstly, it is reasonable to assume that the type of relationship between mother and child during the time the mother is at home is crucial. Hoffman's results regarding the children of satisfied working women tend to corroborate such an assumption. Moreover, this hypothesis is generally supported by clinical experience with mother-child relationships. At the same time, however, it seems clear that good contact-relations are themselves dependent on a number of other factors in the mother's situation; for example, whether she is confident that her child is in safe hands during her absence at work, and that she satisfies other personal needs through her work.

A second factor that must be taken into account is the possibility of conflict within the mother due to her deviation from the conventional maternal role. Such conflict can produce different varying reactions in the child depending upon its sex, environment, the type of work the mother does, etc. And these reactions may be as important as the factor of maternal employment itself.

The third variable is related to the way in which the family functions as a whole. It is here that the role of the father emerges as an important factor. The mother's career can alter the father's role; for instance, he may have more contact with his children than is customary in other homes. In the event, his children will derive certain advantages from his presence—as was suggested by the studies of sailor children—particularly where the children are boys.

Parental Contact and Sexual Development: Cultural Variations

Certain findings of the studies on maternal absence due to work suggested that this tended to produce different effects in boys and girls. Let us examine some. The study by Siegel and others indicated for example that sons of working mothers manifest less masculine attitudes and daughters manifest less characteristically feminine attitudes than other boys and girls [14]. This, it appears, entails greater self-assertiveness and independence on the part of the girls. Conformity and dependence are of course conventionally associated with femininity, while aggressiveness, dominance and independence more typically mark the masculine role.

In order to understand the mechanisms underlying the sexually differentiated effects of maternal absence due to work it is necessary to return to the issues of role structure and identification. The studies which are available suggest that the relationship between the mother and child is particularly important. Without a certain minimum of maternal contact, the growth and development of the child will be seriously obstructed. A healthy ego development presupposes that the child has had an opportunity to identify from the very early stages. However, this identification is more dependent on the quality of the contact than the continuous presence of the mother.

We have also indicated that contact with an adult of the same sex is a pre-condition to a satisfactory adjustment to a sex role: that is, the avoidance of compensatory reactions. We can derive an idea of the universality of this relationship by studying it in other cultures. While there appear to be no direct anthropological studies of the relationship between paternal absence and compensatory masculinity, certain observations have been made in the course of studies of other cultures that appear to throw some light on this phenomenon. Bengt Danielsson [15] mentions that in the old Polynesian community there was a clear division of work between the sexes. The less heavy tasks as well as the duties of the household were allocated to the women, states Danielsson, 'because they bore and reared the children, while the men were assigned the heavier tasks as well as those requiring great freedom of movement and *lengthy absence from the home*'. (Italics mine.) 'The Polynesians adhered very strictly to this traditional division of labour', he continues, 'and it was unthinkable for a woman to assist in the construction of a house.' 'A man would become a laughing-stock and bring upon himself the wrath of the gods were he to attempt to perform a typically female task such as preparing food.'

What is particularly relevant in Danielsson's account for our purposes is the fact that the man's tasks were those requiring freedom of movement and lengthy absence from the home. What was the attitude of Polynesian men to women and to sex differences? Is it possible to discover anything in this culture that is reminiscent of 'compensatory masculinity'? Danielsson, at one point, tells us that 'the relationship between the sexes in the home, as in society in general, was governed to some degree by the religious concept of the impurity and inferiority of the female'. Typical of the Polynesians was the idea, prevalent too among the Maori tribes, that if a man lies down or rests on a woman's sleeping-place or resting-place or if he uses a typical female object, such as a pillow, he will become contaminated by this contact with unclean people. His physical, spiritual and intellectual powers will be damaged and he will run the risk of losing them. Danielsson adds, 'illness, death and defeat in battle were all assumed to originate from a breach of the taboo rules, the only act which the Maoris considered criminal'.

Guttorm Gjessing [16] in his study of puberty rites has suggested that 'the basic feature is that boys are leaving the control of their mothers and the female community to enter the community of the fathers and the men. Consequently, great drama attends the procedure.' Gjessing shows, moreover, that puberty rites are especially prevalent in typically 'male societies' and he suggests that the male society is often based on the division of labour. Even in the most primitive hunting cultures, the man deals more with other men than with women. While the woman stays at home, more or less alone, caring for the children and digging for roots, the man is out hunting and trapping with other men. Gjessing goes on to tell of the clear difference between the spheres of activity and functions of men and women. He observes that 'if we conceive of a division of labour as the corner-stone of the male society, it is much easier to understand why the concept of the "man's house" is first found among certain hunting peoples, particularly those which were semi-agricultural, where the differences between the work of men and that of women were most sharply delineated'.

These and many other observations suggest that where economic or other conditions create a situation where the man is absent from the family for a large part of his lifetime and has relatively little contact with women and children, we will find the 'male society' in its more extreme forms. There will be puberty rites for the boys, taboos in relation to women, etc. In other words, such tendencies appear to be most strong in societies where the mother plays an almost exclusive role in child rearing, even if the rearing process for boys consists in preparing them for their male sex role. It is quite conceivable that where a society of this sort lacks institutionalized puberty rites the transition will be much more difficult for boys. What other forms of expression will be employed to manifest the transition?

It is possible to view much juvenile delinquency and the formation of anti-social 'street gangs' at this age as expressions of a self-created puberty or transitional rite. Through these devices, boys are able to confirm that they have left their dependent, passive role in a female or maternal society and have passed into an adult, male society. In our own society we find illuminating examples of transitional rites. For instance in the sailor culture there are initiation rites during the first voyage for boys coming from predominantly maternalistic sailor families and being accepted into the isolated male society of sailing life. It appears, thus, as if the more tightly the child has been bound to the mother or the more dependent it has been on maternal or female society, the more difficult and demanding will be the ritual which the boy must undergo in order to confirm his masculinity. In the event we are once again confronted by the relationship between the male sex role and delinquent behaviour and the possibility that delinquency may be a means through which the young boy attempts to prove or demonstrate his masculinity. It is, moreover, quite possible that the more insecure the boys feels about his masculinity, i.e. the more insecure his identity, the stronger will be his tendencies to engage in super-masculine behaviour. In this way, it is relatively easy to slide over into delinquent activities. Another, perhaps equally essential, reason for such delinquency may be that the masculine sex role has not been internalized in the boy to the same extent as the norms he has acquired through identification with his mother, that is, he may not have been able to internalize his sex role in the same way as it has been possible for the girl to do. As a result, there can be a partial repression of the feminine values upon which the boy has been reared without the internalization of other, necessary controls for his behaviour. He will thus lack the internal controls or the inner moral mechanism that more or less automatically regulate behaviour and make it possible for him to realize his masculinity without compensating, i.e. without deviating in a delinquent direction. For the young boy this in a sense is a case of throwing the baby out with the bath water. He has a very crude and stereotyped concept of masculinity. His concept of masculinity is based largely on what women and his mother are not. Consequently, he defines his sex role as complementary to the female sex role.

Social disturbances on the part of youths, particularly juvenile delinquency, has often been explained by the use of the concept, 'broken homes'. Commonly, however, no special effort is made to analyse more closely the way in which such a family situation is measured or the psychological factors which underly such a situation.

In the case of divorce, for example, is it the previous bad relations between parents which are the most important factor, or is it the divorce itself which can create grave emotional pressures on the parents, or is it the lack of contact with one or the other parent which is the reason why the child has been unable to adjust properly?

Since, in most cases, children remain with their mother in the event of separation or divorce, it is only reasonable to query whether lack of contact with the father can be a factor contributing to a child's delinquent development. This would be a particularly promising line to pursue if we could assume that contact with the father is especially important for the social and moral development of the boy. Strangely enough, no specific basic studies have been made of this problem. However, Kåre Bødal found that among youthful delinquents (the subjects consisting of 100 reform school pupils) at least half had grown up without any permanent or stable contact with their fathers [17]. Where the mother is rejected as an authority figure and the young boy has no opportunity to establish contact with a father or a permanent father-substitute, it is quite conceivable that the norms and ideals of the gang will be overwhelming in their influence. And of course in many cases the gang itself will consist largely of boys lacking the internal control mechanisms which can best be developed by harmonious, consistent contact with the father. These will be boys who compete to display their 'masculinity' and 'toughness'.

A study by Sears, Maccoby and Levin [18], tends to confirm these assumptions about the development of moral controls in boys and girls. These authors have found that in general, conscience and guilt appear to be more strongly developed in girls than in boys. The American psychologist Bronfenbrenner interprets this finding as a contributing factor in the lower delinquency rate among girls. Girls to a far greater degree than boys, he suggests, have adequate internal controls. Bronfenbrenner goes on to assert that the more 'efficient' rearing methods applied to girls entail the risk that they may result in 'oversocialization' [19]. One is tempted to conclude that the existing family type in our society is such that it pushes boys towards the borderline of delinquency while 'oversocializing' the girls. As is apparent from our discussion, this may be a direct drawback of the traditional parental role division, where girls enjoy a close daily contact with the mother, while boys in effect must construct an imaginary model with which to identify for their sex role. It is not unreasonable to assume that greater participation by mothers in working life could reduce the incidence of 'over-control' of daughters and, moreover, make it quite clear to them that there are alternatives to the traditional female sex role. For many girls, life consists of a development from the role of 'dependent home resident daughter' to the role of 'dependent housewife and mother' without any intervening period of experimentation with and exploration of the society outside the home. In the event, many are unable to develop the independence, initiative or perspective on the conventional views of life that might be gained through such an experience.

Parental Authority and Identification

Thus far we have attempted to throw some light on the way in which participation by men and women in working life can in general influence their roles as child-rearers and their positions within the family. Now let us focus on a specific aspect of this relationship; the development of masculinity and femininity in children.

Given—as we have suggested—that the child identifies with the human individual which in its opinion controls the means to satisfy its needs, it seems likely that the process of masculine identification can also be based on the same mechanism. Masculine identification can be established to the extent that the father—or men in general—is viewed as the source of such control.

In the still prevalent patriarchal family type, the child's contact with the mother is largely determined or regulated by the father. In other words, the father can interpose himself between mother and child by, say, demanding consideration of his own attention, or obedience. When the child becomes aware of sexual differences, it may recognise this power position and perceive it as a sex trait. In this way, the patriarchal father may be perceived by the child as the real source of its means of satisfaction. The position and authority of the father may be communicated to the child by the mother's actions—through her defence of and obedience to the father—or verbal references to the father's regulations. In such families, then, there is a foundation already laid for the development of a secondary identification with the father in boys as well as girls.

This theory has been termed the 'status envy hypothesis' by Roger Burton and John Whiting [20] when applied to the case of identification. (It also to some extent corresponds to Anna Freud's concept of 'identification with the aggressor' [21].) Burton and Whiting maintain that the process of identification is based on the desire to possess the status that entails control of—and the opportunity for—need satisfaction. The more clearly the father's status in this respect appears to the child, the more strongly will be its inclination to identify with the father owing to envy. In the typical patriarchal family, therefore, there will always be good foundation for the development of masculine identification. However, such identification will most frequently be secondary in character, for such families are also marked by relatively little contact between father and child in the early stages of its development. In a typical matriarchal family, by contrast, there will be a good foundation for the development of feminine identification, which is both primary and secondary in character.

According to this view, one might expect to find in our own culture expressions of tendencies in women to play the typical male role. To be sure, the foundation for such role-playing will be difficult to detect. However, one may speculate about the extent to which the endeavours of women to gain equality with men are expressions of their conscious adult insight that the man's role is a privileged one, or reflections of childhood experience of the position of the man in the family.

A third important aspect of this problem is the role of the father as child-rearer and as the one who metes out discipline in the family. Typically, in our society, the father will discharge this function to a larger extent with his son than with his daughter. Consequently, identification with this aspect of the role will most frequently result in masculine identification in boys and feminine identification in girls. Similarly, it appears likely, as was previously suggested, that the mother far more frequently than the father performs the disciplinary role in relation to the son as well as the daughter. Yet it is essential to recognize that we can expect to find deviating identification in girls to the extent that they have been subjected to disciplinary treatment from the father. It seems clear, then, that the more patriarchal the family type, the greater will be the chances for masculine identification in boys as well as girls.

But this takes us back to the general question of sex-differentiated socialization. For it is most likely that the same forms of behaviour by boys and girls will be punished or rewarded differently, whether it is the mother or father who is meting out discipline. It seems fair to assume that in a purely patriarchal society a greater emphasis will be placed on conformity to traditional sex role behaviour than in our own society. For the particularly patriarchal father in the process of rearing the child swiftly puts an end to behaviour deviating from the sex role norms. As far as girls are concerned, aggressiveness, initiative, self-assertiveness and boldness are subjected to negative sanctions. For girls are relegated to a pattern of behaviour developed through early contact with their mother and based on the mother's role. Thus, this form of child-rearing involves a development of relatively clear and 'polarized' sex roles—apart from the possible attempts at secondary identification by girls with their father.

Given the great importance of the mother as the first object of identification for boys and girls, the formulation of her own sex and family roles will clearly be a crucial factor in the child's later adjustment to her sex role. Moreover, the mother's individual personality and character traits will necessarily contribute towards the child's image of femininity and the female sex role. The traits that are typically attributed to the female role, e.g. obedience, compliance, helpfulness, etc. will often be character traits possessed by the mother but this need not necessarily always be the case. It is possible that the traits which become internalized in the child due to identification with the mother, may not correspond to those typical of the female role. In the event, traits will gain a firm internal hold in the child which are not relevant to its adjustment to its sex role. This is particularly evident with boys. For at a later stage in their development boys tend to suppress or inhibit personal traits that have been acquired from the mother through the process of identification.

The problem can also arise with girls, where the mother possesses traits that clearly deviate from the norms of her sex role. Such traits can clash with role characteristics that are later perceived by the girl as important to display. Apparently, many girls can experience conflict between identification and role norms where the mother displays, say, some degree of aggressiveness or independence, traits commonly viewed as 'masculine'. This is particularly applicable to the present time, when so many women—and mothers—are breaking with traditional role expectations to some degree. To the extent that the mother has been able to resolve such conflict in herself there is hope that the girl may not have to suffer unduly the pressures of traditional role expectations, and that the role norms will not necessarily threaten the girl's identity at a deeper level.

However, the girl may feel it to be necessary to behave in a way not consonant with her internal identity in order to achieve recognition and contact. This type of 'acting' can too often inhibit the development and the realization of the personality potential of the individual.

In the same way, as in the case of the boy, an over-controlled and over-protective rearing pattern can lead to excessive dependency on the part of the girl. Such dependence is clearly an obstacle to healthy, mature adjustment, even if it is an accepted characteristic of the female sex role. Under the circumstances, we can expect the girls to develop protesting attitudes towards the mother and, moreover, exaggerated (compensatory) expressions of the need for independence and freedom. In an investigation of the effects of paternal absence during puberty, we found that the daughters of whalers, who were subjected to over-protective and restrictive treatment by their mothers, developed a 'masculine' attitude pattern, characterized by an exaggerated idealization of the male role and aggressive authoritarian attitudes [22]. Since, on the whole, girls are more frequently subjected to over-protective treatment than boys, there is often much protest concealed beneath an external acceptance of the sex role. Erik H. Erikson has found that ambivalent feelings of dependence towards the mother can be expressed in masculine behaviour on the part of girls. As well, in order to experience feelings of independence, a girl can negate her sex role by her behaviour. She may attempt to affect a trait which she feels is either irrelevant to the female role or in an extreme case, manifest traits which she views as unfeminine. Erikson suggests as an illustration that certain masculine forms of play, when engaged in by girls, can represent an over-compensation for ambivalent feelings of dependence towards the mother [23].

This would appear to suggest that masculine traits are manifested in women with a mother-dominated and sexually discriminatory family background. However, it is also conceivable that such a family type— i.e. one marked by a strong mother authority—can also contribute to a change in the traditional pattern of male and female roles.

The increasing influence of women in many spheres—in addition to family life—appears to be a harbinger of a trend towards the gradual assumption of many more 'masculine' functions by women. Of course this tendency may be offset to some extent by an increase in compensatory 'hyper-masculine' adjustment tendencies among men. However, despite this, it does appear that it is becoming increasingly more difficult to maintain stereotyped notions of what is 'feminine' and 'masculine'. The future perhaps holds in store a redefinition of these concepts as individuals of both sexes grow up in a less restrictive social climate. To the extent that children are given greater opportunity to freely express their individuality and to enjoy contact with adults and peers of both sexes according to their needs, we may move closer to discovering the genuine, i.e. biological, differences between masculinity and feminity and no longer be misled by differences which are defined by the social patterns of a particular culture.

Conclusions

Though existing studies may have produced results that tend to be conflicting in other respects, they appear to suggest fairly uniformly that the fact that the mother is working outside the home and not following the traditional maternal role of full-time housewife is not by itself determinative of the child's development and personality adjustment. The decisive factor appears to be whether or not the child, in its early stages of development, experiences sufficient contact to gain a fundamental confidence in itself and its surroundings. Given such an emotional foundation, the child ought to be able to survive the separation and gradual independence which is in any case an innate feature of its development and which involves changes in the mother's role. The mother can thus be progressively freed from the role of protector and need-satisfaction which was necessary when the child was a helpless baby, totally dependent upon other people for its survival. This will mean that the concrete content of the mother's role will change as the child matures. If the mother's occupational role limits her contact with the child, the latter can overcome this as long as it has achieved the necessary degree of independence and emotional security. Whereas, if the traditional housewife-mother role tends to 'over-spill', there is a risk that the child will continue in a dependent relation to the mother and family. This appears to have been a fairly common phenomenon hitherto. As long as the mother's role remains unchanged throughout the course of the child's development, there will be the risk that its later chances for self-realization, as mother or father, in family and professional life will be diminished or lost.

REFERENCES

1. Tiller, P. O., *Nar far er Borte*, Tidsskrift for samfunnsforskning, arg., No. 1.
2. Tiller, P. O., *Father Absence and Personality Development of*

Children in Sailor Families, Nordisk psykologi's monografiserie, No. 9. Einar Munksgaards forlag, København 1958.

3. Spitz, R. A., *Anaclitic Depression. Psychoanalytic Study of Child*, 1, London, Imago, 1945.

4. Spitz, R. A., *Hospitalization. Psychoanalytic Study of Child*, 1, London, Imago, 1945.

5. Bowlby, J., *Child Care and the Growth of Love*, London, Penguin, 1953.

6. Ferguson, T., and Cunnison, J., *The Young Wage-earner*, Oxford University Press, London, 1951.

7. Nye, F., *Employment of Mothers and Adjustment of Adolescent Children*, Marriage and Family Living, 21, 1959, No. 3.

8. Blume-Westerberg, G., *Yrkesarbetande Mödrars Barn i Skolan*, Svenska läkartidningen, 1955, 52: 1575 (no. 24).

9. Blume-Westerberg, G., *Förvärvsarbetande Mödrars Barn i Skolan*, Stockholm, 1962.

10. Cited in Hoffman, L. W., *Recent Research on the Effects of Maternal Employment on the Child*, Unpublished stencil, 1960.

11. Siegel, A. E., Stolz, L. M., Hitchcock, E. A. and Adamson, J., *Dependence and Independence in the Children of Working Mothers*, Child Development, No. 4, 1959.

12. Hoffman, L. W., *Effects of Maternal Employment on the Child*, Child Development, No. 4, 1960.

13. Hoffman, L. W., *op. cit.*

14. Siegel, A. E., m.fl., *op. cit.*

15. Danielsson, B., *Sydhavskjaerlighet*, Oslo, Gyldendal norsk forlag, 1955, pp. 144–148.

16. Gjessing, G., *Individ og Samfunn hos Naturfolk*, Oslo, Norlis, 1948.

17. Bødal, K., *Arbeidsskolen og dens Behandlingsresultater*, Universitetsforlaget, 1962.

18. Sears, R. R., Maccoby, E. E., Levin, H., *Patterns of Child Rearing*, Evanston, 1957.

19. Petruello, L., Bass, B. M., *Studies in Leadership*.

20. Burton, R., and Whiting, J., *The Absent Father: Effects on the Developing Child*, National Institute of Mental Health, 1960.

21. Freud, A., *The Ego and the Mechanisms of Defence.*, London, Hogarth Press, 1937, p. 121.

22. Tiller, P. O., *Father Separation and Adolescence: a Study of Attitudes and Personality of Adolescent Sailor and Whaler Children*, Stencilled report, Institut for samfunnsforskning, Oslo, 1961.

23. Erikson, E. H., *Sex Differences in the Play Configurations of American Pre-Adolescents*, Mead, I. M., and Wolfenstein, M., *Childhood in Contemporary Societies*. University of Chicago Press, 1955.

THE POSITIONS OF MEN AND WOMEN
IN THE LABOUR MARKET

by ANNIKA BAUDE *and* PER HOLMBERG

I. *Sweden in an International Perspective*

ACCORDING to recent publications of the ILO and OECD,[1] participation rates among men of working age in all countries during the 1950–60 period varied between 90% and 95%. By contrast, female participation rates varied between 10% and 70%. Though the statistics of many of these countries are not completely comparable, the data can serve to indicate certain broad trends. Thus, the group of countries with the lowest proportion of women of working age actually at work includes Latin America, South Africa, Spain, Portugal, the Netherlands and the predominantly Mohammedan states in Asia and Africa. Apart from the Eastern European countries, those with the highest rates of female participation are Finland, Denmark, Turkey, Austria, Thailand and Japan. These variations are not merely a reflection of differences in living standards. They are also the product of the varying relative status men and women enjoy under different cultural, political and economic systems.

The majority of Western European countries, the U.S. and Canada, fall somewhere between the two groups of countries towards the extremes. Table I offers a comparison of the proportion of women of working age gainfully occupied in the countries of the Western world.

Viewed in this international perspective, the proportion of women gainfully employed in Sweden exceeds that of the U.S. and Canada but lies close to the mean for Western Europe. The U.K. and Austria have significantly higher female participation rates, while rates in Switzerland and Western Germany are roughly equivalent to those in Sweden. Belgium, France, Ireland, Italy, the Netherlands and Norway all have a lower proportion of women at work.

[1] Manpower statistics 1950–1962. Published by OECD, Paris, 1963. Women workers in a changing world. International labour conference. Report VI (I). Geneva 1963.

Marked disparities can also be observed between the *changes* in the participation rates of women during the post-war period. According to OECD statistics, the proportion of gainfully occupied women decreased in Finland, France, Ireland, Norway and Portugal during the years 1950–1960. Yet, during the same period, there were pronounced increases in Canada, the U.S., the U.K., Italy, Austria and

TABLE I

The Percentage Proportion of Women of Working Age who are Gainfully Occupied, ca. 1960.

With a minimum of half-time work		All part-time work included	
Belgium	37	Canada	32
Canada	28	France	45
Denmark	52	Italy	34
Finland	55	Sweden	50
Ireland	35	Western Germany	49
The Netherlands	29	USA	43
Norway	36		
Switzerland	42		
Sweden	40		
United Kingdom	48		
USA	36		
Austria	56		

Source: Manpower statistics 1950–1962. Published by OECD, Paris, 1963; and Population Censuses.

Sweden. In Western Europe at least, such increases usually coincided with either continuously low or falling unemployment levels. Moreover, in all Western European countries, save Western Germany, there has been a simultaneous decline in birth rates, a factor which would itself tend to raise the proportion of working women.

The ILO Report, 'Women in a Changing World', contained a summary of replies by many member governments to enquiries regarding their official attitudes to female participation in the labour force and the measures employed to promote this end. Most governments with a clearly articulated position on this subject were able to give only heavily qualified support to a policy of encouraging women to work. Thus, the British Government felt that greater female participation should not be induced 'solely to give women with family responsibilities the opportunity of working'. Western Germany expressed the view that female employment should be encouraged only 'in so far as the family responsibilities may permit'. The United

States referred to 'the basic legal principle which places on the husband the primary responsibility for support of his wife and family with secondary liability devolving on the wife'. The Soviet Union maintained that their public measures were applied with the objective of allowing women to assume occupational as well as familial responsibilities, 'without detriment to the interests of their family or to their own health and welfare'. The common thread running through these and a number of other official replies was the attitude that men were the primary family providers, while women were provided for; women and not men were to bear the major responsibility for the care of the child and the home; hence, gainful employment could conflict with the family responsibilities of women but not those of men.

It is rather remarkable to find such a high degree of uniformity of response and adherence to traditional values among the public officials of countries whose political, cultural and economic features and female participation rates vary so widely. A number of other countries—Denmark, Finland, Italy, Yugoslavia and Sweden—indicated that their official position either rejected entirely or modified the traditional view. In this latter group, Sweden appears to deviate most markedly from the international norm regarding female employment. The official Swedish position is that labour legislation should not differentiate between men and women apart from the case of rules relating to childbirth. Responsibility for the care of children and family should devolve upon men as well as women. Society should promote the entry of women and men to the labour market without discrimination. Part-time employment should be arranged for female as well as male applicants desiring such jobs.

This view, which is somewhat unique in the Western context, is partly a consequence of Sweden's relatively high and steadily rising post-war proportion of gainfully occupied women. It reflects the current official opinions of the trade union movement and employer organizations and the recent radically changed public consensus on sex role norms in the family and occupational life. At the same time, however, this approach should be recognized as an expression of a desire to achieve a particular end rather than as a description of currently prevailing conditions.

II. *Working Women in Sweden*

With the onset of industrialization in the late 1800s, Sweden experienced a considerable population increase. Employment, though rising, was unable to keep pace, and the resulting population surplus led to widespread emigration; by the start of the first world war, almost one-fourth of the Swedish people had emigrated. Given the prevailing social norms, legislation and educational conditions, women were more severely affected than men by the acute shortage of jobs.

Industrialization, therefore, brought about no immediate change in the occupational lot of women. The narrow range of female occupations, which had remained restricted since the time of the guilds, was enlarged only gradually, occupation by occupation. Among the forces giving rise to this expansion were the relatively low wage position of female workers and the political and social emancipation of women.

Under the full employment conditions enjoyed by Sweden since 1940, there has been a further widening of vocational opportunities for women. One key factor in this expansion has been the shortage of male workers within an increasing number of industrial and occupational sectors. In addition, the continuing trend towards 'urbanization' has led to more widely differentiated labour markets, providing women with greater job opportunities. Moreover, the growing importance of the service sector, in the total employment field, particularly the social welfare and educational systems, has entailed an increased volume of demand for female employees.

Women in the Labour Force

According to the Swedish census, in which gainful employment is defined as a minimum of half-time employment, the proportion of women in the labour force varied between 31% and 34% during the period, 1910–1960. This proportion rose slightly in the 1910s and 1920s, fell somewhat in the 1930s and remained fairly constant at 31% in the 1940s and 1950s. These movements were characteristic of the labour force of urban labour markets as well as the overall labour force. If the definition of gainful employment is enlarged to include all part-time work, the above picture is altered in one important respect; the number of women workers as a percent of all workers was higher and rose more swiftly from 1940 to 1965, reflecting the great increase in part-time employment among women during the period. At the start of 1966, women constituted 38% of those gainfully employed, under the widened definition of that term. Current, long-term labour force surveys, i.e. to 1980, assume that this fraction will rise even further. According to a labour force survey conducted in May, 1966, the proportions of men and women in the Swedish labour force were the following.

TABLE 2

Composition of the Swedish Labour Force

	Men	%	Women	%	Married women	%	Single widowed or divorced	%
Persons in the labour force	2,389,000	62	1,448,000	38	855,000	59	593,000	41
of which 14–64 years	2,262,000	62	1,399,0c0	38	836,000	60	564,000	40
Persons outside the labour force 14–64 years	389,000	24	1,209,000	76	818,000	68	381,000	32
of which in school or military service	280,000	55	227,000	45				

Source: National Central Bureau of Statistics. Statistical Reports. V 1966: 14. Labour Force Survey in May, 1966, Table 1 (Concepts and definitions are essentially the same as those applied in the Labour Force surveys carried out by the U.S. Bureau of Census).

In 1966, the labour force consisted of approximately 2·4 million men and 1·5 million women of which 855,000 were married and 600,000 unmarried, widowed or divorced. Among the approximately 1·2 million women of working age *outside* the labour force, about 800,000 were married and 380,000 were single. A rather large minority, i.e. about 230,000, of this group were mainly younger women receiving

TABLE 3

Persons at Work by Sex-Marital Status and Full-Time or Part-Time Status

			Women			
Hours of work in thousands	Men	%	Married	%	Single, widowed or divorced	%
1–34	159	7	428	55	104	19
35–44	535	24	204	26	222	42
45–	1,500	69	147	19	209	39
Total	2,194	100	779	100	535	100

Source: National Central Bureau of Statistics; Statistical Reports V 1966: 14. Labour Force Survey, May, 1966. Table 10.

training at the time of the survey. However, the majority of women outside the labour force did housework in their own homes. The latter category consisted of 933,000 married women and about 276,000 single women, including all ages even those above the age of 65.

As is evident from Table 3, men work significantly longer hours than women; on average, men work 45·7 hours while women work 34·1 hours per week. Moreover, 55% of married women work *less than* 35 hours per week, while 19% of single women and only 7% of men have a shorter work week than 35 hours.

TABLE 4

Participation Rates in Different Age Groups among Men and Single Women 1961–1965[1]

Age group	Men %	Single Women %
20–24	79	77
25–54	96	80
55–64	89	54

Source: National Central Bureau of Statistics; Statistical Reports V, 1965: 16.

[1] An average of the data from the labour force surveys in 1961–1965.

Participation rates among *men* are, thus, significantly higher than those among *single women*. This is particularly evident in the higher age groups, where almost 90% of all men are gainfully employed while the corresponding figure for single women is less than 55%. The disparity can at least partly be explained by the difference between the job opportunities available to men and women.

Among *married women*, participation rates have increased in recent years, particularly as far as part-time work is concerned. Table 5 presents a survey of participation rates among married women in different age groups comparing the rates according to labour force surveys (left column) in which all part-time workers are included, with activity rates according to the 1960 census (right column) in which only part-time work in excess of half-time work is included. The difference between the two percentages indicates the percentage of part-time workers working less than half-time.

In Sweden, there are a considerable number of married women with children under school age (7 years) who are working. As is apparent from Table 5, about one-third (i.e. approximately 160,000) of this group are gainfully occupied. These working mothers, moreover, are quite evenly divided between those working more and those working less than a half working day. The limited availability of institutional child care services as well as private help appears to operate as a constraint on increased participation by women with small children.

The strikingly low participation rates among married women in the higher age groups can at least in part be attributed to the difficulty

TABLE 5

Participation Rates among Married Women in Different Age Groups with and without children under 7 years[1]

Married women in age group	Participation rates according to labour force Surveys 1961–65[1]	Activity rates according to the 1960 census
20–24 years		
With children under 7 years	29·4	17·0
Without ,, ,, ,, ,,	79·4	71·3
Total	46·1	34·2
25–34 years		
With children under 7 years	33·4	17·1
Without ,, ,, ,, ,,	70·9	55·0
Total	45·0	28·8
35–44 years		
With children under 7 years	34·2	14·6
Without ,, ,, ,, ,,	58·6	35·8
Total	51·1	28·6
45–54 years	50·4	27·0
55–64 years	32·1	15·6

Source: Central Bureau of Statistics; Forecasting Information 1965: 5. The women in the labour force 1. Table 22.

[1] An average of the data from the surveys in 1961–1965.

these women experience in their attempts to find suitable employment. Yet there is also evidence that many women in this age group tend to lack adequate vocational education and training as well as the will and experience to seek employment actively. Moreover, belonging to a generation with an old-fashioned view of the role of women in society many prefer to stay at home.

Although Sweden is currently confronted by a severe overall shortage of labour, fairly high levels of unemployment can be found in specific geographical and occupational sectors. In these pockets of unemployment, women workers are often the group most severely affected. For throughout much of the labour market, they have been cast in the role of a manpower reserve. Thus, according to labour force surveys carried out in May, 1966, about 116,000 persons were 'latent job applicants', the majority of which, i.e. 99,000, were women (77,000 married, 22,000 single, widowed or divorced).[1] In other words, the official level of unemployment among women, 1·9% of the female labour force taking only registered job applicants into account, amounts to almost 8·1% of the 'gross' supply of female labour. Owing to the difficulties experienced by women in rural areas in obtaining employment there has been a considerable migration of young unmarried women to urban centres.[2] The more elderly single women in rural areas are often prevented from following the example of the younger age groups by gradually acquired duties in the home of parents or relatives. Unemployed married women in these areas are bound geographically by their husbands' job. According to prevailing sex role norms, the husband's unemployment is sufficient reason to change the family's residence. Seldom, however, does the wife's unemployment have such an effect.

The individual's educational level is another important factor bearing on the participation rates of married women. A recent study (Diagram 1) has shown that among female workers with different levels of academic achievement, there is a significant association between the length of time devoted to academic study and the participation rates of married women. For example, in the 30–59 age group, an increased length of time devoted to study of one year was associated with a 7% higher rate of participation.

As is evident from Diagram 1, the proportion of married female dentists and doctors at work is twice that of married women with only a student diploma (G.C.E.). Yet, the fraction of this latter group at work is twice that of married women as a whole. It is noteworthy that participation rates among married women with a university education remain fairly constant throughout all age groups; many women in this category work while rearing children of pre-school age. One possible explanation for this unusual tendency is that greater academic achievement is linked with a higher income level, which in turn allows paid assistance with child care. In the above mentioned study of married women and academic achievement, it has been possible to find an

---

[1] Labour Force Survey, May 1966. 'Latent unemployed' means that the interviewee would have applied for a job, were one available in his or her area of residence.

[2] In the age group, 15–25, almost twice as many women as men moved to urban areas, according to the official statistics on rural–urban migration.

association between participation rates and the income of married women; an increase in income of 100 Sw.kr. per month was associated with an increase in participation rates of 2%.

DIAGRAM I

Participation Rates for Married Women according to Age and Educational Level

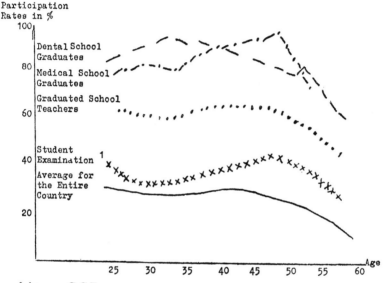

¹ Approx. G.C.E.

Source: Central Bureau of Statistics. Forecasting Information 1965: 7. A survey of the women's participation in the labour force in respect to the number of children and the age of the children. II.

Occupational Structure

As has been observed in preceding sections, the range of job opportunities open to men are often quite different to those available to women. The extent and persistence of these differences suggest that in many sectors there are virtually two separate labour markets, one marked 'male', the other 'female'. In Sweden, as in other countries, there is a tendency to divide occupations by sex. Though some examples of integration can be unearthed in certain areas, the majority of women continue to work in a relatively few number of occupations in which members of their sex predominate. According to the 1960 census

(Table 6) 71% of all gainfully occupied women are concentrated in slightly more than 20 occupations. By contrast, only 11·7% of all male workers are listed in these job categories. The vast majority of occupations are in consequence almost exclusively 'male'.

TABLE 6

Occupations of Women according to 1960 Census[1]

Occupation	Number	Percent of all gainfully occupied women[2]	Women as a percent of all workers in the occupation
Clerical Work (all types)	157,515	16·3	72·8
Shop Assistant	120,825	12·5	78·1
Domestic and Child Nurse	72,823	7·5	99·7
Cleaning Woman	44,701	4·6	92·7
Nurse's Assistant	42,082	4·4	98·8
Clothing Worker	38,283	4·0	97·4
Form Mistress	26,137	2·7	68·8
Waitress	26,726	2·8	87·3
Nurse	20,690	2·1	100·0
Kitchen Help	19,034	2·0	95·8
Farm Labourer	18,839	2·0	18·7
Textile Worker	16,992	1·8	56·2
Hairdresser, etc.	16,942	1·8	72·2
Telephone Operator	14,179	1·5	97·2
Retailer, proprietor	14,773	1·5	28·9
Chef, cook, cold-buffet manageress	12,706	1·3	79·8
Catering	11,138	1·2	81·1
Packing and Wrapping	10,163	1·1	58·1
Total	684,548	71·1	
Other	261,103		

Total Number of Women in the
Labour Force   945,651

Total Number of Men in
Above Occupations   266,647 (11·7% of all men)

Source: Central Bureau of Statistics. Statistical Reports B 1963: 9, Table 2.

[1] All occupations with more than 10,000 female employees.
[2] Gainful occupation defined as a minimum of half time work.

As Table 6 shows, women constitute between 90% and 100% of the membership of certain job categories. If we spread our net to include occupations with less than 10,000 female employees, we encounter several more which are almost exclusively 'female', viz. dental assistants, hospital laboratory assistants, private nurses, beauty parlour assistants, physiotherapists, and receptionists. Not surprisingly, the great majority of these female-intensive occupations women are closely linked to traditional female roles: to nursing, to sewing, to preparing food or to beautifying personal appearance.

Women have also predominated among the recruits to two large 'mixed' occupational groups; clerical work and commerce. However, even in these job categories, there is often a strict division of labour according to sex. In Sweden, as in other countries, working in an office is often a totally different experience for a man than for a woman.

TABLE 6a

Male and Female Salaried Employees in Manufacturing Industry in Different Occupational Groups 1965

Occupational Group	Men %	Women %
Technical	50·2	8·4
Managerial	3·0	0·5
Personnel	1·2	0·8
Commercial	12·7	0·5
Clerical	32·9	89·8
	100·0	100·0

Source: The Organization of Technical and Clerical Employees in Industry. Wage Statistics 1965.

Although women constituted more than a quarter of all salaried employees in manufacturing industry, they were concentrated almost entirely, i.e. 90% in clerical work. That such work consisted mainly of positions of relatively low status and responsibility is shown by Table 6b below. More than 80% of all female salaried employees were placed in the two lowest salary grades, with only 24% of the men so placed. By way of contrast, nearly 50% of the men were clustered in the four highest salary grades while only 6·8% of all female salaried employees attained such heights.[1]

This picture of conditions prevailing in the labour market of salaried employees is equally applicable to that of blue collar workers. In the latter situation the majority of women are classified as unskilled labour with only a small number having attained supervisory positions.

This rather strict, if not complete, division of manpower into separate

[1] To some extent, of course, this striking disparity can be attributed to differences in the average age of female and male salaried employees.

labour markets means that men and women workers are essentially non-competing groups. This is the fundamental reason why it has been possible to describe Sweden as suffering from a persistent shortage of labour during the post-war years, while simultaneously female job seekers have remained unemployed. An automatic market adjustment has not been possible because the labour shortages have primarily occurred in certain skilled, blue collar occupations and highly qualified

TABLE 6b

Male and Female Salaried Employees in Manufacturing Industry in Different Unit Occupational Groups 1965

Unit Occupational Groups[1]	Men %	Women %
2	0·3	0·0
3	3·2	0·1
4	14·1	0·6
5	29·3	3·8
6	29·4	12·9
7	19·8	40·5
8	3·9	42·1
	100·0	100·0

Source: The Organization of Technical and Clerical Employees in Industry. Wage Statistics 1965.

[1] The digits 2–8 are the fourth digits of the numerical code for unit occupational groups. Within each group, this digit denotes, in descending order; degree of difficulty and responsibility (occupational standing).

salaried positions. Since these shortages are growing steadily more acute, the goals of greater social and vocational equality for women now undeniably coincide with the objectives of economic policy. By ending discriminatory recruitment practices in many occupations, strides can simultaneously be made towards both aims. Technical talent is a scarce resource in the Swedish economy, yet a significant reserve of such talent is hardly being tapped.

Such considerations seem particularly applicable to recruitment practices among industrial workers and engineers. Because no real tradition of industrial employment has been fostered among Swedish women, the more highly skilled jobs and technical positions have remained outside the range of their vocational choice. Only in certain exceptional industries such as textiles, confectionary products and chemicals can an appreciable number of female blue collar workers with substantial skills and engineers be found.

The other side of the coin, the problem of recruiting men to traditional female occupations in, say, the public health services, raises difficulties of a different nature. The primary obstacle to the flow of manpower in such a direction is the relatively low pay in these occupations.

Changes in the Occupational Structure

In recent years, there has been some indication of a growing demand for female employees in occupations traditionally recruiting only men. Thus, municipal transit authorities in the larger cities now recruit women as well as men to fill vacancies as bus drivers, ticket collectors and train conductors. Taxi companies have recruited women for almost ten years but in recent years they have considerably increased their intake. In Stockholm, for example, more than 200 taxi-cab drivers, out of a total of 5,000, are women.

Undoubtedly an important catalyst in this process has been the acute shortage of male workers, a shortage that is expected to increase during the remainder of the 1960s and throughout the 1970s. Confronted with this prospect, companies in an increasing number of industries—often prodded by the labour market authorities—have undertaken a systematic review of the potential of female workers in hitherto 'male' job categories.

According to a survey of 146 large and medium sized industrial firms conducted by the National Labour Market Board,[1] in the period 1960–65 women workers had been newly recruited to almost 100 individual job categories previously the exclusive preserve of men. The leaders in this development have been the metal and engineering industries; the jobs now performed by women as well as men include lathe operating, drilling, machining, welding, metal-pressing and casting, and foundry work. Moreover, in these and other industries, women have been recruited as truck drivers, crane operators, sprayers, works carpenters, painters, inspectors, assembly workers, and stock-room and warehouse workers. More than half of the firms in the survey indicated that they plan to take on even more female workers.

In view of the extensive contact between Swedish labour market authorities and private industry, these changes in the pattern of values at the work place can be expected to filter back to vocational guidance, services and vocational training programmes.

[1] Swedish Labour Market Board. Information from the Research Department, no. 13:1, 1965.

In the past, women have moved into new job areas mainly because they were the only workers willing to toil for the low wage 'going' in such fields. This was how women flooded the primary school teaching profession in the mid-1800s as well as certain civil service positions, e.g. clerical workers and telephone operators, two areas still largely dominated by female employees. In order to limit the flow of women into primary school teaching positions, the annual intake of teacher training colleges has long been regulated to ensure that at least 50% of the new students are men. This control will probably be discontinued and therefore the proportion of women amongst primary school teachers will once again rise substantially. Moreover, concentrated vacation courses are being designed to provide teachers with the opportunity to gain sufficient credits to transfer to a higher teaching level. Since it is likely that male teachers will attend these courses in far greater numbers than female teachers, the probable impact of this reform will be to accelerate the 'feminization' of the teaching profession at the lower and middle levels of the comprehensive school.

There are, moreover, strong indications that traditionally male occupations once opened to female recruits, can be progressively 'feminized' where companies concentrate primarily on recruiting women to these positions. Men tend to avoid applying for jobs in certain categories with a high and growing female contingent. Such a tendency has been found among truck drivers and crane operators in certain garages and on certain sites.

Certain low paid civil service and municipal positions can be affected by the same type of change. Today, municipal transit authorities in certain large cities are experiencing difficulties in recruiting men as ticket collectors, conductors and bus drivers. The GPO in Stockholm now directs much of its advertising for postmen especially to 'housewives'. Parking meter wardens are recruited exclusively among women, etc. The process strongly reminds one of a similar development in the American labour market in which non-white workers are able to move into occupations which have become less attractive to white workers.

III. *The Wage Structure and Wages Policy*

In 1962, Sweden was a signatory to the ILO Convention on Equal Pay for Men and Women. Yet, a comparison of the actual wage positions of men and women in the Swedish labour market in 1965 discloses relatively few examples of wage equality even where similar jobs are held. According to a 1964 study, average hourly pay for women in all occupations was 40% less than that for men.

Table 7 below indicates the average wage earning for adult men and women in different industries in 1964. Since then, though average hourly earnings have risen considerably, the gap between male and female wage earnings has remained roughly the same.

TABLE 7

Industry	Wage Earnings in 1964		Women's Wage Earnings as a % of Men's Wage Earnings	
	Men	Women	1964	1954
Manufacturing Industry				
Salaried Employees (kr/month)	2,216	1,162	52·4	53·0
Wage Employees (kr/hour)	8·57	6·31	73·6	69·0
Agriculture				
Farm Worker (kr/hour)[1]	6·86	5·67	82·7	75·7
Garden Worker (kr/hour)	(5·94)[2]	(4·89)[2]	(82·3)[2]	76·0
Commerce				
Clerical Personnel (kr/month)	2,014	1,132	56·2	62·6
Sales Personnel (kr/month)	1,381	1,004	72·7	68·8
Finance				
Permanent Clerk (kr/month)	2,580	2,373	92·0	
Restaurants				
Head Waiter (kr/month)	1,604	1,486	92·6	87·9
Cooks (kr/month)	1,185	998	84·2	92·0
Cashier (kr/month)	783	715	91·3	92·9

[1] Regards those farm workers who have a standard wage rate.
[2] Regards 1962.

It is readily apparent from this table that the narrowest wage differentials between men and women are found in areas characterized by a similarity of job content and qualification (e.g. bank clerks, head waiters). The widest wage differences exist in occupational categories with a widely varying job content (e.g. technical and clerical personnel). Yet another phenomenon, indirectly illustrated by Table 7, is the wage policy of Swedish trade unions. The occupations with narrow or recently narrowed wage differentials have been the target of a conscious trade union policy of wage equality. Again, those occupations with constantly wide or widening wage differentials have been those where the trade union policy has been least successful.

Commonly, the sectors with a wide gap between male and female wage earnings are those in which female employees are largely concentrated in a narrow range of occupations while men are relatively evenly distributed throughout the remaining job spectrum. Often, these sectors have special positions 'reserved' for women to which few if any men are actively recruited. The effect of such an occupational distribution on relative wage earnings is demonstrated in the following table of the salaries of government employees, a sector which has for

TABLE 8

Salary grades of civil service employees 1965 (excludes teachers)

Salary grade[1]	Men %	Women %
A 1–8	6·3	55·2
A 9–12	40·3	26·3
A13–19	34·3	13·4
A20–27	15·8	4·9
B 1–10	3·3	0·2
	100·0	100·0

Source: National Central Bureau of Statistics.

[1] A 1 is the lowest salary grade. The different grades naturally reflect differences in responsibility and qualifications. Salary grade B is that of the highest ranked government employees.

TABLE 9

State school system. Teachers in different salary grades 1965

Salary grade[1]	Men %	Women %
A 7–13	8·7	56·4
A14–16	65·2	37·4
A17–23	22·8	6·2
A24–27	3·3	0·0
	100·0	100·0

Source: National Central Bureau of Statistics, Am. 1966: 45.

many years formally applied the principle, 'equal wages for equal work'.

The notable feature of the pay structure of civil service employees is that, although it is formally governed by the principle of equal pay, its distribution of jobs among men and women and the difference

[1] A 7 is the lowest salary grade for teachers. A 13 is the highest salary grade for the preparatory-school teachers and the initial salary grade for primary school teachers. The highest salary grade for primary school teachers is A 18.

between their average wage levels are strikingly similar to those in
the pay structure of salaried employees in private industry, a sector
that has *not* committed itself to the equality principle. With women
concentrated in certain occupational categories and a female job zone
virtually isolated from the male job zone, it has been possible to pursue
a policy of setting women's salaries without reference to those of men.
Thus, wage *differentials* have been established between male and
female occupational areas largely without regard to the relative requirements of skills, responsibility etc. of the different areas.

Often in the course of discussion about the appreciable gaps between
the wage earnings of men and women in the civil service and in the
white collar positions in private industry, mention is made of the fact
that the lower wage position of women is linked with their relatively
lower average age, as well as their relatively smaller share of the more
responsible positions. Thus, while about 51 to 52% of all women
salaried employees in private industry are under 30 years of age, the
corresponding proportion for men in that sector is about 20 to 21%.
Of course, under white collar pay schemes differences in the age
distribution and often the attendant differences in experience will be
expressed directly as well as indirectly in differences in average wage
earnings.

It seems important here, however, to separate cause from effect.
That the average age of women white collar workers in industry and
civil servants is significantly lower than that of men may well be
linked to the fact that employers in these sectors apply different wage,
training, recruitment and promotion policies to men than to women.
Discriminatory company practices are often partly responsible for the
higher turnover among female employees. State training and education
policies must also bear their share of responsibility. Sectors with
relatively small differences between the wage earnings of men and
women and with non-discriminatory salary, training, recruitment and
promotion policies (for example in banking and certain levels of
teaching) often have, in consequence, a rather similar age distribution
for men and women employees. Apparently, in these sectors, married
women tend more often than in other sectors to continue to work
while rearing children.

Thus upon closer scrutiny differences between the pay of men and
women workers in Sweden suggest a strong inter-relationship between
the pay structure and the structure of the labour market. The significantly narrower range of occupational choice exercised by women

as well as the frequently differentiated recruitment and promotion policies of management have led to sizeable gaps between the wage earnings of men and those of women. These gaps, in their turn, have made many occupations unacceptable to male job applicants. In the event, the low wage occupations have become predominantly staffed by younger women who because of the unfavourable conditions of employment either move to other occupations or leave the labour force altogether. It has been estimated that the current 40% differential between the earnings of men and women is largely, i.e. about 3/4ths, owing to an unequal distribution of men and women occupationally and industrially and only to a relatively small extent, i.e. about 1/4 a reflection of differences in pay for similar job categories.

In the event, it appears that the scope for a wage policy, as traditionally conceived, to reduce the wage gap between men and women workers is rather limited. Even were the principle of 'equal pay for men and women in equal positions' to be universally adopted—and the equal wage principle goes no further—only a small proportion of the sex-wage differential would be eliminated. This has been empirically demonstrated by the efforts of the Swedish Employers' Confederation and the Confederation of Swedish Trade Unions to implement their 1962 agreement on equality of wages for men and women. According to the agreement, the practice of setting special hourly or piece rates for women blue collar workers was to be wholly discontinued by 1965. Although this was accomplished, during the three year period 1962-65 the wage gap between male and female blue collar wage earnings was only slightly affected. Thus, women's wage earnings rose from 70% to 75% of men's. To be sure, the reduced differential represents a success for this joint wage policy. At the same time, however, this development confirms that the major problem in removing the sex-wage differential is to change the pronounced difference in the occupational structure of men and women, i.e. to widen the range of occupational choice for men as well as women through public education and manpower policies and management recruitment, training and promotion policies. Again, such a widening presupposes certain changes in wage policies primarily to raise the wage levels in traditional female job zones.

IV. *Education in Sweden*

The Swedish school system is currently undergoing an almost total transformation. Many basic reforms have been introduced in an effort to ensure that all students, regardless of social background, sex or locality, shall enjoy equality of educational opportunity. That such factors can seriously affect access to higher levels of study had been clearly indicated by the results of research connected with the government's commission on the schools.[1]

The former system was highly selective; all pupils were streamed after four years of primary education—usually at age 11—into three different types of institution. One group would remain at the 'folk school' for another three or four years under conditions resembling those of English secondary modern schools; a second group would enter special girls schools for four years; a third group would be channelled into a four year course in a pre-grammar school. This elite would then be eligible for three or four more years in a grammar school.

In 1962, after many years of experimentation, this was replaced by a comprehensive school system in which all children attend the same type of school for their first nine years. Those who choose to specialize in the more theoretical subjects during their final year in the comprehensive school become eligible to enter a three year secondary school or a two year training college. Many new secondary schools have been established in the attempt to remove the geographical barriers to further studies.

A recent trend in the secondary schools has been the increasing proliferation of natural science and technical subjects at the expense of the humanities. The forthcoming merger of the previously independent commercial and technical schools into the new, integrated secondary school is expected to accentuate this trend. In the event, the transition from school to working life will be considerably smoothed.

A guiding precept in the new school reform is that all courses should be provided in one school premises wherever possible; all children in any one area should have the opportunity to receive an education according to their ability and inclination in one school. The nine year comprehensive school, the new two year training colleges, three year secondary schools, and in the near future the new vocational schools will

---

[1] Härnquist and Grahn have shown that the children of blue collar workers in manufacturing as well as those of workers in farming and forestry, etc., have been clearly under-represented in the student group accepted into the grammar schools (gymnasiums). They also indicated that girls, to a far greater extent than boys, have been discouraged and prevented from continuing with their education by socio-economic and geographical factors. (Härnquist, K., & Grahn, A., *Vägen genom gymnasiet*, Stockholm, SOU 1963: 15.)

together constitute an 11 or 12 year basic education for all Swedish children.

To ensure that pupils' career choices are guided by interest and ability and to offset the influence of essentially irrelevant factors such as locality, social background and traditional sex role an extensive programme of vocational guidance is conducted by the schools in conjunction with the national employment service. One feature of the programme is that all pupils in their eighth year spend three weeks with industrial firms observing two or three different occupations.

Another feature of the vocational guidance programme, one that is also characteristic of the school programme in general, is that the authorities have adopted an emphatic policy of not only refusing to perpetuate but actively counteracting the traditional view of sex roles. Thus, the following instructions can be found in the official teachers' guide for the comprehensive school: 'When receiving career guidance, girls should be clearly instructed that women can make important contributions in scientific, mathematical and technical fields. Girls displaying natural talent or interest in such subjects ought to be positively encouraged to cultivate their ability and interest.'

As a practical matter, however, guidance teachers and counsellors do not have sufficient authority greatly to influence pupils. Moreover, many are themselves often too unaware of the adverse effects of mutually exclusive male and female job sectors to overcome long standing prejudices when presenting career information. To make things worse, many of the guidance materials now circulated in the school are out-dated and continue to reflect traditional notions of different occupational roles for men and women. New guidance materials, however, are carefully scrutinized by a committee of representatives from private industry, the Board of Education and the National Labour Market Board which has been made responsible for screening text and illustrations.

Another feature of the new school reforms has been a general programme of financial assistance to secondary school and university students. The object is to allow students to make their career choice independent of their parents' desire or ability to finance their pursuit of further studies. As has been shown, the career choice of female students is often influenced by their parents' economic station. The newly expanded financial assistance programme should result in an increase in the number of women obtaining advanced education.

Under the new school reform, the minimum school leaving age has been raised to 16. The reforms together with the rising standard of living have led to considerable increases in the number of students continuing to attend school beyond the compulsory period. In 1965, 50% of the 15–19 age group were pursuing studies, compared to 37% in 1960. According to expectations, the rise should continue to the point where some time in the 1970s about 70% of those completing the comprehensive school will continue until at least the age of 19. A similar trend is observable in the 20–24 age group which consists largely of university students. In 1965, the proportion of students in the 20–24 age group was only 13% but during the 1970s it is expected to climb to 25%.

Accompanying this increase in the overall level of education, has been a slight narrowing of the considerable gap between the average educational levels of men and women. The number of younger women attending secondary schools is equal that of men and the flow of female students to university has increased recently not only in absolute terms but also relatively to men. In 1955, the proportion of women among all university students was 29%. By 1965 it had risen to 38%.

Interestingly, there seems to be a difference between the motivation of girls and that of boys in going on to secondary school. Härnquist and Grahm found that boys far more often than girls indicated that their decision to carry on with their studies was dictated by the need to prepare themselves for their chosen career.[1] Girls were more often inclined than boys to claim that they enjoyed school and didn't wish to discontinue their studies, that they were uncertain about their choice of occupation, or that a secondary school education would be useful as a general background. Many girls, however, refrained from continuing their studies beyond the primary level because they had relatively low career ambitions not requiring a secondary school education, or they felt that there wasn't much point in girls sitting for the G.C.E.

The girls' different approach to secondary school studies is also reflected in their choice of speciality: in general they prefer the humanities or languages, while boys more often select 'practical' specialities such as the natural sciences or technical courses.

In 1960, approximately 60% of the male secondary school graduates had concentrated their studies in the natural sciences or technical subjects while only 20% of the female graduates had pursued such courses. Five years later, in 1965, there was little change in these proportions. And if one accepts the estimates of education forecasts

[1] Härnquist and Grahn, *op. cit.*

there will be little change in the foreseeable future. In the new two year training colleges, which offer courses of study similar to those offered by the secondary schools, there is a similar differentiation between the course concentrations of boys and girls.

TABLE 10

Courses of Study of Swedish Secondary School Graduates 1960 and 1965

	Languages and Humanities		Natural Sciences		Commercial Secondary School		Technical Secondary School		Total	
	Men	Women	Men	Women	Men	Women	Men	Women	Men	Women
1960	2,065	3,353	2,779	939	538	514	1,147	46	6,529	4,848
%	32	69	43	19	8	11	17	1		
1965	3,384	6,586	6,084	2,538	1,076	1,299	2,892	264	13,436	10,687
%	25	62	45	24	8	12	22	2		

Source: National Central Bureau of Statistics. Forecasting Institute. Figures are for June, 1965.

There is a marked tendency among girl students, far more than boys, to select course concentrations that are not directly career-oriented. This is apparent not only at the secondary level, as we have seen, but at all levels of education. In the universities, for example, women are predominant in the humanities and social science faculties. This tendency is also evident in the following table (Table 11) which contains

TABLE 11

The Proportion of Women among Gainfully Occupied University Graduates and Newly Registered Students

	Women	
Faculty	Percent of gainfully occupied university graduates	Percent of new registered students
Law	9	19
Medicine	14	21
Humanities and Social Sciences	50	58
Natural Sciences	22	24
Colleges of Technology	2	5
Colleges of Business Administration	7	14
Dentistry	27	40
Pharmacy	27	47
Chemical Prescription	90	100

Source: Census of the Population in 1960. Vol. IX.

the proportion of women in the total number of employed university graduates and among new students. The only exceptions to the rule at the university level appear to be found in the law and dental faculties.

Consequently, though the expansion of the educational system is creating a growing number of educated women, it appears to presage no pronounced change in the occupational structure in the foreseeable future.

In the vocational schools, career choice is subject to an even greater degree to the traditional view of different occupational roles for men and women (Table 12). The relatively small proportion of girls that select a technical speciality are concentrated in courses in which few boys are found, probably because these courses lead to careers of a more clearly subordinate nature. Thus, girls in technical courses are evenly divided between two specialities: laboratory assistant and drafting.

TABLE 12

Full-Time Students in Vocational School Courses

Sex	Technical	Industrial	Clerical	Household	Nursing	Other	Total
Men	7,197	32,349	3,673	713	42	2,173	46,147
Women	880	3,713	11,835	9,303	3,389	422	29,542

Source: National Central Bureau of Statistics. Statistical Reports, V 1965: 5.

Almost one-half of the 4,000 girls taking industrial training courses were concentrated in textile and needle-work while most of the remainder were in training as hairdressers. Much of the training received by girls in vocational schools is not intended to be used to further a career but rather in their own home.

The continuing expansion of the education programme in Sweden will undoubtedly give young people a certain advantage over older individuals on the labour market; that is, younger men in relation to older men; younger women in relation to older women. However, it is questionable whether the rising educational level of women will lead to a reduction of the distributional disparities between men and women in the present occupational structure.

There is a growing demand for highly qualified and technically educated individuals in private industry. Yet the technical courses are dominated by men. The proportion of women studying these subjects remains fairly constant although there are no objective obstacles to a shift. It appears that young girls today often lack interest in work in private industry—a sector that is swiftly expanding and a source of responsible and independent positions. Moreover, many young women are prevented from obtaining vocational experience and hence the necessary background for higher positions by early family formation and the shortage of child care centres.

Perhaps the seeds of change are contained in the growth of the adult education programme and the subsidized adult retraining programmes —a notable feature of the new, active national manpower policy.

V. *Swedish Labour Market Policy*

Prior to World War II, the dominant objectives of public policy in the Swedish labour market were employment creation and unemployment relief. Public works programmes, state subsidies for housing construction, unemployment insurance, expansive government budgets and a network of municipal labour exchanges were the primary policy measures. For the first ten post-war years, such measures continued to figure prominently in the public arsenal though a slight shift in policy aims created a new emphasis on the prevention as well as the mitigation of the employment effects of the trade cycle. It was only towards the end of the 1950s that a truly 'active labour market policy' began to evolve. Under this new approach the government not only undertook to combat unemployment and counter cyclical variations in employment, but also addressed itself to the problems of facilitating the adjustment of manpower and management to a continuously changing economy and technology and improving the utilization of manpower resources.[1]

Even though occasional examples of policy measures applicable solely to female workers—such as the 1939 legal prohibition of the discharge of women employees on the grounds of engagement, marriage or pregnancy—can be detected on the whole labour market, measures were applied without special regard to sex until the early 1960s. Such 'neutrality', however, meant in practice that the benefits of public measures were directed to the male sector of the labour force. Thus, the extensive public works programmes and the state subsidies for

[1] A survey of Swedish manpower policy is provided by *Labour Market Policy in Sweden*, OECD (1963) and Olsson, Bertil, *Employment Policy in Sweden*, International Labour Review No. 5 (1963).

housing construction resulted mainly in increased employment for male workers.

During the early 1960s, the increasingly acute shortage of male workers as well as a heated public debate on the social implications of sex role differences helped to awaken interest in the possibilities of improving the employment position of women within the framework of an active manpower policy.

The measures urged and adopted to improve the vocational lot of women have not been confined to reforms in the public employment services (i.e. the National Labour Market Board, the 25 County Labour Boards and the network of local employment exchanges). They have also reached into such areas as vocational guidance given in the schools, vocational education, family taxation and municipal programmes for child care.

One tangible result of these efforts has been the greater measure of co-operation, at local as well as central levels, between labour market authorities and the school and child welfare systems in the attempt to provide women and girls with a wider range of occupational and training choices and ease the burden of families with both parents gainfully occupied.[1] Other gains have been the Swedish Parliament's discontinuance of its prohibition against night shift work for women in private industry in 1962 and its introduction of a more favourable tax scheme for working married couples in 1965.[2] These changes represent the first returns of a movement to introduce many other reforms of social and taxation legislation and manpower policy.

If we focus our attention on the current programmes run by the Swedish labour market authorities pertaining especially to women, we can compile the following list:

(a) The Public Employment Service

In recent years, more than one million job vacancies have been registered annually with the public labour exchanges (private employment agencies are illegal); almost 80% of these vacancies have been filled each year by registered job seekers. The proportion of women among

---

[1] The budget appropriation to municipal day nurseries rose from 20 million Sw.kr. (about £1·3 million) in 1963 to 48 million Sw.kr. (about £3·2 million) in 1966.
[2] A new tax policy of separate taxation for married couples with both partners working has been mooted as a measure to stimulate the return of married women to the labour market. The Minister of Finance has appointed a special committee to study the problem. The current system of joint taxation acts as an economic dis-incentive to married women wishing to work.

I   *Changing Roles*

all job applicants as well as the total number of filled vacancies has been roughly similar to their share of the overall Swedish labour force, i.e. 35 to 40% including part-time workers. According to these figures it would appear that on the whole women have resorted to the exchanges and have enjoyed exchange services to the same extent as men. Other investigations suggest, however, that unemployed men use the labour exchanges considerably more often than unemployed women.

Marked differences, too, can be found between the proportions of men and women placed in certain occupational categories. For instance, in 1964 women were placed by the exchanges in 98% of all vacancies in domestic work, 93% of all positions in the nursing field, 91% in textile industry and 85% in clerical positions. By contrast, women managed to fill only 10% of all blue collar jobs. Since this pattern of placement, if continued, would perpetuate the present containment of women to a significantly smaller number of occupations than men, directives have been issued to the labour exchanges to limit sex discrimination in their services. As well, the prevailing practice of dividing certain sections within the exchanges according to sex is to be discontinued. This reorganization will be completed in the next few years.

(b) Vocational Guidance

Vocational guidance courses are provided in all comprehensive schools by teachers and school administrators specially trained by the National Labour Market Board. In addition, the County Labour Boards have special sections in their vocational guidance divisions, one devoted to providing career guidance in the higher school grades and another to industrial guidance both within and without the school system. Though the largest proportion of those receiving vocational guidance are young people, increasing numbers of middle-aged and elderly persons have applied for and received guidance services in recent years. These services in certain cases included gratuitous, psycho-technical and vocational aptitude tests.

The proportions of men and women receiving vocational guidance have remained more in line in most of the lower age groups in recent years. In the age groups over 40, however, women—whose ranks are increased by those married women returning to gainful employment after a period of child rearing—become the preponderant majority of recipients. In the vocational guidance services, as in employment exchange services, the problems of removing sex discrimination have not been readily solved. Though the teacher's instruction manual in the new comprehensive school urges teachers to encourage those girls who display an interest in technical, mathematical and scientific fields, a more conventional view continues to hold sway among parents as well as teachers.

(c) Adult Training and Education

Sweden's adult training programme, conducted either by or in conjunction with the labour market administration, has greatly expanded since the late 1950s. The programme is divided into beginner, further training and retraining courses varying from 2 weeks to 20 months in length. The courses are given in small rural communities, large training centres in cities, as part of the curriculum of the vocational schools and in private firms. Training is offered in almost 100 different occupations most of which are currently suffering from a shortage of labour. The course content has been designed to give trainees a fairly wide background, extending into related occupations. Before the late 1950s, subsidized adult training was restricted to only a few hundred persons yearly. Since that time, however, such training has been recognized as a vital part of the new labour market policy and the resources allocated to the programmes have swiftly multiplied. Thus, by 1965, almost 46,000 individuals, i.e. more than 1% of the Swedish labour force, were receiving subsidized vocational training.

The adult vocational training programme is financed entirely by public funds; training courses run by private firms are subsidized. The courses are open to everyone and are generally filled through the employment service. Tax-free, training grants are also given to trainees by the public employment service. To qualify, individuals must be unemployed or faced with the prospect of unemployment in the immediate future. Housewives are deemed to be 'unemployed', and single women with young children are eligible for training grants. The grant consists of 410 Sw.kr. (about £27) per month; married women usually receive only half that amount. In addition, trainees may receive a rent subsidy, a dependants allowance, and compensation for travel, training material and work clothes expenses.

In the first few years of the burgeoning training programme, the proportion of women was exceedingly low. However, by 1965, it had risen to 45%. As with other manpower policy activities, the vocational training programme tends in practice to provide quite different services to men than to women. Training courses with female participants are largely concentrated in traditional female occupations (health and medical services, clerical work, etc.); in practice women have continued to choose among a decidedly narrower range of occupations; and generally their courses are amongst those of shortest duration.

The Swedish labour market administration has employed several devices to encourage women participating in the adult training programme to apply for courses outside the traditional range. Short introductory courses in hitherto exclusively or predominantly male occupations have been offered especially to female workers. These have often been followed by more advanced and intensive courses. In addition, special courses have been instituted to assist women to overcome their inadequate background in certain theoretical subjects such as physics, mathematics and chemistry.

(d) Transfer Allowances

The adjustment of the individual worker to a continuously changing labour market often involves movement to a new area. To encourage such geographical labour mobility, a system of cash grants to moving workers was developed in the late 1950s as part of the new active manpower policy programme. The grants, disbursed by the public employment service, consist of a starting bonus of 150–500 Sw.kr. (£10–£34), travel and removal expense allowances and a family allowance where the migrating worker finds it necessary to live separately from his family for a transitional period. In certain distressed areas, unemployed workers can be encouraged to move to expanding communities by the prospect of receiving a special allowance of 2,000 Sw.kr. (£134). Moreover, the labour market administration is authorized to help a moving worker with the sale of his old house and the acquisition of housing in his new community. These forms of assistance and grants are restricted to approximately the same categories of persons eligible for training grants. (Indeed, transfer allowances are often given in conjunction with retraining.)

In 1965, more than 30,000 persons received grants covering their travel expenses in the process of job seeking; 3,000 received removal allowances; more than 21,000 obtained starting bonuses and almost 2,000 were given special incentive allowances.

In the past, transfer allowances were taken up largely by male workers, though the proportion of women receiving grants has risen steadily since 1960; the proportion of women receiving starting bonuses, for example, rose from 5% in 1960 to 28% in 1965. In this way it has been possible to reduce unemployment, both registered and concealed, especially among single women in rural communities.

(e) *Vocational Rehabilitation Services*

Vocational rehabilitation services for disabled persons have long figured among the measures used by the public employment service to assist job applicants. In Sweden, this service is essentially non-medical and concerns itself with such measures as placement, testing, training, 'sheltered employment', and assistance to disabled persons starting their own small business. During the period 1960–64, the number of disabled persons referred to jobs by the Vocational Rehabilitation Division of the National Employment Service rose from about 14,000 to 30,000. The factors underlying this striking increase, in addition to the greater resources allocated to vocational testing and training, have been the increased assignment of disabled persons to adult training courses and the reorganization of emergency public works to serve as sheltered employment for difficult to place workers.

The proportion of women referred to public works projects as part of the rehabilitation process has declined from 20% in 1960 to less than 16% in 1965. The decline is closely related to the emphasis on male jobs in the emergency public works projects—usually of the construction variety—which have increasingly served as 'sheltered employment'. In other words, it is evident that differences in the treatment of workers of different sex characterize the vocational rehabilitation service as well as the employment service, vocational guidance and adult training programmes.

(f) *Conclusions*

The overall impression one receives from the current Swedish manpower policy programme is that it has attempted to alter the bias towards male workers so typical of earlier public policies. It has also effected an increase in the number and proportion of gainfully occupied women. However, though there have been official pronouncements about the need to counteract discrimination according to sex on the labour market and a few occupations provide specific examples of a more enlightened view, it is difficult to discern any pronounced trend towards wider career and training choice among women. Perhaps, certain conventions have become so well established that many more years of concerted effort will be required before they loosen their hold.

The need for a new and more rational set of conventions to encourage men to enter traditional female occupations, is an issue practically ignored so far in the policy debate. Whether men can be persuaded to include such occupations in their career selections cannot be answered at this stage; few, if any, public policy measures have attempted to promote this practice. However, if such steps are not taken, it seems likely that conditions of employment in the predominantly male labour market will continue to improve, while those in the female occupations will continue to become relatively less favourable. A factor of great importance in this connection will be the behaviour of wage differentials between different occupations. If, as is likely, the Swedish wage structure remains as rigid as in the past—a rigidity which has persisted even over the long terms—there will be a continuing income incentive for women to enter male occupations. On the other hand, the movement of men into traditional female occupations will be discouraged by the prospect of lower wage earnings.

EMPLOYER ATTITUDES
TO FEMALE EMPLOYEES

by SIV THORSELL

Introduction

THE way in which sex differences have permeated the labour market
in Sweden was described in the preceding chapter. There it
was shown that more than 70% of all working women were concentrated in 20 occupations; a range which included only 12% of the
total number of working men. It was also shown that the distribution of
men and women amongst the various job categories and salary levels
was highly uneven in many occupational sectors. A good example was
that of the white collar employees in private industry and the civil
service. Almost three-fourths of the male salaried employees in private
industry were placed in jobs of a technical, supervisory or commercial
nature while only 9% of the female salaried employees held such
positions. Almost 90% of the women white collar employees in private
industry were concentrated in clerical work, a job sector which claimed
only one-fourth of all male salaried employees in industry. Broadly,
then, women white collar employees in the civil service as well as private
industry are concentrated in the lowest job levels; a significantly higher
proportion of men enjoy the positions at the medium-high and highest
levels.

The distribution of men and women by industry (Table 1) gives
further evidence of the pervasive influence of sex differences in working
life.

The first three chapters of this book, which described the content
and meaning of 'sex roles' and the firm hold they have gained in
different social contexts, help to explain how this cleavage has arisen
and how it can persist over such a long period. The great majority
of the population follow the conventional pattern, which in turn
influences the career decisions of boys and girls. Furthermore the
traditonal outlook appears to be the accepted view of employers in

TABLE 1a

Distribution of Women and Men in Industry

Industry	Women		Men	
	No.	%	No.	%
Agriculture, Forestry, Fishing, etc.	38,865	4·0	408,087	17·91
Total Manufacturing	247,743	25·7	861,184	37·80
Building and Construction	9,621	1·0	285,372	12·53
Electric, Gas and Waterworks	3,128	0·3	32,210	1·4
Trade	209,366	21·7	229,160	10·06
Transport and Communications	43,321	4·5	198,537	8·72
Services[1]	410,094	42·5	233,221	10·24
Miscellaneous	2,556	0·3	8,007	0·35
Total	966,027	100·0	2,278,057	

[1] Services include clerical and office workers in national and local government.

TABLE 1b

Distribution of Male and Female Manual Workers in Manufacturing Industries[1]

Manufacturing Industry	Women		Men	
	No.	%	No.	%
Food and Beverages	21,806	14·1	40,505	6·6
Textile and Clothing	45,229	29·3	14,947	2·4
Wool	1,750	1·1	52,451	8·5
Paper and Pulp	6,712	4·4	49,757	8·1
Metal	9,624	6·2	107,720	17·5
Engineering and Electrical Equipment	15,413	10·0	129,941	21·1
Transport Vehicles	1,524	1·0	82,222	13·3
Others	52,425	33·9	138,804	22·5
Total	154,583	100·0	616,347	100·0

[1] The seven industries listed employ a total of 3/4ths of all blue collar workers in manufacturing industries.

TABLE 1c

Distribution of Men and Women among Manual Workers, Salaried Employees and Self-employed persons in Manufacturing Industries

	Women		Men	
	No.	%	No.	%
Manual Workers	154,583	62·4	616,347	71·6
Salaried Employees	86,004	34·7	193,905	22·5
Self-employed	7,146	2·9	50,932	5·9
Total	247,743	100·0	861,184	100·0

Source: 1960 National Census.

their recruiting policies. Many factors, all closely interwoven, have combined to conserve the division of the labour market into male and female job sectors. To assume that employers alone are responsible for this development would probably be as narrow an approach as to suppose that fellow employees—men and women—are the sole cause.

Because firms are the immediate decision takers in hiring, promotion and other personnel matters, a study of their attitudes towards female employees can be of great interest. In this chapter, we shall first examine the explanations given by employers for their present policies and procedures. Secondly, we shall analyse these stated reasons to determine the extent to which they have been rationally conceived and based on factual information and the extent to which they have tended merely to follow established customs and traditions which already have or could conceivably become fossilized.

We can then consider the cost-benefit case for the individual employer changing his current personnel policies in so far as they are based on prejudice against female employees. Would more rational personnel practices lead to a worsening or improvement of the profit position of the firm? Unfortunately there are no studies that have attempted to tackle this problem. Surely a necessary condition for such a study would be an investigation of employer as well as employee actions. But since there are few if any examples of employers seriously breaching conventional recruiting patterns it would be extremely difficult to measure the effects of unconventional personnel policies.

One of the basic sources of information in this field is a study carried out by Stina Thyberg for S.N.S. in the late 1950s. The objective of this case study was to bring new ideas as well as an informational base into an area that had hitherto hardly been subjected to serious research.

In retrospect we can see rather clearly how traditional thinking implicitly influenced the formulation of the main lines of this study. Thus, in a study of the prevailing cleavage in the labour market it would have been equally relevant to take the position of men as the point of departure and ask why there were so few men employed as, say, typists, nurses and primary school teachers?

The Format of the S.N.S. Study

For the purpose of this study, discussion groups were formed at six different locations throughout the country. Altogether about seventy managerial staff from medium and large firms participated in these groups; with about sixty holding high production and administrative positions in manufacturing, retailing, shipping, hotel and restaurant services, banking and insurance, and about ten officials in the national employment service and the labour market organizations. The discussions were held throughout the course of one year (1958–59) and complemented by personal interviews.[1]

This was essentially an exploratory study undertaken partly to discover whether firms consciously pursue discriminatory recruitment and personnel policies with respect to male and female employees and partly to clarify the predominant motives prompting such policies.

Inevitably, the majority of the statements made fell into the category of 'apologias' for existing personnel policies. Interviewees tended strongly to defend their companies' reasons for recruiting women and men to separate job categories. Moreover, many statements were tentative and unclear, owing largely to the novel and unexpected nature of the questions. In many cases managerial staff had not begun to consider the reasons underlying the existing sex differences in the job structure of their own firm. Another point worth mentioning is that the views on women personnel discussed and analysed in the study were all those of men. Few women were to be found holding leading managerial positions.

The Strict Division of Jobs by Sex

The S.N.S. study gave a detailed picture of the range of jobs open and closed to women. To what extent are women and men employed in the same branches of industry in the same occupations and in the same job categories? To answer these questions satisfactorily it was necessary carefully to dissect the sex differentiated labour market. Were there even more subtle dividing lines for the male and female personnel than those shown by the statistics and if so what were the reasons asserted for such a differentiation?

It was possible to sift out certain individual occupations that were typically 'male' or typically 'female'. When men and women worked together in the same firm or branch, men almost entirely dominated the highly skilled and supervisory positions, whilst women were largely relegated to unskilled or low skilled positions. Thus, women in the textile industry were most commonly found employed as seamstresses and sewing machine operators and those in the engineering, electrical and chemical industries mainly worked as joiners and fitters,

---

[1] Of the 72 participants, 60 were representatives of specific companies. These covered 41 firms. Interviews were held at 27 of these companies.

inspectors and packers of lighter products. Further, women pre-dominated among the workers in such occupational categories as cleaners, newspaper carriers, cold buffet manageresses, shop assistants, punched card machine operators, cashiers, secretaries, office and draughtsman's assistants, telephone operators and as cooks and serving personnel in catering establishments and small restaurants.

Women were almost entirely excluded from skilled manual job categories such as toolworkers, cutters, typographers, restaurant chefs, etc., as well as heavy or dirty work in manufacturing, warehousing or transport. Extremely few women held positions as technicians, econo-mists or commercial travellers. Rare indeed was a female foreman or department supervisor. And only in family firms could a woman be found in the higher echelons of management.

According to the available data, certain branches and occupations were classifiable as 'mixed' in the sense that the work force comprised men and women in roughly similar proportions. Upon closer scrutiny, however, a strict division of positions could be detected even in these sectors. Thus, even in mixed branches men and women tended to be employed in totally different occupations. And in mixed occupations women were concentrated in particular firms, areas, or work on certain types of products, etc.

The matchstick industry was a typical 'mixed' industry. About 40% of its employees were women and yet most job categories were strictly divided according to sex. Thus, veneer lathe operation, woodstick chopping and drying were entirely 'male' jobs. Women worked mainly at assembling and filling matchboxes.

A similar division prevailed in the textile industry where almost half of the employees were female. The work force consisted of three main types of workers: semi-skilled production workers, highly skilled maintenance workers such as loom mechanics, and 'special' workers. The latter two categories were almost exclusively men while almost all women could be classified as semi-skilled workers.

Yet even in the semi-skilled workers category, there was a marked division of jobs according to sex. In one weaving mill, women were almost entirely employed as rollers, winders, spoolers, twiners, warpers, threaders, etc., whilst men occupied such positions as weavers and loom operators, set-up men and inspectors. The same company had never employed women as weavers or loom operators for wool products but did so for silk products.

Cutters and graders, the 'aristocrats' of the ready-made clothing industry were exclusively men. Women were employed largely as sorters, markers, selectors and in the sewing and ironing departments.

Restaurants, laboratories, shops, banking and insurance, personnel work and journalism are all 'mixed' occupational sectors. Again we find a more subtle differentiation of positions according to sex. The following quotation, the second part of which is obtained from a department store, suggests how finely the distinctions can be drawn.

'Male staff should be dealt with by male personnel consultants and female staff by female personnel consultants.'

Only male sales staff should sell carpets, sporting goods, automobile appliances, and gentlemen's clothing. Male and female staff can sell furniture, electrical appliances and kitchen articles. Only female staff should sell children's and women's clothing.'

In the field of personnel work it was generally found that women held positions as consultants which meant that they were largely involved with the firm's social and human relations problems with its staff. Men were the preponderant majority in the personnel administrative positions such as personnel manager, etc.

Amongst the editors and journalists of the newspaper firms covered by this study, almost all women were working as general sub-editors or general reporters with a few scattered exceptions among the foreign correspondents. Few women could be found in the ranks of the political reporters, the editorial writers, sports reporters, and the city desk editors. One spokesman for the newspaper world stated:

'In the field of journalism, we recognize no difference in principle between men and women. In practice, however, certain types of reporting lend themselves best to men, for example crime and accidents, technical reporting, etc., while other types are most appropriate for women, such as women's pages on clothing, fashion, and food, etc.'

In the laboratories, women workers were employed largely at checking and control tasks. While men advanced to research and development work. This is only one example among many of how in certain mixed professions men and women are placed at entirely different levels. At the outset men and women can be appointed to the same level and do identical work. However, men often tend to have lengthier educational backgrounds and greater opportunities for education and training during the course of their professional career. As well, they appear to have the desire to advance, while women tend to be less 'career-minded'.

The finer the breakdown one makes in branches, occupations and job categories the stronger is one's impression of the sex cleavage in working life. Few occupations are really 'mixed'. To be sure, there are some exceptions, i.e. the pressers in the engineering industry, some types of semi-skilled machine operators and stock workers in other industries, but these are insufficient to disprove the rule.

Employer Motives

The S.N.S. Study produced a rich variety of reasons why employers on the whole recruited men and women to different job categories. The interviewees were often not content with giving only one explanation but tended to marshall several reasons as if to strengthen their cases.

Thus, the strict division of jobs according to sex in the matchstick industry was explained by one of the industry's spokesmen in the following way.

'According to established custom dating back to the time when they made matchboxes by hand originally at home, women have performed these tasks in the industry. Even today, they appear to be particularly well suited to this repetitive and physically light work with its requirements of manual dexterity, speed and patience. Although it is true that women draw lower wages, the key factor is their exceptional suitability for this type of work. This offsets the added labour costs caused by their more frequent absence, higher turnover, etc., and were they to receive wages equal to those of men it would still pay us to employ them at these tasks. To place a few men in this women's work would be almost as difficult an operation as the reverse, largely because the men would find it difficult to accept women's work. Such a step too, would create higher labour costs and thus we attempt it only as an emergency solution to the problem of temporary shortages of female employees.'

It is readily apparent from this statement that a division of labour, plainly a vestige of custom, can also be considered economically justifiable because of certain special qualities attributed to women workers, which make them particularly well suited for such work. Moreover, it is implied that it is as difficult to place women in work now performed by men—no reason is given for this though perhaps an analogy is implicitly drawn between the reactions of the two sexes—as it is to recruit men to 'female' jobs.

One firm stated that women were not recruited for plastics work (pressing, polishing, rinsing, etc.) because they had less technical ability, more frequent absence and higher turnover. Also, such work was considered dirty and unpleasant by comparison with other work in the company; it was not the firm's policy to offer such work to women as long as it was possible to allocate them to more agreeable tasks.

Often, however, the reason for the current recruitment policy was quite simply that it continued the customary way of doing things; there was no rational explanation for the prevailing division of jobs according to sex.

The most common explanation for the concentrated employment of women in certain 'female' job categories was the twofold idea that female labour was relatively cheaper and better suited to the job. The most often heard case against the employment of women in 'male' positions in production work was that all available male manpower in the area should first be employed, that it was not possible to transfer a few women into all-male departments and that the factory lacked the necessary changing facilities for women.

The higher frequency of absence of women and their greater horizontal job mobility—between different work places, and between home and gainful employment—were often asserted to be the determining factors for a 'men only' recruitment policy where no other reasons could be adduced. Thus, in one firm it was said that the increase of 'automation' of foundry processes had already begun to lessen the requirement of physical strength. This, it was felt would have made the company more interested in offering foundry employment to women workers were it not that the newer technological process increased the need for low employee absence rates and long and continuous service.

Another recurrent theme in the case of skilled work was that few women could be found with the requisite training and interest. However, it was often the case that the same firms had not invested in training schemes for women comparable to those they offered to men. Among industrial workers in general, few if any women had attempted to apply to apprentice schools. One firm which had had female applicants had refused them, a course of action that met with the approval of other firms that had not had female applicants. Companies were unwilling to underwrite the risk entailed in an expensive investment in training for women workers. Even though the high turnover rates among women derived from those working in menial and highly routine jobs, the same behaviour pattern was attributed to all women.

The reasons put forward for discriminatory recruitment can be summarized under three main headings:

Cost, i.e. that hiring women instead of men resulted in relatively higher or lower labour costs.

Role Preconceptions, i.e. attitudes in working life that men and women should discharge different functions in our society—that the right place for a woman is in the home! Men were viewed as family breadwinners and as such entitled to first priority in respect of employment. Women should not work at jobs that are dirty, involve pressure or entail responsibility. These opinions were based on the assumption that men and women are basically different in many physical, sociological and psychological respects.

Physical and Mental Differences. It was generally assumed that such differences are great, though this was not verified. It was often asserted that such differences are inherited characteristics. Such an explanation was often put forward to emphasize that women are more suitable for certain jobs while men are for others.

Role preconceptions were also frequently based on social or family needs, i.e., someone must be home to care for the children, the husband and the home and responsibility for such functions has traditionally devolved upon women. Occasionally it was suggested that 'this was the way things should be' but in a majority of cases such ideas were expressed as a statement that this was the current division of family responsibilities and that such a division adversely affected women in their vocational role.

Let us examine more closely these three basic types of reasons put forward by company spokesmen to explain and justify the present cleavage of the labour market into 'male' and 'female' job sectors.

Costs

With few exceptions, companies claimed that routine work requiring a short period of training and inherently less sensitive to high rates of absence and labour turnover was eminently suited for recruitment amongst women from the standpoint of labour costs. As far as more highly skilled work was concerned however, i.e. work sensitive to frequent absence and high turnover and requiring a protracted training period, they felt that it was altogether too risky to hire female personnel.

In the former case, women were regarded as a cheaper source of manpower than men, partly because they could be paid relatively lower wages and partly because it was assumed that they perform such work more acceptably than men.[1]

Thus, within the engineering industry, women performed and were assumed to perform best such tasks as routine inspection, control, electrical testing and adjustment. In one firm it was reported that,

'Such work is light and requires care and cleanliness, rather than muscular strength or training. For economic reasons, we should employ more women in such jobs than we do at present.'

Another company representative suggested that:

'As far as winding and insulation work are concerned, women and men are equally efficient and consequently we employ women for economic reasons.'

In one firm in which women constituted almost half of the employees working in the assembly of medium- and light-weight electrical products the following view was put forward:

'They (the women) are cheaper, both under the collective bargaining agreement and in the labour market; they are better at this particular type of work.'

Here as in many other cases, other assumptions were implicitly entwined with the economic and suitability arguments, assumptions that women are easier to deal with, more agreeable and have less need for promotion or wage equity than men.

In many cases, however, it appeared that some quite light jobs were reserved for men. This was explained by the fact that certain elements of the job were too heavy for women. Further, certain light work was reserved for partially disabled male workers; this was particularly true in heavy industry. A number of firms in areas with a small population concentration thought that they should give priority to employing men. Often, the reason given for the refusal to hire female staff for physically light work was that the firm wanted to have a sufficient recruitment base for its foremen and technicians.

It was commonly felt that even given equal pay for equal work, women would be preferred for certain repetitive and routine work. The following two statements, the first related to inspection, the second to packing work, were made by spokesmen of chemical companies.

[1] The principle of equal pay for equal work has been accepted in Sweden since 1962 upon adherence to the convention on Equal Pay for Men and Women. As indicated in Chapter 4, present practice is somewhat at variance with this principle. For as long as men and women continue to work in different types of jobs, the equal pay principle will have only a very limited significance.

'Plainly, the lower wages of women affect our decision, but the suitability factor is so influential that even were women's wages equal to those of men we should prefer women inspectors.'

'For purely manual packing, the manual dexterity of women as well as their patience are the decisive factors in our choice. Even given conditions of equal pay, it would not be profitable to resort to male workers for such work. We might, however, use male workers for machine work under such conditions, since men are better at this sort of thing.'

In most industries, the decisive motives for the division of jobs according to sex appear to be relative costs and suitability. The former factor is often strongly affected by the local labour market conditions. There is generally stiff competition for male manpower in the high wage industries, while women are employed largely in low wage industries.

Women are employed in all lower clerical positions for reasons already mentioned, i.e., they are cheaper, quicker and more contented with their lot.

'. . . They leave the labour force so early that we need pay only youth's wages; they do not require the same promotion opportunities and wage rises as men even if they remain with the firm for the same period of time. It is not surprising, then, that wage differences tend to widen with age. And, in this type of work, the higher labour costs of women due to their higher absence and turnover rates does not offset the male–female wage differential. As a consequence, we have begun to rely almost exclusively on female staff for general office work.'

All four insurance companies participating in the study hired only female school leavers just above the minimum school leaving age. With few exceptions men were recruited directly to higher positions after acquiring a good education. One reason put forward for this disparate treatment was that:

'given our starting wages at the lowest training levels we cannot compete for boys with other branches.'

As far as the traditional female clerical positions were concerned, it appeared that there was widespread agreement throughout firms, industries and branches as to the underlying causes. A large proportion of cashiers were women (even in banking). In industry, however, women were mainly employed as assistant cashiers and paymasters though there were cases where they had attained positions as head cashiers. It was said that:

K   *Changing Roles*

'For skilled repetitive work such as that performed by cashiers and paymasters, there seems to be little difference between the effectiveness of men and women. Women do the work equally well for lower wages.'

The cost factor was often mixed with the suitability factor in the case of skilled jobs at all levels. In general, men were considered more suitable for such jobs particularly as far as supervisory work was concerned. Moreover, women were considered to be a more expensive form of labour because of their higher absence and turnover rates. In the following example from an insurance firm, it also appeared that the fact that women's relatively poorer chances to obtain higher positions stems from the firm's general recruiting policy:

'Since men and women are paid equal salaries, and men have lower absence and turnover rates, greater willingness to train, and are more highly motivated in their work, we always take a man before a woman to fill a higher position, if we have the choice. This policy does tend to worsen the chances for women to obtain highly skilled and responsible positions.'

The opinion that women on the average are absent more frequently and the uncertainty about the length of their service resulted in an unwillingness on the part of firms to take a chance on women employees at the higher level. Yet the following point was made during the course of the discussion:

'If women were promoted more often there would probably be less turnover amongst them and a consequent increase in male turnover, due to the increased competition. Were we to advance to this point, many of the presently observed differences between male and female employee behaviour would disappear.'

Yet the more common reaction was that contained in the following statement:

'Where training qualifications and merits are equal, men are preferable since employers must take into account the economic factor.'

As far as work which is almost entirely 'female' was concerned it was said that:

'Those that want to have a *stenographer* who is satisfactory from the start and stays with the job, should choose a woman. A man will soon advance to a higher position.'

It is not possible to draw any clear economic conclusions from such reasoning. The statements are not based on factual information but simply beliefs and general preconceptions. One tendency pervading such statements is worthy of note. Certain firms appeared to have a vested interest in maintaining the sexual division in the labour market. As long as the female labour market was limited to a few occupations, the wage level for those occupations would be lower because of the large supply of labour relative to the demand for it. In the male labour market, a larger and more widely differentiated market, employees enjoyed a stronger bargaining position.

It is also worth observing in this context that firms in the manual and white collar sectors which stated their unwillingness to invest in the training and promotion of women added that the women themselves were unwilling to be trained and promoted. The fear was expressed too that women would tend to 'stop up' the promotion system by staying in jobs which were meant to be transitional positions. Yet paradoxically these were the same persons who felt that women tended to have higher turnover rates and hence were more uncertain investments with respect to promotion and training. Since firms actually invested in women to such a small extent, it was difficult to determine the extent to which the firms' doubts were factually grounded. The category of manpower to which most women belonged, the unskilled, is in general (i.e. including men) the most mobile skill category of all. In other words we may have here simply another case of a vicious cycle. Since the firm will not take a chance on training and promoting women the women have no expectations that they will be given the opportunity to advance with the firm. The current situation, in which women are less interested in training and promotion and more mobile horizontally, is partly a foreseeable consequence of prevailing personnel policies.

The higher turnover rates amongst women can in certain cases be viewed as a cost advantage, and considered as such by the firm's personnel policy. This is evidenced by some of the above quotations on female clerical staff.

Recent history suggests that many of the reasons asserted for the current discrimination against women in the labour market are not based on factual grounds. During the two World Wars, women demonstrated their competence in many jobs that had previously been reserved solely for men. With the advent of peace, the old occupational division was restored. Sweden has experienced full employment and labour shortages for almost the whole of the post-war period. Under such economic conditions firms have again been compelled to change

their recruiting policy and begin to employ women in jobs that previously were more or less reserved to men. It is difficult to be certain
about the ultimate outcome of this development. As we shall see from
the material in subsequent sections, it is quite probable that factors
other than the state of the economy have affected the firms' behaviour.
One such factor has been the attitudes towards the roles of men and
women in the family and working life held by the decision-takers in
the companies as well as by society at large. As was readily apparent
in the above statements of company spokesmen the economic reasons
for discrimination against women were based on preconceptions about
the relative suitability of men and women for different work tasks.

Another important factor—one however which cannot be dealt with
in this chapter—is the education and family welfare policies of the state.

Role Preconceptions

'The Woman's Place'

Although the S.N.S. study was orientated to women and working life,
it soon emerged that views on the subject were strongly influenced by
the interviewees' preconceptions about the social roles of men and women.
Thus, many statements were more an expression of general attitudes
to the sex roles than a rationally considered view of manpower problems.

Many interviewees felt that the traditional role division between
men and women should not be questioned—the right place for women
was in the home, while the man's function was to be the family breadwinner. One personnel manager in a shipping firm stated: 'Stone Age
men hunted while women stayed at home. Hasn't this always been the
case? The woman's efforts in the home are of great value, but can this
value be reduced to monetary terms? Should we attempt to train
women to be mechanics? Wouldn't it be wiser to accept that there are
typical male jobs, that men are in the majority in the labour market and
that they, as family supporters, are entitled to higher wages. If a man
succeeds in his work it is often as a result of teamwork with a housewife
who has been an important member of the team.'

The following two examples suggest that the desire for personal
comfort and convenience cannot be discounted as a factor in men's
attitudes to women's work participation.

'It is a good idea for women to remain in the home. I would not like
to come home tired and worn out from work and then wait for my wife
to come home a bit later, even more weary.'

'One wants to live reasonably comfortably and the essential thing is to have a wife at home to take care of one. I want to set my wife on a pedestal.' (Foreman in the same firm.)

Several company representatives took a more moderate line. They thought that the woman should remain at home at least while the children were small. At the same time, they recognized that this was bound to create difficulties once women attempted to resume vocational roles.

A personnel manager in an engineering firm was one of the few with a more progressive outlook.

'In principle, I am for the idea of helping women as much as possible. . . . In the end however it depends upon them to help themselves. They cannot merely sit and feel sorry for themselves; they must take each other by the scruff of the neck and attempt to improve their position. Women are widely thought to lack the courage to pull themselves up. I have repeatedly tried to get them to take on responsible positions, but even with a bayonet in the back they are unwilling to take a step up the promotional ladder. Intensive propaganda might help if it is spread at several different levels; in the home—where the father, mother and brother must encourage girls so that they will be more interested in education, training and work, and not only in getting married; in managerial circles; and, not least, amongst women themselves.'

These statements on the woman's place have not been included simply to show that the attitudes of company management to women are particularly conservative. The view that the right place for the woman is in the home and that her career is something secondary is one that is widely shared. The important thing about the personal opinions of management however is that they tend to colour the personnel policy of the firm. Thus, an employer with a less traditional approach is probably more inclined to turn to female employees than an employer with a more conservative outlook.

A local manager in an engineering firm made the following statement—indicating that he personally had a highly negative attitude to working mothers but at the same time felt that the problem could be viewed differently from the firm's standpoint:

'The question of female employees is inevitably entwined with that of family relations—a woman with small children should have nothing to do with a factory. Seen purely from the employer's angle however, there is no important difference between selecting men or women—only that the workers concerned do their jobs satisfactorily!!'

The S.N.S. study shows also that the role division currently prevailing in society can be put forward as a kind of social defence for the fact that men have and are given a better position in working life. It was pointed out in the study that the majority of firms acutely feel a greater responsibility to promote men than to promote women.

In general, it is assumed that all working women are engaged in 'dual work', and that this is a handicap particularly in the more highly skilled positions. In many cases, it was said that such work is too difficult to be combined with home and family. The above quotations demonstrate too that higher wages for men can be justified by the fact that the man is the family supporter.

In one insurance company the practice of recruiting only women staff to its lower clerical positions, and taking men with more advanced education directly into higher positions, was explained by the idea that it would be almost criminal to attract boys with such a low education to the office side.

Opinions About the Differences in the Vocational Behaviour of Men and Women

Prejudice or Fact?

In one chapter of the original version of this book Harriet Holter examined the question of whether existing opinions about the vocational behaviour of women were based on facts or stereotyped thinking. She thought that the great majority of people had a strong need to simplify and that this need inevitably gave rise to prejudices, to the attribution of certain characteristics to a person simply because he or she belonged to a category of persons, e.g., a given race or sex, in which such traits were common, without any attempt to discover whether the person in question actually had such traits. She further emphasized the fact that stereotypes made it possible to 'simplify' socially and psychologically, and that this facilitated evaluations and decisions in many situations.

On the basis of her own investigation Harriet Holter compiled a list of the most common opinions of women's vocational behaviour. These were given in Chapter I (p. 49). She felt that in many cases there were good grounds for assuming that such opinions were based on prejudices and stereotyped thinking. Though she stressed that this did not preclude the possibility that factual differences actually existed. It was thus conceivable that there were certain average sex differences even given a fairly wide dispersion around each mean. To confirm the validity of such views it would be necessary to resort to empirical research. And were sex differences to emerge from such a study, the next step in the analysis would be to determine their causes.

The S.N.S. study gives us the opportunity to distinguish between two different kinds of existing stereotypes with respect to women at work.

Certain jobs are viewed as typically woman's work, i.e., certain jobs are assumed to be appropriate for women (or men) while other jobs are assumed not to be suited to women (men). This view plainly stems from traditional role preconceptions which in turn are based largely on prejudice. The exponents of such views neither explicitly acknowledged nor appeared conscious of the fact that they felt that certain vocational traits were sex-linked.

The second type of stereotyped thinking, i.e. the type analysed by Harriet Holter, was the view that men and women have certain (innate or acquired) characteristics which express themselves in differences in behaviour in certain situations and which justify the recruitment of men and women to different types of work. Let us take a closer look at some of the stated views of the mental and physical differences between the sexes.

In general these statements were marked by either the absence of an ideal range of vocational behaviour, i.e. the basis for a comparison, or the tendency to employ the vocational behaviour of men as the norm for comparison. 'Masculine' traits were preferred for 'masculine' jobs but such a conclusion strongly suggested the possibility that it was based on traditions that had evolved in an occupation that had hitherto been performed only by men.

'Certain jobs are appropriate for women, certain jobs are not!'

Work to which women are the predominant recruits is often characterized as 'typically female work'. The implication is that such work is what the speaker feels is 'appropriate for women'.

Referring to plastics rinsing, one company spokesman declared, 'This is typical women's work, light and clean. Indeed we shall have more women here because they are cheaper'.

Electrical winding was also considered to be 'a light and traditionally female job reminding one of sewing'.

In the case of secretarial work—almost exclusively a female occupation—it was said that, 'It is more natural for women to work in such an occupation because it involves hostess-type functions.'

'A typically female occupation! The perfect secretary should be the manager's daytime wife—take care of him, correct and keep track of all that he does.'

Sales assistants in large department stores are predominantly women. In one store, this was explained by the fact that this type of selling is more attractive to women than to men.

'It is work that brings one into contact with people, is generally light and reasonably neat and is, moreover, traditionally accepted as women's work.'

A representative from one engineering firm which employed no women as machinists stated that 'such work was not as nice as other work we could offer our female staff'. In that firm women were employed in assembly work, which was assumed to be acceptable to them because it was 'neat and tidy'. He added that,

'many firms use women on heavy and dirty jobs, but we think that our work division strikes a more congenial note at the workplace'.

In one department store only women staff were assigned to the buffet. Besides the suitability and labour market factors, it was stated

'that it is the nicest and neatest way. We have never considered men for such work.'

There are many other examples of situations where employers could not imagine men in jobs considered to be 'typically female'.

In the preceding chapter, it was observed that the 20 occupations in which more than 70% of the female labour force were placed and predominated, were largely occupations associated in some way with 'traditional female tasks' such as cooking, sewing, nursing, etc. The S.N.S. investigation showed that firms were more inclined to employ women in positions which had such an association. Thus, in one statement above, winding work in the electrical industry was characterized as a typically female job because of its resemblance to sewing. And commercial travelling was considered by most spokesmen to be clearly a male occupation. One company representative pointed out however, that 'there are certain sales lines that would be well suited to women—buttons and ribbons, etc.'.

Certain occupations have become predominantly female because they were originally handicraft work that was subsequently 'industrialized'. There are good examples of this in the textile and matchstick industries (see p. 141). In the latter industry, the study found that the traditional views of women as well as men about what are appropriate male and female tasks had influenced the job division.

Many company representatives expressed surprise at the fact that women were not found in certain types of work which were palpably 'good for women'. Thus, in the textile industry surprise was registered that there were no women technicians on production work despite the large female share of the overall work force. The absence of women technicians in male-dominated industries was however never questioned. Another example was that of skilled bookkeeping and accounting work where the firms in the investigation employed no women. In one firm it was said that,

'The more routine aspects of bookkeeping work are particularly well suited to women.'

The feeling that certain types of work were not appropriate for women was expressed in a sort of chivalrous solicitude for women. Women should not be subjected to work that was too dirty, heavy, responsible or straining. In one food laboratory in which 60% of the staff were women, a proportion explained by their relative cheapness, it was thought that it was not possible to employ women for all jobs

'since some employees must travel around to take tests and we did not want to send women out on such tasks during the dark winter afternoons and evenings'.

All thought that porters in office buildings should be men because the position could entail much work that was too heavy, unpleasant and risky for women.

'We do not want to subject women to the risks connected with, for example, the transport of money, and the women themselves are reluctant to undertake such tasks.'

'Women are appropriate for some jobs and not for others'

Many of the opinions of female and male work behaviour noted by Harriet Holter in her Norwegian study (see Chapter I) appeared to be shared by the subjects of the Swedish study.

One explanation of why women industrial workers were placed in unskilled, routine and closely supervised work tasks frequently recurred: women were more appropriate for such jobs than men. This conclusion was based on the assumptions that women had greater manual dexterity, were more orderly and service-minded than men.

It was often remarked that women more easily accept the repetitiveness, lack of opportunity for advancement and lack of independence that characterize such work.

Similar reasoning was put forward to explain use of women in certain jobs in the medical and welfare sector. It was inconceivable that anyone other than women would perform the nursing functions because women had the disposition necessary for such work.

Even in the case of the secretarial occupation, many of the interviewees stated that women were more suitable than men because of their feminine characteristics. It was thought that women in this work were more co-operative and found it easier to accept supervision than men.

'It is easy to work together with a clever woman secretary. No man can compare with one.'

'It is much easier to get along with a woman secretary; one finds it harder to deal with a man.'

A department store had experimented with both male and female interpreters and found that as a rule the latter had 'an easier and milder manner. Besides, they are more decorative.'

Department store sale clerks are, as was mentioned, predominantly female. At one store it was said that

'Female characteristics are best; gentleness and the ability to adjust are most appropriate for such sales work.'

In such jobs, the characteristics attributed to women may have been positive factors but in other types of work the same qualities were felt to be disadvantageous. Thus, the asserted lack of independence of women workers excluded them from more highly skilled work. The notion that they were more able to accept repetitive work and more willing to take orders was interpreted to mean that they could not assume responsibility and discharge supervisory functions.

The restriction of women to a narrow range of job categories in private industry was often explained by the fact that most of the other jobs were too heavy or dirty for women. No company however, had attempted to investigate whether all jobs performed only by men actually required great physical strength. It was felt that even in jobs that were usually light there were occasional heavy tasks to be performed requiring male bodily strength. It was often suggested that as long as there were more agreeable jobs available, i.e. jobs that were not heavy and dirty, women should be first used for such jobs. It was generally agreed that women were more suited to the lighter and stationary jobs because of their greater patience and dexterity.

A common argument against the use of women in technical work was that they were not technically gifted. Women were also thought to be inappropriate for positions which, though not requiring particular technical ability, did require the ability to direct machine adjustments and the repair of technical faults, etc. One works superintendent stated that,

'We see this very clearly in comparisons of men and women in the same routine tasks and with equally little training. In routine work the difference is not great, but once the machines make trouble it becomes more obvious. Then the men will themselves look for the fault and in many instances succeed in repairing it; while the women simply sit down and wait for help.'

Occasionally interviewees suspected that the lesser technical ability of women was innate:

'. . . There are no women inventors in the purely technical areas and that cannot be explained simply by environmental differences.'

In one chemical firm with women providing a considerable proportion of its laboratory work force, there were no women in supervisory posts. A partial explanation was that,

'Women have accepted the tradition that they shall not educate or train for technical areas and as long as this tradition prevails the likelihood of finding a woman with suitable technical qualifications is practically nil.'

It was also observed that:

'Women are unwilling to take chances. This is related to the fact that they are less independent and more conservative and tend more to resist new developments than men. They are also clearly more unwilling to take on positions of responsibility.'

In the same company women were thought to be particularly well suited to control analysis—a skilled repetitive job where their care and patience were regarded as an asset. 'That is one job where one does not have to be a risk-taker.'

The reasons put forward to account for the paucity of female supervisors—in addition to their lack of training and relatively high turnover rates—were largely psychological. Women in general were thought to lack leadership qualities. It appeared from the study however, that those firms that had had some experience with female supervisors were more approving than the others.

One spokesman for a printing firm that had no female supervisors stated:

'Foremen must exercise a certain degree of authority over the workers. Women are too weak and lack sufficient general background. Most firms are convinced that women would find it difficult to supervise large groups of personnel particularly where the staff included male employees. A male supervisor can speak plainly to male workers. Even women prefer male supervisors. We have seen evidence of greater rivalry between women.'

One firm explained that women were excluded from its higher managerial positions because it thought that they could not bear the brunt of such heavy responsibilities and that they would not be able to master the range of human relations skills required by the job. Another industrial firm thought that women were fine as section heads but,

'Women seldom have the physical and psychological reserves or the organizational and leadership abilities required to manage a large department, a job which is probably the most difficult going.'

Female supervisors can be found primarily in the ready-made clothing and chemical industries, in banking and insurance firms, and in retailing. Among these firms women were felt to be acceptable as supervisors. The following statement was made by the spokesman for a chemical firm for which 25% of its supervisory staff and 60% of its total work force were women.

'We have many women who have proved themselves to be capable supervisors, who have won acceptance in their shops as well as men and who have worked exceedingly well with their male department heads.'

The interviewees had the greatest difficulty imagining a woman as a supervisor of male staff. Yet there was some gradation of opinion on this issue. One company representative who at first thought it to be out of the question to have women supervisors placed over men staff, began to speculate during the interview about the relative advantages of women supervisors for men and vice versa. A number of interviewees thought it best to have women supervisors for women, while others thought it obvious that a man should supervise women.

One firm said that 'it is easier for women to control women, more difficult for men to have female supervisors'.

A bank representative indicated that it had had rather favourable experience of women supervising male personnel.

'We have women group supervisors—the groups consisting of anywhere from 5 to 24 persons including men. It is often said that women are afraid to assume positions of responsibility; and it may be true that they are reluctant to take the leap to managerial positions, but once having done so they are capable of discharging heavy responsibilities as satisfactorily as male managers.'

What are the qualities required in a good supervisor? Commercial traveller? personnel worker? The answers to these questions varied greatly depending on the interviewee. Sales were considered by many to demand 'male' characteristics, i.e. aggressiveness, pushfulness, etc. On the other hand, some wondered whether modern selling techniques did not require more of the talents of a woman, neatness, pleasant manner, etc.

Two firms with female personnel consultants rendered different accounts of their experiences. One firm generalized that,

'Women not only find it difficult to avoid showing their feelings but also are less successful in stamping their authority on other staff. They are too spontaneous in their dealings. Men tend to think things out beforehand.'

However, the other firm, a textile company, stated that,

'They [women] have an exceptional ability to plan their exchanges and employ a fine psychological strategy. They get people to talk and they listen.'

Several interviewees thought that effective supervision required authoritativeness and firmness, etc., qualities which men possessed but women lacked. Others felt however, that good supervision required psychological insight, an ability more characteristic of women. Opinions were rather divided about the requirements for different occupations and the extent to which women and men correspond to these qualities.

One argument often raised against women was that they would not be accepted by employees or customers. Male employees would not accept a woman amongst them let alone a woman supervisor. Supervisors opposed the firm's hiring of women. The bank's customers often 'wanted a man in extreme cases to talk things over with when something needed to be cleared up'. Male customers expect to be sold to by male salesmen, there is a 'certain preference among customers to buy meat from male shop assistants', etc. One banking spokesman stated:

'Female staff can handle all counter services duties with the one exception of loans. These are negotiated in private and require a detailed discussion of personal problems and it is surely easier for men and women to confide in men. Perhaps too, it would be more difficult for women officials to withstand the charms of male customers.'

In some cases, the integration of men and women at the same work place was thought to create disciplinary problems, with occasional moral overtones. In other cases it was felt that the mixture might have a favourable effect on discipline. The gravest reservations about the integration of personnel were held by firms which had never attempted it. Among all the pioneer cases, not one had reported disciplinary problems due to integration. One of the firms which had a female worker in a fairly large male section explained away the favourable experience by the fact that 'the woman was just the sort that could carry it off. If younger women were transferred there would surely be some disorder.' At work places, however, where men and women had worked together for a long while, disciplinary problems due to integration were unheard of. In one firm with mixed personnel in several workshop sections, certain benefits were seen to be derived from the integration:

'The young, attractive and well groomed girls that we always have had and will have in the work shop have had an exceedingly favourable effect on morale and the somewhat older women often provide a kind of motherly stability in the plant.'

In many statements, it was emphasized that women placed in skilled positions which had previously been filled by men are often closely scrutinized and subjected to particularly exacting demands. A woman in a 'man's' position, becomes a representative of her sex, a sort of 'guinea pig'.

'Suitability depends largely on personal motivation, and not on a person's sex. Men and women get the same information about training opportunities. If women could only raise themselves vocationally and technically they could be supervisors even over men. But plainly the pioneers must be keener than their male colleagues if they are to break the ice.'

In another engineering firm, the thought of employing women as work study experts evoked the following response:

'The first women on that job will have to overcome an extra dose of scepticism.'

A representative of an insurance firm shared this view. He felt that women who advanced to higher managerial positions would meet with relatively greater critical resistance from the people they encountered.

Women who are reasonably successful at 'men's' jobs are often suspected of not being 'real women' or else the phenomenon is explained by the fact that they are 'exceptional women'.

A few engineering firms had employed a small number of women as stock-room workers. One firm reported that, 'they perform jobs which are plainly men's jobs and they perform them well'. The women however were considered to be 'exceptionally mannish for women', even though some were small and slender.

One company spokesman had met two female saleswomen during the course of a business journey to Poland and had made the following personal discovery.

'One woman bore the authority of a division head and yet in no way appeared forced. She wasn't even a chemist but had begun as a secretary for the firm. Both women appeared to be highly normal and not particularly mannish.'

Are There Differences in the Vocational Behaviour of Men and Women?

How do the foregoing employer beliefs, attitudes and reasons relate to reality? Is it true for example, that turnover and absence rates are relatively higher among women workers when comparisons are made between truly comparable groups, i.e. when such factors as age, training, education, qualifications and experience are taken into account?

Recent studies of worker absence have consistently found that a relatively small fraction of the work force accounts for the preponderant part of total absences. In addition, such studies have indicated that there is a fairly clear relationship between absence due to illness and age, salary level and job status. Thus, younger workers tend to be absent more frequently than older workers, low paid workers more frequently than high paid workers and those performing unskilled and repetitive tasks more frequently than those holding highly skilled and responsible positions. Since women in the labour market are on the average considerably younger and lower paid, and tend to be employed in unskilled jobs more often than men, their absence rates are often particularly high.

Similarly, there is some empirical evidence to suggest that the average labour turnover rates of women are relatively higher than those of men. This was the finding of a study jointly performed by the Swedish Employers' Confederation and the Swedish Industrial Salaried Employees' Association. However, an unfinished but partly published study by Magnus Hedberg indicated that there is no direct relationship between turnover rates and sex. Rather, differences in rates of turnover appeared to be a function of age differences, with turnover rates tending to decrease markedly with increasing age. In view of this finding, the relatively higher turnover amongst the salaried women employees can be 'explained' largely by their relatively lower age level; the median age for female salaried workers was 25 as opposed to that of 40 for their male colleagues.

The comparisons made by the interviewees in the S.N.S. study were rarely based on systematic investigations. It was inherent in the nature of the exercise that the statements made about such factors as interest in training, managerial qualities, technical competence, independence, etc., were fairly subjective, i.e., based largely on personal experience. Whenever statistical data was referred to to make a point about, say, differential absence and turnover rates, almost inevitably the mean was quoted without reference to the dispersion around it.

The available statistical findings demonstrate that in most respects differences between different individuals of the same sex are greater than those between the means for the two sexes. The statistical dispersion is such that the two distribution curves cover areas that largely coincide, i.e. there are some women who are physically stronger and more interested in technical matters than the average man, while there are some men who exhibit greater manual dexterity and interest in languages than the average woman. In other words the mean values give data which are too crude to be applied to the behaviour of individual men or women. The wide dispersion from the mean indicates that other factors play a prominent role.

How should we interpret the finding that the physical capacity of women corresponds to about two-thirds of that of men in comparable age groups? For a start, drawing upon the reasoning above, we know that the mean offers no certain guidance in the allocation of work tasks. Further, we must determine the real importance of physical strength in an industrial context characterized by accelerating mechanization and automation of production processes. For surely one conclusion implied by technological developments is that differences in the physical strength of men and women are decreasing in practical importance.

Research in occupational physiology has demonstrated that the special measures designed to protect women workers, in many countries enshrined in legislation, are without medical foundation. The results of such research have recently begun to win acceptance among many firms particularly in the assessment of job requirements. Job requirement analysis helps to determine recruitment requirements and provides a basis for ergonomic measures as well as job evaluation.

In recent years, studies made in Swedish firms in the paper and pulp, engineering and mining industries have indicated that many jobs can be adequately performed by women. In studies of the physical load involved in mining work—a type of work which is generally considered among the heaviest—it was found that 75 to 80% of all work tasks did not require above average physical strength. A similar study in a large engineering firm showed that all work tasks in the firm could readily be performed by women!

As far as technical background was concerned, the investigations found that differences between men and women tended to increase with increasing age. Women's lesser interest and background in technical matters is thus essentially a result of environmental influence which take their toll at a fairly early stage. In Eastern European countries, for example, there is a far greater proportion of women involved in technical work.

A Sociologist's Hypothesis

It is exceedingly difficult either to refute or support most of the statements made about the differences in the vocational behaviour of men and women given the available empirical data. For as Harriet Holter has shown most of the research having scientific pretensions has tended to draw unwarranted conclusions from its findings. In some cases, stereotyped thinking has been paraded as scientific findings. In other cases, the datum itself has had inherent limitations, i.e. only women were studied. Finally, there has been a tendency both in the Norwegian and Swedish literature to assume that the actual vocational behaviour of men was the ideal vocational behaviour, though the criteria set were extremely imprecise.

However, even if we cannot satisfactorily determine the reasonableness of many of the assertions about the behaviour of women in working life, it might be interesting to attempt to explain why they exist at all and the significance of their existence.

Let us assume for the moment that certain opinions about differences in the vocational behaviour of the sexes are correct. How can we explain such differences? Harriet Holter has put forward the hypothesis, summarized in Chapter I, that women are subjected from the start to a 'training' that is quite different from that given to men. Thus, women are orientated largely to primary group norms and consequently carry over such norms into working life. These in many cases conflict with the prevailing norms in industry which must be adhered to in order to be successful in that context.[1]

Harriet Holter has also observed that certain groups gain materially from the continued effect of certain stereotypes. In certain cases employers have demonstrable interest in maintaining the idea that it is equitable to pay lower wages to a certain group of workers. Similarly, fellow employees who have reached a certain position or who hope to advance to certain positions have a vested interest in limiting competition; a step which can be taken most effectively by excluding all members of one sex.

Swedish and Norwegian investigations have shown that certain features of feminine vocational behaviour, while normally unappreciated, can in certain instances be considered desirable for economic and administrative reasons. In general, such qualities as forwardness, independence and solidarity were highly prized. However, employers were not dissatisfied with the thought that some part of the work force did not require promotion, accepted repetitive work and did not display overtly solidaristic leanings, etc.

Holter also observed that such economic and personnel policy considerations were mixed with the more diffuse, psychological needs of individuals at all levels of industry, e.g. the need to maintain the prevailing norms for manliness and feminity and the norms for the job division in family and working life. The latter need, Holter suggested, was linked to the basic psychological mechanisms for preserving the ego and psychic balance.

This hypothesis is given some support by Swedish and Norwegian studies. It has been found, for example, that competent women in

---

[1] A study cited in the Harvard Business Review July, 1965 found that younger men 'on their way up' were particularly strongly against the promotion of women.

work that is widely accepted as 'men's work' run the risk of being considered 'de-sexed' or mannish.

Women in working life are thus confronted by the widespread expectations that they will be docile, unambitious, and uninterested in technical matters, etc., because these are regarded as feminine traits in our culture. They are further expected to marry and make the family their predominant interest. Women who pursue successful careers must be 'a special type of extremely vocationally orientated woman with no thought for home or children', as one spokesman in the S.N.S. study expressed it.

Holter denotes such expectations as *informal expectations*, i.e. expectations that are rarely overtly expressed and not always consciously held. They derive from the general woman's role in our society and it appears that the sex role often exerts a greater force than the formal, official vocational role and the expectations associated with it.

This means that women will encounter conflicting expectations in the norms for their work performance to a far greater extent than men. Moreover, the sanctions attached to the woman's role often appear to be stronger than those attached to the man's role. Thus, when a woman bases her behaviour in vocational life on a 'masculine pattern', she is punished by being considered 'unfeminine'.

The Strength of Tradition

Even if the opinions put forward by the interviewees in the Swedish and Norwegian studies cannot be dismissed as entirely unwarranted, it is nevertheless possible to establish that sex differentiation in working life can largely be attributed to the strength of traditional notions amongst employees and employers. Indeed, many company spokesmen have been quite conscious of this. Some accept it as natural, while others react against the inherent sluggishness of the system. In the case of sex differentiation in office work, one spokesman said,

'It is undoubtedly true that all positions that are jumping off posts to higher managerial jobs are reserved to men, and are advertised in the male-job vacancy columns. This is largely because of tradition. When a man leaves, another man is sought. When a woman leaves another woman is sought.'

Some firms however, were fully prepared to experiment,

'Since recruiting policies over the years have tended to promote men and not women, it will take a long time before women come forward

who can successfully compete with men for the higher positions. . . .
But were we to get a male and a female applicant with the same qualifications we would certainly choose the woman to give her a try.'

In general, however, the statements gave a clear impression of
passive acceptance of or resignation to the force of tradition. Those
who wanted to introduce changes said that they would encounter
resistance either from the managing director or their subordinates.
Many felt too that much of this was due to the tendency of women
themselves to aim only for 'female occupations'. 'There are no women
with the required training.' 'No women apply', etc.

The Employers' Problems

Management are responsible for recruiting and promoting the firm's
employees or at least indicating the policy guidelines for such activities.
On the surface therefore they appear to be the key people affecting
the opportunities of women in the labour market. Yet what real
possibilities does any one firm have to influence the overall development? Is it in their interests actively to work to reduce sex discrimination in working life?

The preceding material has provided a rich variety of managerial
attitudes to female employees. It has also established that some of
these attitudes are demonstrably based on prejudices. In general,
however, it appears to be impossible on the basis of the available
research findings to test the realism of such attitudes. It has also
appeared that management are not alone in holding fixed views about
how women conduct themselves at the workplace, their vocational
capabilities, efficiency and morale, etc. Not only supervisors but also
employees of both sexes regard and treat one another quite differently
depending upon the sex of the individual. There are no grounds, therefore, for singling out any one group as more prejudiced than another
towards women and their role in working life.

The primary task of management is to promote 'the interests of
the firm'. For the individual manager, sex discrimination in working
life is a given institutional factor, which he or she has only very limited
possibilities of affecting. The attitudes of others—including women—
are *realities* which must be taken into account in practical transactions.
The rational manager would be as equally unwilling to pay wages to
women above those rates stipulated in collective bargaining agreements
or dictated by market conditions as to pay voluntarily a higher rate of
interest than that charged by the bank.

What are the factors that determine the position of women in working life and what is the relative importance of each? Our knowledge in this area is unfortunately extremely limited. Experience with attempts to introduce reforms in other, analogous, areas such as the male wage structure with its division into low and high wage occupations suggests that only small strides can be made by actions at the national and central labour market confederation levels. For it appears to be true that ultimately the market mechanism exercises a decisive influence over wage differentials.

Plainly, too, any hopes of an eventual central agreement by the employers and trade union confederations on the position of women in working life must be tempered by the knowledge that such general regulations can easily be circumvented as personnel move and job content changes. An individual employer might have reason to introduce reforms in his own firm while at the same time delaying or preventing similar reforms in other firms. Yet, managers as a group have no collective interest in preserving existing conditions. The most suitable personnel policies for the firm are dictated by its location and the particular branch of industry to which it belongs. It was clearly indicated in the answers to questionnaires that expanding firms in a full employment economy often felt themselves constrained by preconceptions of the suitability of certain types of jobs for women. Such firms have rather strong reasons to question the prevailing views of sex differentiation in industry and to demand to know to what extent such views are based on tradition and to what extent on empirically ascertainable facts as well as to work to bring about changes where they appear feasible. Of course, private firms cannot be expected to agitate for social reforms out of pure altruism. It should be recognized that measures manifesting a progressive attitude to women in working life can be competitive weapons in the market for a basic factor of production labour.

Current Trends

The S.N.S. investigation in the late 1950s, indicated that many management officials responsible for the formulation and practical administration of personnel policies were rather prejudiced and extremely unclear in their thinking about the position of women in industrial life. In the debate following the publication of the results of this study in 1962, no voices were raised to defend these views. The study created an insight into the thinking of firms on this issue and thus a foundation for various parties to analyse more thoroughly and question the treatment of women in industry. Moreover, academics, journalists and other outside parties received both an opportunity and a prodding to study the problem area and evaluate and criticize the views that were aired in the study.

Sweden's experience of full employment for the past two decades must be recognized as the decisive factor producing the changes that occurred not only in the climate of discussion but also at the work place. Our long term economic plans indicate that married women constitute the largest unutilized manpower resource available to mitigate the predicted increase in the severity of our overall labour shortage. The proportion of married women at work is officially expected to increase by 27% from 1965 to 1970. Yet in order for married women to enter the labour market in such numbers certain minimum reforms of tax policy, family services, and national manpower and training policies are required.

It cannot be too strongly emphasized that the problem is not simply a quantitative one. Recognition must be given to its important qualitative implications. Thus, it is vital to ascertain the vocational areas where the new women workers can be best employed and whether the existing female manpower resources are optimally or even rationally allocated. For it is not merely in traditional female occupations that the demand for labour has exceeded and will continue to exceed the supply of it. It seems difficult to avoid the conclusion that it is in the national interest that women be given a greater stimulus as well as opportunity to enter occupations outside the range of traditionally 'female' job categories.

The foremost agents of change in the transformation of industrial attitudes have thus far been the central employer and trade union confederations and affiliated industrial employees associations and trade unions. These have actively campaigned amongst their members to break with tradition. One employer group, for example, the Swedish Metal Trades Employer Association, has attempted to persuade its members to employ more women in positions hitherto thought to be 'typically male'. In a 1965 circular to its members, the Association pointed out that 'the myth that women are not suitable for mechanical work ought now to be laid to rest'. Insufficient knowledge and uncertainty of entry into industrial work have often put off married women who wanted to take up employment. It falls within the province of the individual firm, the Association stressed, to apply the measures necessary to interest women in applying for industrial work and those firms that were prepared to change their approach to female employees and apply the necessary measures will have a head start as competition for manpower stiffens.

The Association recommended that members consider increasing the number of their part-time positions and the opportunities for women to train, as well as improving their circulation of specific information concerning training schemes and job vacancies and general information about industrial work. It also suggested certain concrete measures such as introductory courses and study visits for women.

The employers organizations appear, too, to have accepted the need to interest young girls in technical training and education both at the theoretical and practical levels. This is evident from their vocational information pamphlets and brochures (Chapter IV).

That there has been considerable pressure from above therefore can be readily established. What changes have evidenced themselves in individual firms during recent years? Ideally, to answer this question we should like to have a new investigation along the same, comprehensive lines of the S.N.S. study. Unfortunately, none has yet been forthcoming. In 1965, however, the National Labour Market Board made an investigation among a sample of large industrial firms which had begun to recruit women to work previously performed only by men.[1] It found that a large number of firms that had previously not recruited women had begun to open their doors to them. The study also threw light on the types of jobs that have recently been opened to women employees. The 146 firms studied were mainly in the metal trades and engineering, wood, paper and pulp, and chemical industries.

The most obvious breakthrough of female workers in industry has occurred in the metal trades and engineering. An indication of the strength of this trend is offered by the membership figures of the Swedish Metal Workers' Union. In 1964, women accounted for more than 95% of new members.

The National Labour Market Board investigation suggested, however, that the overall change in the pattern of male and female employment has not been great. The number of women in jobs previously considered 'male' was relatively small and the average number of job categories per firm performed by women was minimal. In general, the work tasks to which the great majority of new female recruits were

[1] Paper No. 13, Research Bureau, 1965, National Labour Market Board.

assigned were basically similar in type to those traditionally allocated to female employees; i.e. highly repetitive tasks.

In sum, it appears as though companies as well as trade union and employer organizations in Sweden have accepted in principle and to some extent in practice the notion that women constitute an under-utilized and needed manpower resource. The changed view however, has not progressed to a stage of reasonable refinement. The problem is still thought of rather narrowly in quantitative terms, i.e. man-power shortage is regarded as soluble by resorting to greater numbers of female reserves. The importance of promotion and training measures for female employees both presently at work and newcomers appears to have been played down or disregarded.

Several points appear apposite here. First, it is quite clear that the allocation of manpower without regard to training and suitability and based on such criteria as traditional restrictions, sex, age, race, religion tends to reduce the flexibility and adjustability of the labour force. This is not only inconsistent with the objectives of national manpower and training policies; it detracts from the economic and social benefits to be gained from a rationally allocated labour supply.

Secondly, the interviewed firms claimed that their lack of interest in training and promoting women was prompted largely by lack of ambition on the part of women employees. Yet a study recently made in a large Swedish insurance company disclosed that a large proportion of the unpromoted women in that company desired to advance to super-visory positions. It also appeared that the women interested in promotion in that company were far more sceptical about their opportunities to advance than the men. Further, a significantly greater number of un-promoted women were dissatisfied with their opportunities for advance-ment within the firm than unpromoted men. There is thus some support for the assumption that the low expectations of firms in respect of their female employees contribute to the maintenance of their employees' ambitions at a low level.

In recent years, the problems of promotion and training have begun to attract greater attention in Swedish firms. If we put aside for the moment the question of whether or not it would 'pay' firms to promote and train women and, instead, accept the idea that women should be given better opportunities to advance, the following measures would be called for. The promotion structure within the individual firm and the requirements for promotion such as training and capabilities should be clearly indicated to all personnel. These measures would fall within the province of general personnel policy. In addition, firms should take a special interest in forming and providing a vocational stimulus to their female employees, individually and collectively. An important prerequisite to the success of such a programme would be a greater awareness on the part of managers and supervisors at all levels of the consequences of sex discrimination in the job market and the problems stemming from this discrimination.

It would probably be impossible for firms to calculate the economic profit to be gained by investing in women as a group. However, there is good reason for them to catalogue the resources constituted by women and discover how much will be lost if the problem of women's equal opportunity in the labour market is not tackled.

ANALYSIS OF THE DEBATE ON
SEX ROLES

by EDMUND DAHLSTRÖM

I N this paper we shall examine the general debate on sex roles in its wider sociological and ideological setting. Some may prefer a more 'realistic' discussion of concrete social measures from the start. Yet a study of the general assumptions and values regarding the status of the sexes in society as a whole can be equally useful. For, all the practical proposals made concerning the gainful employment of women contain in fact implicit assumptions and values regarding the positions of the sexes in family life and in society.

The debate among the experts has often been marked by a some-what limited perspective. But the sex role question is one which affects a wide variety of spheres, within which particular measures are taken that influence the status of the sexes in society, viz. family legislation, the statutes regulating the public rights and duties of citizens, family welfare policy, labour market policy, building and housing policy, other social policy, education policy, tax policy and policy on the location of industries. What is often lacking is an overall perspective on the combined effect of such measures.

Earlier Ideological Positions on Sex Roles

Let us start by glancing at some of the earlier ideologies on sex roles. An analysis of these must start from the view of men and women held by Western society before the industrial revolution.

The *traditional* ideological position on sex roles was anchored in the Judaic/Christian religion and in talismanic concepts. It can be summarized as follows: [1]

God created men and women as essentially different types of being. Woman is weaker. Man is woman's lord and master. This difference between the sexes must reflect itself in their relative status in society; they must enjoy different rights and be required to fulfil different duties. Only the man can be given full rights. Society must assign men and women to different occupations and fields of activity. Women must be sheltered. By being a virtuous and gentle wife, and a pious, fertile mother, a woman could gain respect.

The *early liberal* ideological position on sex roles had its roots in the doctrine of 'natural rights' and the age of reason. It evolved towards the end of the 18th century and can be summarized as follows:

All individuals are unique but of equal value. Women and men are essentially alike. They have the same 'natural rights'. There shall therefore be equality between the sexes. Women shall have the right to equal treatment in all spheres, e.g. in education, in inheritance, before the law, within marriage, occupationally, politically and in appointments or elections to public positions.

The early liberal ideology particularly emphasized the need for legal and political equality for women. This, it was thought, would automatically lead to emancipation in other fields. The leading liberal theoreticians, such as John Stuart Mill, thought that married women would continue to discharge their duties as mothers and housewives and that they would thus cease to be gainfully employed when they married and had children. No change was envisaged in women's status in the home, apart from the right to legal equality [2].

The *romantic* ideological position on sex roles involved both a rejection and a synthesis of elements in the traditional and early liberal attitudes. It can be summarized as follows: [3]

Men and women are essentially different. Yet society needs both and assigns them equal value. In love, the sexes complement each other.

The woman graces the home with her motherliness, virtue, innocence, submissiveness, self-sacrifice, charm, softness, piety, intuition, naturalness, etc. Society must guard these virtues of women and protect them as wives and mothers. In certain respects, women should be allowed to enjoy a greater degree of equality with man, e.g. in education and in marital status. Functions outside the home, however, such as gainful employment, public positions and the exercise of political rights, are best left to men.

The ideological position of *Marxism* on sex roles is reminiscent in its principles and aims of the early liberal view. Men and women are of equal value socially and the emancipation and equality of women are goals to pursue. The Marxist view, however, differs from the liberal view in the means it proposes to realize these objectives [4].

According to Marxist ideology, family life has developed into a patriarchal system in which woman is enslaved, suppressed and isolated from the public life of the community. Her status involves a form of domestic slavery and in effect 'legalised prostitution'. In a capitalist society, she is forced to choose between an enslaved and dependent status as mother-wife and an independent existence as a single person.

Once emancipated, women will be reintroduced to work in the community. Only when both sexes jointly participate in such work can they achieve real equality. Complete freedom can only be realized when the capitalist system of production and property has been replaced by a socialist system. Then and only then can marriage involve a free choice based on love and full equality; for the economic aspects of marriage will no longer be relevant; women will no longer be regarded as unpaid labour in the home.

Different Levels in the Current Debate

Legal and social reforms in the Scandinavian countries up to the present day have promoted many rights advocated in the early liberal programme; the right to equal education; equal inheritance rights; legal equality in marriage; equal rights in working life; access to public positions and equal political rights. However, the formal legal equality gained through these reforms has not yet resulted in real social, vocational or even political equality. In reality, women have only limited opportunity to exercise their rights in many areas, e.g. vocational training and occupational choice, political and organizational influence.

Many of the *external* barriers have been removed. The remaining barriers are of a somewhat different type; they are intertwined with deeply rooted attitudes, role expectations, role ideals, value and habits on the part of employers, supervisors and co-workers, husbands and above all women themselves. These barriers are continually reinforced by the mass media and are strongly anchored in the pattern of relationships within the primary groups, particularly the family. Earlier, when the problem was one of removing the external barriers, the forces of feminism could preserve a united front. There is today, however, much less unanimity among women concerning the aims and means of further social and vocational emancipation.

The current debate on the sex roles is no longer a controversy between women and men; it has become one between 'housewives' and 'working women'. Both groups can find male support for their opinions. The degree of emotional involvement seems to be almost as great as when the suffragettes attacked the masculine society.

I think that it is possible to distinguish three different levels in today's debate. We shall focus on the first, the 'ideological' debate, in which the parties articulate more or less systematic and coherent assumptions and concepts. This debate most frequently finds expression in the publications and public talks of the feminist movement or the political parties. It is at this level more than any other that attempts have been made comprehensively to consider the question of the sex roles.

The second level I have already touched upon, the 'expert' or 'technical' debate on particular aspects of the overall problem, e.g. the need for day nurseries and kindergartens, the principle of equal pay, regulations regarding women in the legislation on worker's protection, the rationalisation of household work and tax policy. These separate spheres are actively guarded by the organizations of the various interest groups, e.g. the employers' associations and trade unions, the organizations of working women, housewives' associations and consumer associations.

The third level appears in the mass media in the form of more personal and less pretentious contributions to the debate; on the women's pages of newspapers and magazines, in letters to the editor and articles, in stories and novels, films, plays, revues and popular songs.

At the ideological level there can be discerned a wide range of views, from extreme conservatism to extreme radicalism. The words 'conservative' and 'radical' are not to be read in the light of their current political usage but rather refer to a desire respectively to preserve and change the traditional functions and structure of the family.

The 'structure of the family' in this context can refer to *relationships within the family,* in which event the focus is on the distribution of roles within the home. The extreme conservative attitude views as an ideal the bourgeois family of an earlier period, when the wife devoted herself exclusively to the home and the man was the sole means of support for the family. The extreme radical position is marked by an attempt to redistribute work within the family, so that tasks previously assigned to the wife are assumed or shared by the husband and vice versa.

The structure of the family can also refer to the *relationships* between the family and society, in which case the focus is on the need to have the institutions of society assume functions that were previously discharged by the family.

Industrialization has undeniably led to a number of functions that were previously the responsibility of the family—production, education, medical care, care of the aged, social assistance—being wholly or entirely transferred to the public sector. The radicals wish to increase the contribution by society by expanding and introducing institutions for child care, collective services for household work etc. The conservatives wish to maintain the autonomy of the family in relation to other social institutions and therefore struggle to retain as many duties as possible within the family.

The reduction of certain previous family functions does not automatically entail that the family diminishes in importance. For the loss of—or liberation from—certain traditional functions could allow other remaining or new functions to become more important or more meaningful. The 'quantity' of contact between parents and children should not be confused with the 'quality' of such contact.

The radical ideology is formulated in slightly different ways depending on the social framework within which it is incorporated, that is, its general political-ideological context.

Radical arguments on the sex roles in Sweden—an essentially capitalistic system—have emphasized the need for a redistribution of roles and duties within the family to increase the opportunity for women to assert their equality in a 'free' labour market. In the event, the role of the husband has become the focus of attention. The radicals have stressed the need for the husband to share equally the responsibilities of educating the children and maintaining the household. They have pointed to the favourable consequences for men who contribute more actively to child care and household work and whose wives—on more equal terms—shoulder their own share of the strains of working life. Parallel demands have naturally been made for support from the community with child care and the creation of various types of organized services.

In states which are predominantly socialist, discussion has tended to exclude the distribution of roles and tasks within the family, for society has already replaced a large part of women's traditional work with communal facilities for child care and private consumption. Similarly the politically and culturally radical movements of the 'twenties considered this to be a necessary step on the path to the emancipation of women. The Kibbutz system, for instance, and the changes in the structure of the family introduced in Soviet Russia and China are variations on the radical theme of transferring the family duties of the mother to new social institutions, thus placing women on an equal footing with men without disrupting the role of the latter [5].

As a rule, it is easier to obtain a clear picture of the radical view. For it has been put forward in books and programmes, while the conservative ideology has been less systematically formulated and has often appeared in the guise of concealed assumptions. Traditional and romantic viewpoints are seldom championed at the 'expert' level of debate. They tend rather to be represented implicitly or explicitly in the letters to the editors of weekly magazines and in the views expressed by employees, supervisory personnel and employers.

Since I have limited myself to analysing the debate at a more 'initiated' level, the conservative ideology of the sex roles will inevitably occupy a subordinate position. When I speak of 'conservative' ideas, I am referring without any great precision to those flowing from a traditional or romantic attitude.

Since my analysis will be limited to the more advanced level of debate, the conservative ideology will unavoidably be under-represented. By conservative ideas I mean those flowing from a traditional or romantic attitude. The hall-mark—signal—of such an attitude is a preoccupation with the woman-housewife role and a conviction that such a role is a lifelong pursuit.

Current Ideologies

In the current debate, there has been a pronounced shift towards the radical viewpoint. With few to champion the conservative ideology, the debate has been dominated by radical and moderate thinking. The latter is essentially an attempted compromise between the two ideologies, or perhaps more correctly stated, between the ideologies and their feasibility. Typically, the moderates will abstain from defending the 'housewife role' while continuing to adhere to the notion that women have a greater responsibility for the care of their children, particularly during their early years. The major objective of this ideology is as a consequence the discovery of ways and means for women to combine a career with their role as mother either by a division of the latter's lives into periods devoted to one of the roles at a time or by practical arrangements to lighten the burden of child care and supervision of the working mother. The moderate ideology—with its focus on women's two roles—has tended to dominate government commissions on family policy from the 1930s to the present day and to some extent the positions taken by the feminist organizations as reflected in their official reactions to proposed legislative reforms.

The radical ideology in contrast asserts that the emancipation of women cannot become a reality until women actively pursue lifelong careers and reject the housewife ideal and the idea that the family is a means of financial support. As has been mentioned above, it is possible to distinguish between two versions of radicalism. We shall concentrate on the variant that starts from the Swedish ideological background of social democracy and social liberalism. Its most consistent champion is a young liberal, Eva Moberg, who published in 1961 a pamphlet called 'The Conditional Emancipation of Woman'. It was this article that provoked the intensive debate of later years on the facts and mythology of motherhood.

The other variant based on Marxist ideas will be represented briefly by certain aspects of the Communist sex role ideology in the Soviet Union [6].

The Moderate Ideological Position on the Sex Roles

This ideology endeavours to bridge the gap between woman's two roles as mother and working woman. The most common pattern proposed is for the wife to work while young, leave her job and devote herself to children and home during the years of active motherhood and then pick up the threads of her occupation when the children have grown up.

However, the two roles can conflict and women are often torn between conflicting aims and functions. The decision between being a housewife and pursuing a career is often dictated by external circumstances. A number of women are compelled to take work for economic reasons, while others are prevented from continuing or resuming their work owing to a shortage of day nurseries and other facilities, by the shape of tax policy or by the required hours of work.

The aim of feminist policy according to the 'moderates' should be to secure for every woman the right to draw the line freely between housework and career. The primary aim of family policy should be to remove as far as possible the conflict between these two roles and to give women a possibility of choosing both or either of them, without their choice unfavourably affecting their performance in either role.

The two roles of women present certain problems of adaptation and transition which can only be overcome with the assistance of social policies. Such policies should not attempt to direct women's choice between them, i.e. should not give priority to the working woman or to the housewife. For the members of the family are the ones most competent to decide upon the desirable role distribution.

At present, women include in their future plans thoughts of marriage and motherhood. Their choice of work and their ambitions are influenced by their probable future role of housewife and mother. Their potential maternal role influences their status in working life and they usually choose to stay at home and look after their children during pre-school age. None of these things will change in the near future. They are natural and have to be accepted. In a family with small children, the care of the household and the children is a full day's work. The mother is usually the person best suited to such work, which is on a par with any other form of occupation.

There is no reason to couple the demand for emancipation and equality with a requirement that the married mothers of small children should combine their occupation as housewives with gainful employment outside the home. But modern society should give housework a status equivalent to that of other occupations. To achieve this the following social policies should be promoted:

Girls should be made aware that their role as mother and wife is not their sole function in life. They should be stimulated to take a more serious interest in a career, and obtain a better basic education and vocational training. They should be encouraged to train for occupations over a wider range than they now tend to do. Girls should be encouraged—upon completion of their vocational training—to compete with men in different areas and to take their occupations seriously. Married women should be given an opportunity to keep up with their field, maintain their contact with the labour market during early motherhood.

Housing and collective services for distribution and consumption should be so designed as to reduce the volume of housework. Labour-saving aids should be introduced to a greater extent. Most important of all, facilities should be organized for the care of the children: institutions for semi-open child care, kindergartens, day nurseries, afternoon schools and family day nurseries.

Married women at work should not be 'punished' by excessively heavy taxation, as is now the case in Sweden for highly qualified women with husbands in middle or high income brackets.

The discriminatory treatment of women in the labour market—through segregated occupational sectors, different rates of pay for men and women and special stipulations in the legislation on worker's protection—should be eliminated.

Conditions on the labour market and at places of work should be so organized as to facilitate the 'dual' career of women, e.g. by part-time jobs, longer periods of paid leave in connection with childbirth and increased opportunities for further training and retraining, particularly for middle-aged women desiring to re-enter the labour market. The government's policy for the location of industries should be improved to make it possible for wives as well as husbands to obtain gainful employment in most geographic areas.

Increased support should be given to families with children, so that mothers are not obliged to take work for financial reasons.

The status of housewives can be improved in several ways: by arranging training in housework; by recognizing their right to house and pocket money; and by assessing the financial value of house work. The economic security of housewives should be increased by providing them with improved sickness and pension benefits and recognized leisure and holidays. The isolation of housewives in domestic work should be reduced by facilities for studies and club activities, and by the husband and other members of the family assuming a greater share of the work in the home.

The Radical Ideological Position on the Roles of the Sexes in Sweden

The objective of this ideology is absolute equality between the sexes. Formal legal equality alone is an insufficient means to attain this goal. Discrimination between the sexes should be fought until men and women are treated equally as regards vocational training, employment, pay and promotion. Moreover, women must consciously aim at making a career for themselves and becoming socially and financially independent of men. Equality must also be extended *within* the family.

The Liberal-Radical View

Equality cannot be realized as long as the majority of women are content to bear by themselves the main responsibility for the care of the home and children. Emphasis is given to the man's participation and co-responsibility within the family. Both the men and the women have an occupational role and a family role. It is the woman who bears and breast-feeds the child, but there is no biological connection between pregnancy and breast-feeding, and washing, cooking and other household work. In the present system, motherhood and woman's love of her child are exploited to restrict her freedom as an individual. She must have fulfilled her main duty as guardian of the children and the home before she is accepted as a working woman. This system of conditional emancipation leads to girls as they grow up regarding their occupation as something secondary and marriage as a legitimate and comfortable livelihood.

The concept of 'the two roles of women' is dismissed as untenable. Both men and women have *one* main role, that of a human being. For both sexes, this role would include child care.

Under the existing family system, the husband-father is regarded as the main source of support and the wife as the person entitled to support. This notion is reflected in the relatively higher wages received by men for the same work. The difference is a 'maintenance factor', based on a sort of concealed needs principle: the husband as family provider earns more. From the employers' point of view such a differential is justifiable, for there are usually special costs associated with female employees, due to their major responsibilities for the home and children, (higher turnover, higher absenteeism and lower ambitions etc.).

According to the liberal-radical ideology, measures of family policy are at least as important as those of labour market policy. As long as the family maintains its character as an institution to support mothers, the status of women in the labour market cannot be greatly altered. The liberal-radicals object strongly to those aspects of the law which tend to preserve and reinforce this view of the family, e.g. maintenance to divorced wives and widows' pensions. They attack the traditional structure of the family with a permanent housewife labelling it 'legal prostitution'. The housewife lives 'the humiliating existence of a parasite' and her isolation in the home makes her a 'spiritual cripple'.

The radical ideology stresses the importance of a more active role of the husband in the family, particularly his responsibility to his children. It therefore combats practices that tend to give the wife a more prominent role *vis-à-vis* the children, e.g. the custody of the children following a divorce. The demand for equality between the sexes means that certain advantages and privileges previously enjoyed by women should no longer be reserved for them alone, e.g. their protected position and their right to be supported through marriage. Financial support for the family should be a shared undertaking by husband and wife and both should share the pleasure of caring for the children and maintaining intimate contact with them. Men have been brought up according to a tougher, more impersonal credo in working life and in large secondary groups, while women have been groomed for and given a more protected position in the family, with its more personal atmosphere. Equality implies that men and women should share more equally not only the satisfaction of living in close contact with the children but also the strains of competition outside the home.

The measures to promote the employment of women that were listed under the moderate ideology quite naturally find support among the radicals. The latter give special emphasis to the following points:

Boys and girls must be reared and educated in as similar a manner as possible. Both must be prepared for their occupational family roles and be made aware of their shared responsibility for the children and the home. Domestic work and care of children must be shared freely between husband and wife.

The time taken by housework and child care should be radically reduced by different measures, such as the rationalization of domestic work, improved housing, the expansion of collective services and more suitable consumer goods. Most important of all is the provision of facilities for child care during the day, or part of the day.

The costs of childbirth and child care should be shared by all employees and not be borne by working women alone. A deduction should be made from all incomes and allocated to a child allowance fund. Allowances from this fund should be paid to the parents of small children to be used as required. The allowance should be sufficiently large for the family to be able to afford to have one parent at home with the child during its early years (according to one proposal at least the first three years) or to pay for domestic help or a day nursery.

Conditions on the labour market should be so arranged as to make it easier to combine gainful employment with care of the home. An expansion of part-time work has been indicated as a suitable measure. The planned reduction of the standard work-week will also make it easier for parents to manage their jobs and households at the same time.

This should help to increase the parents' freedom of choice. They should both be able to combine work in the home with gainful employment, full-time or part-time, in the proportions that best suit their individual needs.

A more widespread acceptance of the notion of child care as a

shared responsibility of both parents should help to reduce much of
the existing discrimination on the labour market. Moreover, were the
financial or conventional barriers against the father reducing his
gainful employment to spend more time with the children to be
removed, it is quite possible that many men would take this step.

The Radical Ideological Position on the Role of the Sexes in the Soviet Union

Since 1918, different 'official lines' can be traced. The emancipation
and equality of women is one of the corner-stones of the communist
ideology. Women should enjoy political, economic and legal equality
and be given an opportunity to participate in the work of the community. They must be liberated from 'domestic slavery' by collective
housing facilities and treated as equals on the labour market.

The communist ideology has imprinted on the communist society
the 'dual role' of woman as worker and as housewife-mother. Society
must create the proper conditions to allow her to fulfil both roles. A
career for women is to be promoted by a number of measures, such
as identical education and job opportunities, equal wages and promotion
opportunities, the creation of suitable housing, collective services,
consumer goods and distribution systems to reduce domestic work
(above all day nurseries, kindergartens and boarding schools), together
with an ideological pressure on the mother to return to gainful employment fairly shortly after the birth of her child. The year of childbirth
is not viewed as a break in continuous service and there is no loss of
rights or pay.

The role of the woman as mother must be assisted by expanded
maternity and child welfare services, leave with pay in conjunction
with childbirth, child allowances, the provision of suitable housing
and collective services, stipulations in the legislation on workers'
protection that take into account the woman's role as mother or
potential mother, regulations in family law that protect the mother
vis-à-vis neglectful fathers, and a full recognition of the status of unmarried mothers, with the same rights of support and assistance.

In the period after the Soviet revolution there was a division of
opinion as to the future nature of the family in communist society.
In the mid-twenties, ideas about the dissolution of the family and
free love were replaced by those of the 'socialist family' based on the
writings of Marx and Engels. Admittedly the community was to
assume the educational, protective and productive functions, but the

monogamous family was to be retained, with its reproductive, fostering
and erotico-sexual functions.

Great freedom was nevertheless allowed and *de facto* marriages
were accorded the same status as legitimate marriages, unmarried
mothers the same status as married. Divorces were easy to obtain,
as was abortion. With the advent of the Stalinist era, however, a
stronger guard was thrown around the socialist family, without this
detracting from the central idea that women have a main function in
the working life of the community in addition to their roles as mothers.
During this period the legislation on marriage and abortion was
tightened and *de facto* marriages viewed with disfavour.

Apparently it has been possible to suppress sex discrimination at
the work place, in part owing to the devices available to a totalitarian
system and in part to the way in which labour costs are calculated in a
socialist economy. The extra costs of female labour related to their
role as mothers according to the communist ideology, are a burden
to be borne by the community as a whole.

The difference between the liberal and communist radical ideologies
can be traced partly to differences in the underlying economic system.
The liberal ideology has emphasized more strongly the necessity of
family duties being shared more equitably by men and women largely
in order to end the present situation in which a woman's family role
results in higher labour costs. For, in the labour market of a predominantly private enterprise economy a differential labour cost entails
the risk of discrimination. In socialist economies it has been easier
to obtain employer acceptance of the idea that the higher cost of female
labour is one to be distributed throughout society as a whole; all forms
of discrimination have been made offences and the rules have been
strictly applied. By contrast, liberal ideologies have had to be wary
of discriminatory treatment even in the legislation on workers' protection, e.g. prohibitions against women participating in different kinds
of work and lower retirement ages for women. For this too, can be
translated into relatively higher labour costs for female workers and
hence discriminatory treatment in a private profit labour market.

Arguments in the Debate on Sex Roles

Let us now consider some of the arguments put forward in the current
debate. Broadly, differences have consisted of *disagreement over facts*
or *disagreement over values.*

Factual disagreement involves a dispute over whether or not a particular assumption is true. Disagreement over values, by contrast, presupposes a difference in attitudes, with one side viewing a given situation as desirable (good), and the other viewing the same situation as undesirable (bad). Factual assumptions and attitudes are often inextricably intertwined. The ideologies that value equality between the sexes (old liberalism and Marxism) assume that there is a basic equality between the sexes, while those ideologies that prescribe different social functions for the sexes (the traditional and romantic ideologies) assume that there are essential differences between the sexes.

The parties can also disagree about certain aspects of the current situation. One side can maintain, for instance, that the majority of housewives with small children are satisfied with their lot, while the other considers the majority to be basically maladjusted, e.g. isolated, excessively dependent and retarded in their development.

The parties can also have differing opinions about the future *situation*. One side may consider that participation by married women on the labour market will rapidly increase during the 'sixties, while the other does not accept that such an increase will occur.

The parties can also disagree about the *causes of a given phenomenon*. Some maintain that the increase in the gainful employment of women is due mainly to a change of attitude on the part of women while others believe that the increase is attributable mainly to a change in the structure of industry and current levels of business activity.

Disagreement can also be expressed about the *effect of conceivable changes and measures*. Some maintain that the increased employment of married women leads to increased marital instability, while others deny this. Some maintain that the realization of the principle of equal pay in industry will lead to a reduced demand for female labour, while others deny this.

Disagreement, finally, can be felt about *the necessary conditions for effecting certain changes*. Some maintain that a necessary condition for married women attaining parity of influence with men is their pursuit of a career, while others maintain that women can acquire an equal level of influence as housewives.

The arguments can be divided according to the type of basic value systems cited. One group focus on the positions of men and women in society and their opportunities to attain these things are generally sought after in our culture, e.g. income, influence, good social relationships, social intercourse and psychologically harmonious adjustment to their work and leisure. A just division of these benefits exists when the individual's chances of asserting himself in different fields is dependent solely on his or her personal merits, and is independent of sex. Starting from this point, the degree of equality between the sexes can be discussed with reference to the barriers which confront men and women respectively. I have called these *arguments on the equality (and freedom) of the sexes.*

Another group of arguments start from a consideration of the family and the contribution made by the family to society as a whole: marital harmony, reproduction, and child adjustment. I have called these *arguments bearing on the family.*

A third group of arguments focus on the overall economic aspects of the problem, e.g. the manpower situation on the labour market, an efficient utilization of labour resources by industry. I have called these *economic arguments.*

Arguments bearing upon Equality and Freedom

Equality and Freedom in General

Arguments concerning the equality and freedom of the sexes are without objective meaning unless the terms of reference of freedom and equality are clearly specified. Argument must be based on the extent to which women and men have access to a particular value, e.g. influence or power. Let us therefore make a rough breakdown of the values referred to in the discussion on the freedom and equality of men and women. There are five categories that are analytically discrete, though partly overlapping. The last category can be said to include all the others.

The benefits of vocational life: These include pay, fringe benefits, promotion, responsibility, power and influence, human contact, solidarity and community of interests with co-workers, identification with lower and higher organizational units, solidarity within trade unions and above all the satisfaction given by the job itself in certain respects (variety, change of pace, self-development, opportunity to express different needs etc.).

The benefits of family life: Work and leisure in the home are separate from the competition, strain and anonymous discipline of outside work. Domestic work is carried out independently and includes many different fostering and curative functions, together with a variety of practical duties of both a routine and creative character. 'Relations on the job', i.e. between husband and wife, are intimate and personal. Contact with the children and promotion of their harmonious development are a deep source of satisfaction.

Power and influence: Influence and power are in relationship to a definite social system, e.g. within the family, at the place of work, in associations, and in local and central government. Power is in the hands of the persons exercising control over the things valued by the members of such a social system.

An important source of power in our society consists of expert knowledge and skill.

Esteem and prestige must—like power and influence—presuppose a system, a particular context. The esteem enjoyed by an individual depends e.g. on his status in the family, in working life, in the town, society at large, internationally. The individual's self-esteem depends on how his position or positions are viewed by other individuals.

The discussion of freedom and equality is naturally most difficult to pin down when it is extended to cover all goals, values such as *happiness, social adjustment, satisfaction* and *self-realization*. Often a change in the status of women in any given respect increases their opportunity to achieve certain goals but reduces their chances of attaining others. An assessment of the total increase (or decrease) in women's freedom presupposes a weighting of the different aims against one other. The result is often a lapse from the realm of the descriptive into that of the normative.

The demand for equality in respect of all the advantages listed above has on the whole played a more important role in the radical ideology. Those of conservative bent have been inclined to accept a differentiation of roles, i.e. men and women should admittedly reap the fruits of the social system to an equal extent, but men should receive a greater share of the benefits of business or public life, and women those of family life. The radical view rejects this and maintains that women should share the benefits of family life as well as those of working life.

In the discussion of freedom and equality between the sexes we can distinguish the following areas of disagreement between the radical and moderate ideologies. The radicals stress the benefits that women can win by gainful employment. They implicitly assume that by asserting herself outside the home woman can achieve other benefits such as influence within the family, happiness, self-realization and social prestige, and that by remaining a housewife she loses numerous advantages and becomes 'economically under-age' and a 'spiritual cripple'. Various circumstances limit the opportunities of women to join the labour market and force them to become housewives. These obstacles must be removed. In the event, increasing emphasis must be given to the problem of 'freedom'.

The radicals point to the inconsistency between policies encouraging mothers to remain at home and those attempting to remove the obstacles to women competing with men in working life. For as long as married women continue to leave their occupations and enter careers on a temporary basis, female labour will inevitably involve a higher cost. And, in a profit-motive economy, this will increase the risk of discrimination. A policy that makes it easier for women to be housewives leads to a devaluation of female labour input and a reduction of women's opportunities on the labour market.

Pay and Conditions of Employment of Women in Working Life

The demand for equality as regards pay and treatment in working life is to be found in both the moderate and radical ideologies. Criticism has been voiced against the traditional attitudes assumed to enjoy currency in private industry, particularly but not exclusively amongst management.

Moderate and radical critics have attacked the problem from several different angles. *Firstly* they have demanded the introduction of the principle of equality at all stages, i.e. in recruitment, training, promotion and wage setting. They have not denied that differences exist on the average between men and women and no goals of the 'equal distribution' type have been set up. Attention has been drawn to the error of grouping according to sex and an attack has been launched on thinking based on categories or sex types. A person's sex cannot be of decisive importance for his or her efficiency in working life; treatment should be based on an assessment of the individual employee. In several important respects there is no great difference between the sexes; at most the differences are only marginal. Even in sectors where men are on the average more efficient than women, some women are more efficient than the average man and some men are less efficient than the average woman.

Secondly, the correctness of certain assumptions, i.e. that men are on the average more efficient, has been questioned.

Thirdly, measures have been promoted that are designed to reduce differences between the efficiency of men and women, e.g. measures that can stimulate women to a more serious interest in working life or can facilitate the gainful employment of married women. Any reduction in the difference between the efficiency of men and women would further reduce the causes of differentiated treatment and pay.

Criticism of traditional thinking on the labour market has attempted to throw into bold relief the feedback effect on women's behaviour on the market of the discriminatory treatment of female labour. The relatively poorer opportunities of women on the labour market—the fact that they are referred to fewer types of occupation, that they are usually less qualified, worse paid and receive less encouragement to seek training and promotion—affects their attitudes to their careers and their tendency to continue in their job after marriage. More equal treatment it has been suggested would increase women's motivation in working life.

It seems clear that traditional thinking on the labour market, like discrimination of any kind, is essentially what sociologists term a self-fulfilling prophecy [7]. Women are regarded as less reliable workers in many sectors and treated accordingly. This treatment results in less efficiency on the average in the work in question, which, in turn, gives further confirmation of traditional views. This confirmation, is more apparent than real, however, since the traditional view is often that 'women are on the average less efficient in this occupation than men, regardless of how they are treated', while the actual behaviour of women on the labour market suggests that 'women are on the average less effective in this job because of discriminatory treatment on the labour market and other environmental influences'. The object is to break the vicious circle and achieve some sort of cumulative effect in the opposite direction.

In the labour market context it has thus far proved rather difficult to state with precision the context and meaning of the term, 'equality'. This emerges clearly in the debate on the equal pay principles. Private as well as public committees of inquiry have been unable to agree on any clear objectives. Should the principle of equal pay, for instance, mean *equal pay for equivalent jobs* or *equal pay for equal work performance*? In the latter case, any discernible differences between overall efficiency of the sexes, e.g. in the duration of their working life, their absenteeism and their relative mobility, will be taken into consideration.

Much of the difficulty experienced in defining equality has been due to the system of wage negotiation. In principle and in the long term it has been generally agreed that an individual's chance of obtaining a particular job and the pay for this job should depend entirely on merit, i.e. probable efficiency rather than sex. The fact that a number of indices of efficiency give different average values for men and women, and that the division into two sexes has been so firmly anchored in the system of wage negotiation, has made it difficult to decide on the ultimate aims of equality and even more on the policy to be adopted in the short term.

It appears that the central employer and trade union organizations have now reached agreement that discriminatory treatment should be abolished, though they seem to disagree about the speed at which, and the means by which they are to accomplish this. Central recommendations for equal pay for equal work have resulted in a gradual abolition of special female pay rates. Such measures, however, seem to be having only a limited impact. For 'unequal pay' tends to be preserved by the division of occupations into 'male' and 'female' sub-labour markets and discrimination in training, recruitment, employment and promotion in different sectors.

The criticism of traditional views has occasionally attempted to place the concepts of work and efficiency in a wider social perspective. The lower average efficiency shown by women on the labour market, due largely to the shorter duration of their working life, higher absenteeism and less permanent interest in their occupation, is largely a result of their greater contribution in the home. There is nothing to suggest that their total working contribution is lower or that their work as a whole is less efficient from the viewpoint of society. It appears inequitable to reward the contribution of women in the labour market less when their total social contribution is probably equal to that of men. Housewives indirectly help their husbands and any adult sons who are gainfully employed by running the household. Women must always count on dealing with this work 'in their free time', while men can count on female service in the home. The greater costs of female labour should be borne by society as a whole and not affect only working women. Equal treatment of men and women would mean that everyone, employers and employees alike, would share such extra costs.

Discrimination affects the sex roles in marriage and the division of labour between husband and wife. The fact that the husband usually earns more than his wife and enjoys other benefits on the labour market preserves the traditional role division. The radical line that husband and wife should share both housework and gainful employment presupposes a labour market policy that gives women an equal opportunity to contribute to the family's economy.

Power and Influence

One of the most important objectives of the feminist movement has been to remove various external barriers to equal influence and participation in decision-making by women in the family, in working life, in organizations and in public life. Few would dispute any longer the right of women to participate in decision-making and in public life. Yet the contribution actually made by women has proved to be relatively modest. Women M.P.s are still relatively uncommon and the predominance of men in the 'corridors of power' is striking.

Opinion differs as to the reasons for this state of affairs. Some have suggested that the number of politically active women is too small and as a consequence parties have had difficulty in finding women candidates who are sufficiently qualified. Others have maintained that politically interested and capable women are still required to stand aside for men. Occasionally women are brought into decision-making bodies for tactical reasons, i.e. to satisfy different 'pressure groups'.

All political parties recognize that there are both tactical and objective reasons to include a certain number of women on their lists of Parliamentary candidates. However, female candidates are often placed just below the level where they will probably be elected.

An analysis of participation by women in public life reveals close parallels with their participation on the labour market. There is strong evidence that early role learning in the socializing process is relevant to women's lack of interest in exploiting their political possibilities as well as their lack of initiative on the labour market. Here, too, we can distinguish between two 'explanations' for this female behaviour; the discrimination they encounter and their orientation which is a product of prevailing sex role norms and a differentiated socialization process.

It appears likely that a more determined pursuit of career and a longer working lifetime among women will lead to the attainment of influential positions to a greater extent than is now the case, in firms, trade unions and professional associations. It is difficult to say, however, what the effect of the increased participation by women in working life will be on *their influence in other public contexts*. An increase in the activity of women in trade unions and in the administrative sector should lead automatically to increased political influence as both sectors are important steps in a political career. Conceivably, the greater experience gained by the working woman will tend to make her more politically active. She will learn how to function in a public and less personal context. Against this, however, it has been maintained that housewives should have more time and strength left over to devote themselves to politics or similar activities, as compared with women with 'two' jobs.

Prestige and Esteem

The debate on prestige and esteem closely corresponds to that on power and influence. Everyone agrees in principle that men and women should enjoy the same degree of esteem and prestige and that barriers preventing the competition of women and men for these psychological rewards should be removed.

The concepts of prestige and esteem are even more ambiguous than power and influence. We can distinguish between three different meanings.

1. Esteem and prestige accorded to the individual's personal qualities and character, i.e. *personal prestige*.
2. Prestige accorded to certain inherent qualities of the individual e.g. age and sex. We shall refer to this as *assigned social prestige*.
3. Prestige accorded to performance and the positions attained by the individual in competition with others. We shall refer to this as *earned social prestige*.

Personal prestige. All individuals demonstrate both 'masculine' and 'feminine' traits. Women win personal esteem by being feminine and men by being masculine. This can lead to conflicts for the members of a sex that according to the cultural pattern should show traits that adversely affect their opportunities to achieve earned social prestige. This appears to be the case in our society. According to traditional sex role norms, women should be weaker than men, require protection, be passive, patient, self-sacrificing, sensitive etc., i.e. possess qualities that cannot be regarded as qualifying them for the more important positions in industry or public life. Women win esteem by being women, but at the same time this reduces their chances of competing for the jobs that offer earned social prestige. The dilemma of women thus consists of a choice between appearing effective and unfeminine or feminine and ineffective. This dilemma has led both moderates and radicals to campaign against all sex role norms that present a direct obstacle to women in their competition for jobs. No conscious champion of the traditional sex roles has appeared. Instead, the reaction has tended to take the form of jokes, personal comments and semi-conscious trends in the mass media. Thus, sarcastic comments have been made as to the lack of femininity in the feminist movement. And it has often been insinuated that equality of the sexes on the labour market involves a threat to the sex differences in the erotico-sexual context. No evidence of such consequences, however, has been adduced.

American studies illustrating role conflicts among female college students have shown that girls act out an unintelligent role in order to win prestige among their friends, predominantly their male friends. No systematic study has been made as to how far the esteem of women is due to their purely personal 'womanliness' and how far to their external success (earned social prestige). The way in which the mass media portray women suggests that a woman who desires a certain measure of esteem should not only be occupationally successful but also give evidence of 'femininity'.

There is a tendency for women who are successful in business or politics to demonstrate their 'femininity'; to show that they dress well, are beautiful, are wives and mothers or fond of children.

Clearly the man earns prestige in a different way from the woman's. There is less conflict between the personal qualities that qualify him as masculine and those that qualify him for important positions. On the other hand, he does not enjoy the same opportunity to acquire prestige by 'charm'. Nor can he make a career directly through his marriage.

Earned social prestige. There is general agreement to the proposition that men and women should have an equal opportunity to earn prestige. Views diverge, however, over the issue of the way in which women should be able to win prestige. The radical view has been that women can only earn the same prestige as men by pursuing a career, while the moderate ideology has maintained that women enjoy an alternative route to respect via motherhood and care of the children and the home.

The debate is analogous to that on the influence of women; it too is marked by a considerable lack of clarity with regard to factual assumptions. The moderates and the radicals differ in their estimates of the prestige women actually enjoy as housewives. The radicals have suggested that the roles of mother and housewife have been over-publicized (the 'mother-cult'), while the moderate and conservative view has been that the role of housewives enjoys insufficient respect and that measures should be taken to increase their prestige, e.g. by the introduction of training and pay for housewives. It is conceivable, moreover, that different values prevail in different contexts, e.g. that 'official' opinion values the working woman more highly, while private opinion among friends assigns greater value to the housewife. A study of such value structures would be highly interesting. A number of statements of the 'only a housewife' variety suggest that the role of housewife is sometimes perceived as inadequate. Indeed, the current discussion itself appears to have aroused feelings of inadequacy among a number of housewives.

Satisfaction and Adjustment

A comparison between men and women with respect to their average careers, average positions and average opportunity to satisfy different needs etc., reveals a number of differences. We find among men no counterpart to the double burden born by earning mothers or to the dependent and isolated status of those women who work only at home. The discussion has also emphasized the specific adjustment problems of women and the conceivable measures that can be applied in this context. Thus far, less attention has been paid to the problems of men and measures needed to solve such problems.

The radical view has been that greater equality between the sexes will bring both costs and benefits to women. Woman's privileged position with regard to the rewards of family life—protection from the faster pace and competitive pressures of earning life, greater contact with the family and an opportunity for interests and relaxation in the home—would be modified and family benefits would be more equally shared. Women would have to make a more effective contribution in the labour market.

The debate of recent years, however, has not regarded happiness and adjustments as dependent solely on the distribution of the rewards of gainful employment and family life. Attention has also been drawn to the socialization process in the formative years. Both men and women are faced with problems of adjustment specific to their sex. The conflicts experienced by women have been mentioned above. The stronger demand on the boy/man to assert himself, to push forward, to be hard and aggressive and not to show his feelings, creates problems of adjustment that emerge in a relatively higher rate of criminality, higher mortality, a greater risk of stress and certain symptoms of over-strain, and a higher suicide rate. It leads in other words to increased physical and psychic illness, repression of feelings, inhibitions in establishing intimate contact with others or developing certain types of emotional relationships. Certain masculine traits, such as toughness and authoritarian tendencies, have become devaluated by the 'feminization' of society; this may have eased the pressure and created an increased opportunity for men to experience 'feminine' values. There are signs, however, that special problems of adjustment still exist for growing young men and that 'compensated femininity' can be an important contributory factor to the high rate of criminal offences among young people.

All agree that men and women should have an equal chance to be happy. Agreement has not been reached, however, as to whether the alternative of working woman or that of housewife, the complementary or the equivalent roles, gives men and women the greatest opportunity to live a fulfilling life.

The arguments adduced *against* the gainful employment of married women are based on the following assumptions. The combination of outside employment with care of the home and children involves an excessive strain. Women tend to become tired. They also tend to burden the man with functions in the home. The woman with two jobs can handle neither successfully. Moreover, neglect of children and husband tend to create serious guilt feelings. Double work leads to friction in the home. Woman's free time is reduced and with it her opportunity to engage in valuable leisure pursuits and develop her personality.

The arguments presented *for* the gainful employment of women contain the following assumptions. Women working entirely at home are almost totally dependent on their husbands. They experience social isolation, confinement to the home, lack of prestige, a lack of contact with outside events and undeveloped impulses. Work in the home cannot give the same satisfaction as a career. When the children mature, the mother becomes underemployed and feels superfluous. By that time, unfortunately, it is often too late to obtain rewarding work.

In assessing the correctness of these assumptions, we can find individual cases where problems of adjustment have arisen among working women and housewives. There is evidence to suggest that gainful employment by the wife can create friction in the marriage and that women confined to the home can experience feelings of isolation.

Adjustment and happiness seem to depend on a variety of circumstances. In certain cases, e.g. when the wife has pronounced ambitions and a responsible position, when the children are at an age where they can more or less manage for themselves, when the wife has a husband who expects her to continue working or when marital relationships are unsatisfactory, the employment of the woman can lead to better adjustment. In other cases, outside employment can have a negative effect, e.g. when the children are small, when the attitude of the husband is negative, when the occupation of the wife is of a routine nature or monotonous, and she is not interested in her job.

A striking feature of this debate is the tendency to generalize from specific cases. The argument *for* the gainful employment of women usually starts from the case where the wife has access to a highly responsible position. The argument *against* outside employment usually starts from the assumption that the position of the wife is one of low responsibility while that of the husband is one of great responsibility.

Disagreement is also due partly to the fact that different sides of the argument refer to different points in time. The more conservative ideology is focused on the present situation and the reactions currently revealed by women. This allows them to quote the problems of a double job and the fact that the majority of families seem to prefer to have the wife at home. The radical ideology addresses itself more to the future, with equality on the labour market, less work in the home (thanks e.g. to collective services and family-conscious fathers) and well educated and career-conscious women. Radical writers speak more frequently of the situation ultimately aimed at, while the moderates have tended to concentrate on what they consider to be practical under present conditions.

Arguments bearing on the Family

The views presented in the name of the family usually start from the premise that the family is a passive institution which has to adjust to the requirements made by changes in economic structure. It is seldom assumed that the reforms demanded would influence the structure of society's economic and political institutions.

The Birth-rate

In the past, the low fertility rate was an argument frequently levelled against the gainful employment of married women. A number of studies were cited indicating that fertility rates among working married women were lower than those of housewives, and attention was drawn to the fact that the steady decline in fertility rates in Sweden since the 1870's has been associated with an increase in the participation rates of women in the labour market.

A closer investigation, however, reveals that there was no marked association between the birth-rate and participation rates on the labour market during the 30's, 40's and 50's. Moreover, the public statistics do not allow a comprehensive study of the co-variance between these two factors among women in different age groups and different marital status groups in recent decades.

Even where studies indicate a tendency for earning women to have fewer children than housewives, moreover, the association is by no means a causal one. To be sure, it is possible to interpret the relation to show that women hesitate to bear more children in view of their working career and their 'double' work burden. However, it is equally conceivable that the absence of children in a marriage owing e.g. to sterility, tends to make the wife more inclined to seek employment. It can also be true that both the wife's employment and lack of interest in more children stem from dissatisfaction in marriage.

A study comparing gainfully employed married women with two children and a similar group of housewives shows no marked difference in the desire to have children or in the use of birth control [8]. This suggests that the correlation between fertility and employment is more complicated than is assumed by those concluding that there is a strong and direct effect of employment on the fertility rate.

The risk that career interest on the part of women might result in a limited family has not always been cited as a reason for creating obstacles to the gainful employment of married women; it has also given rise to demands for measures designed to facilitate the combination of motherhood with employment, e.g. such measures as the establishment of day and afternoon nurseries, the prohibition of dismissals of women in the event of marriage or childbirth, the right to leave in conjunction with childbirth, different measures to reduce the work load in the home, the creation of part-time jobs and measures to facilitate the return of married women to the labour market. Those measures have been promoted under the assumption that the easier it is for women to combine an occupation with motherhood, the less reason there will be for them to limit the family out of interest in their careers.

There is reason here to distinguish between arguments based on

the present situation and those based on the future social structure.
Even if we find today that a number of women hesitate to bear children
because of their careers and a consciousness of the double work involved,
we cannot deduce from this what the situation would be in a society
in which more had been done to facilitate the combination of an
occupation with motherhood.

Child Adjustment and Development

The effect of the gainful employment of the mother on the adjustment
and development of the child has clearly been an important dividing
line between different sex role ideologies. Conservative writers have
pointed to the increase in juvenile crime and lack of discipline flowing
from increased maternal employment. Radical writers have rejected
these arguments and emphasized the injurious consequences of full-
time motherhood; i.e. the tendency for such mothers to become
dominating and overprotective; the tendency for their children in post-
adolescence to show a striking immaturity, dependence and lack of
initiative.

At present there is no adequate data available with which to assess
the effects of maternal employment. A great deal of further research
needs to be done. Studies are required that would take into account
the wide variety of different factors that impinge upon the effects of
maternal employment on the children.

It has too often been forgotten that the effects of maternal employment will differ widely depending on:

1. The age of the child.
2. The quality of the alternative care of the child.
3. The importance of the father.
4. The mother's motives in choosing her occupation and the satisfaction she finds in it.

Family Harmony

The conservatives have occasionally maintained that maternal employment has a negative effect on family life, contributing to the dissolution
of the family and increased asociality among the children.

Attempts to study the effect of the wife's gainful employment on
marital harmony and adjustment encounter somewhat the same
difficulties as attempts to study the effects that we have already considered. It is possible to compare, for instance, a group of marriages in

which the wife works outside the home with another group in which she does not and record the relative frequency of divorce in each group after a given time period. Or we can compare a group of married couples with a group of divorced couples, both groups having married at the same time, and compare the number of marriages in which the wife continued to work after marriage in each group. Neither of these investigations, however, would indicate causality. It would not be possible to determine whether the fact that the wife continued to work affected her marital relations or whether her marital relations prompted her to take a job. Nor can we be certain of the possible interrelationship between those two factors or whether other intervening variables were present.

The results of certain studies suggest that the gainful employment of the wife in families with several children, with some in the pre-school age group, can create problems and role conflicts. There is some evidence that husbands with income above a certain level prefer to have a wife at home partly because her employment would increase the need for his participation in household work. The reaction of the husband depends on his role expectations and the nature of the marital relationship. A number of writers have stressed the risk of prestige conflicts between husband and wife when the latter is gainfully employed. Yet we lack systematic studies of the effects on social relations within the marriage of such factors as role expectations, division of work in the home, etc. The extreme conservative view that has occasionally been articulated is that the working woman's demand for equality involves a rejection of her own sex and leads to frigidity; for full sexual experience it is thought necessary that the women play a subordinate role, i.e. remain a housewife.

On the radical side it has been suggested that the price of a somewhat higher divorce rate is worth paying to ensure that the wife has the resources through employment to divorce her husband when the marriage is a source of deep and persistent discord. Life-long marriage is not an absolute virtue. The present and future structure of our society, a society in which husband and wife have long life expectancies and in which they can easily—owing to their separate careers—grow apart from each other, necessitates a modified view of marriage and greater tolerance of divorce.

On the other hand, the radicals and moderates have pointed to the positive effects that the gainful employment of the wife can have on the marriage. The wife's employment can lead to greater equality; a sharing of the burdens of earning and housework and a consequent increase in common interests.

There is reason, too, to distinguish between the present and the future perspectives as regards the effect of gainful employment on marital harmony. Today when so many men and women have come to accept a traditional role division within the family, an attempt to create a partly new pattern, with husband and wife sharing bread-winning and housework functions, would be bound to lead to problems of adjustment. Tomorrow, however, when this new pattern becomes part of the established order, the gainful employment of married women would have a different effect. The radical and moderate ideology argues that it is impossible to cite the disgruntled reactions of today's husband to his wife's occupation as support for the conservative viewpoint. For this, they suggest, merely indicates a need to re-educate men and boys.

Economic Arguments

The point of departure for this aspect of the debate is the value of the work input of women. The working hours of women—and thus indirectly of men—can be utilized in different ways, both as regards the distribution of women's time between home and job and in the choice of gainful occupations for women. Which approach will lead—under certain economic assumptions—to the most desirable results, as measured in some way by the value of women's productivity?

The starting point for the economic evaluation can vary. The entire matter can be regarded from the viewpoint of the individual firm, and the evaluation of a woman's input can be limited to what she does for the firm. This is *a business economics approach*. We can also assess the value of the contribution made by women in the wider context of the labour market and production as a whole, excluding only the contribution she makes in the home which is never subjected to a market evaluation. This is *a labour market economics approach*. Finally, we can widen our perspective still further and include the work done by women in the home. This we can call *the overall economic approach*.

The currently accepted sex role ideologies are largely in agreement that working women are vitally important from the standpoint of labour market economics and that a variety of measures should be taken to utilize female labour resources in a more satisfactory manner.

They differ, however, in certain respects. The more conservative maintain that the work of married women in the home is at least as important as their paid employment and that we cannot assume that much is to be gained from the overall economic standpoint by transferring more married women from work in the home to the labour market. On the radical and moderate side it is asserted that a considerable proportion of the 'hours of work' now devoted to the home is inefficiently utilized and that the transfer of more women to the labour market would produce a considerable overall gain.

The radicals and moderates also criticize the tendency to regard women as a 'labour reserve'. When labour is short women are enticed into the market, and the value of their contribution is stressed. When jobs are in short supply, values change and every attempt is made to remove women from the market. In this way women are relegated to the role of an unskilled manpower reserve, closely resembling a surplus of labour and leading to the depression of wages and other terms of employment for women.

To assess the value of alternative methods of utilizing female labour resources, certain assumptions must be made as to the efficiency and productivity of women relative to that of men both in terms of average levels of efficiency and productivity and in terms of the distribution of these differences over different age groups, etc.

A distinction is worth making in this context. Let us take *productivity* to mean the value of an individual's output in the short term, say the output of an individual per week in a given job. We can then take *efficiency* to mean something of a more long-term nature taking into consideration not only the output of an individual in one job in a given time period but also the value of the individual over his or her career. In the latter case we can include such factors as absenteeism, span of working life, interest and ambition, willingness to undergo further training and to take such jobs as have to be done, capacity to cooperate etc. Productivity then becomes only one of the factors determining efficiency.

Let us now compare the productivity and efficiency of men and women in different occupations, from the business economic and the labour market economic standpoints.

1. In many if not most of the sectors of the labour market, there is a division of jobs into 'male' and 'female' occupations. The more carefully occupational sectors are scrutinized, the more strikingly evident becomes this division. Consequently, it is often difficult, if not impossible, to compare the productivity and efficiency of men and women in most occupations.

2. The relatively widespread belief in many sectors that women are inferior in productivity and efficiency seems largely based on traditional assumptions rather than evidence. Seldom can we find any reliable data upon which to base a comparison of the productivity and efficiency of men and women in the same job working on the same terms of employment, or a study of relative differences in costs to the firm.

3. The psychological studies made of the skill (productivity) of men and women in different respects indicate only marginal differences in comparison with the similarities. In certain sectors women are more skilful than men, in other sectors the contrary is true. Studies show that no foundation exists for the sort of thinking in 'sex types' that characterizes current conceptions on the labour market as to the relative productivity of men and women.

4. There is probably a greater male-female 'differential' in respect of efficiency than of productivity. There is evidence that women *on the average* have a higher rate of absenteeism, a shorter span of working life, a lesser propensity to pursue a career actively by undergoing training, etc. In the event, female labour tends on the whole to be more costly. This tendency is accentuated by the fact that part-time work often involves a higher labour cost than full-time work.

The question of whether the current utilization of female labour is satisfactory has two aspects. One relates to how women divide their working time between the home and an outside occupation; the other to the distribution of women among different occupations. If we approach the question from the overall economic standpoint, the former aspect is most important. We must take into account work that is performed by women in the home, which cannot be evaluated on a market basis. An increase in the work done by women outside the home will mean an increase in some kind of production but it may also entail increased costs and less efficient results in the 'production' of the family. If we approach the question from the labour market economics standpoint, the question of the actual distribution of jobs between men and women naturally becomes more important.

To arrive at any objective conclusion we require much more data than is now available. What for example is the distribution between men and women regarding efficiency and productivity in different occupational sectors? What is the economic importance of such variables as absenteeism, span of working life and the existence of part-time jobs in different sectors? How will the labour market develop? What level of employment can be expected? How will growth affect the different branches of our economy? How will demographic conditions affect the labour supply?

In general, it is accepted that we should utilize female labour resources more effectively than hitherto from the labour market economics standpoint. The state of our present knowledge of and the forecasts that we can make about economic growth in the next ten years indicate a need for the abolition of sex discrimination on the labour market, a more even distribution of men and women occupationally and an overall increase in the number of women participating in the labour market. The 1959 Long-term Planning Commission argues along just these lines, though it does not support this position by an analysis of the alternative uses of female labour. The Commission recommends a greater allocation of public researches to measure such as day and afternoon nurseries and other collective services to assist gainfully employed women.

The waste involved in the present system has been most striking in the professions and in certain typically feminine occupations, e.g. nursing, where the low degree of participation on the labour market by married women has helped to create a marked shortage of labour. As an ever-increasing proportion of gifted persons are given a higher education, recruitment must be from both sexes and a greater number of highly educated women must continue with their careers. The need to recruit both men and women applies not only to the most qualified jobs but in theory to all sectors requiring skills to be found only among a limited proportion of the total labour force.

In the discussion on 'recruitment by sex' there is again reason to distinguish between the arguments based on the present situation and those directed to conditions in the future. Criticism of the present use of female labour is often based on the assumption that the relative efficiency of women will be greater in the future. To be sure, the lower average efficiency of women on the labour market in some respects is linked with discriminatory treatment [on the labour market], their greater contribution in the home and the influence of different general sex and family standards. If the gainful employment of housewives is stimulated in the future by equal pay and job opportunities, a smaller work load in the home, more help in the home from men, a greater orientation of women in the direction of a career and e.g. higher tax deductions for the expenses incurred, then the average differences in efficiency between men and women will be reduced and with this reduction will diminish the reasons for predominantly male recruitment in certain sectors. Yet, the question of the optimum use of female labour resources in the long term cannot be discussed without making certain assumptions as to future housing policy, tax policy, family policy, educational policy etc.

Disagreement over the economically most efficient use of female labour resource has been greatest when such use is considered from the overall economic standpoint. There has been no systematic attempt to assess the implications of alternative uses from this standpoint. This is due to the difficulty of measuring the value of the working contribution of a given group of housewives in the home in such a way that it can be compared with the value of their alternative contribution on the labour market. It has thus far been impossible to assess home services and products, e.g. care of the children, on a market basis. We have had to content ourselves with noting the net gains in industrial production etc. created by a certain transfer of female labour from the household to the labour market, without offsetting this gain by a satisfactory estimate of the loss created in the household. Yet it is precisely the size of this latter cost that has been called into question, particularly as regards the gainful employment of mothers with young children. A number of costs incurred by such gainful employment are borne by the community, e.g. child care, in such a form (social services) that no market evaluation has yet been made.

On certain points it is possible to find some degree of unanimity. Mothers whose children have reached school age or are in their teens, constitute a labour force whose incorporation into the labour market would be a distinct benefit to society. The measurable costs in the form of retraining and part-time work seem small in comparison. Measures are being taken to stimulate labour market participation by this group.

The decision of a household on the question 'housewife or working woman' is influenced by a number of circumstances, e.g. taxation policy, family policy, housing policy, labour market policy, rearing ideals etc. Social policy provides the framework within which such a decision is made, but this gives us little guidance as to the type of framework society *should* provide. Society must adopt a conscious position with respect to the extent to which and in the direction in which the choice of the households is to be influenced. Since social measures help to form this 'framework of decision', society should investigate whether or not the present framework is a reasonable one.

The question is whether the authorities are aware of how this framework functions or whether they are certain how they want it to function. The present system of taxation tends to encourage certain categories of mothers to stay at home. Greater deductions for expenses would create a different situation by encouraging wives to devote a greater proportion of their time to gainful employment. The establishment of day nurseries would have a similar effect. The costs of caring for and supervising children would be subsidized and this would support the decisions of mothers to take on or continue employment. The small coverage of the day nursery system at present, however, means that the effect of this measure is negligible.

In the economic debate, disagreement seems to be largely over questions of fact. Yet it is surprising how little economic research has been carried out to elucidate the value of alternative uses of male and female labour from the labour market and the overall economic standpoints. The question of overall utility is considered by many to be of decisive importance. But not even the simplest efforts have been made to study the situation in this way.

Some Concluding Views

In the current debate on the role of women in the labour market, there is disagreement not only with respect to values but also as regards factual assumptions: the present situation and how it has developed, the consequences of previous changes, the conceivable effects of new measures and the question of ultimate goals.

There is a notable lack of basic data and an obvious need for further investigation to test many basic assumptions.

Moreover, the need for an 'agonizing reappraisal' and improved co-ordination of social policy in this field is painfully evident. The attitude of women to gainful employment is influenced by many different policy measures applied in different sectors for specific purposes. The total effect of these on the position of women is frequently disregarded. Nor has any satisfactory study been made of the extent to which these different measures are consistent with each other.

Certain measures appear to promote 'equality' of men and women on the labour market. Thus conditions are created to give men and women an equal opportunity to obtain a general education and equal treatment on the labour market. At the same time certain social policy measures give women a special status from the standpoint of maintenance and thus tend to confirm the image and reality of the married woman as a supported housekeeper.

Tax policy acts as a direct deterrent to certain categories of women continuing in their careers.

The lack of consistency and co-ordination of the present system has sometimes been defended on the grounds of the need to preserve the 'freedom' of the family and of women. Families must decide for themselves how to employ their labour and women and this decision should not be subjected to pressure. This argument is not entirely invalid but it ignores the fact that social policy in different fields necessarily creates the framework within which each family makes such decisions. Current social policy is already exercising an influence and its present structure means that different categories of mother are being influenced in certain ways in their choice between remaining housewives and taking outside employment. Such decisions by the family are also influenced from other quarters, e.g. the sex role norms imprinted during the rearing process and the female ideal projected by the mass media. Taken together these influences hardly make for 'greater freedom'.

In order to cite the 'freedom of the family' as an argument, one must first be reasonably clear about the degree of freedom currently enjoyed by the family. Radical writers have often claimed that, at present, women are strongly influenced against combining their roles as housewives with outside work. They point to the 'cult of the mother', tax policy, the prevailing division of work in the home and discrimination on the labour market. It is possible that this argument is somewhat overstated, but at the same time it seems fair to conclude that the present system does not provide maximum freedom to women or to families. What is required here is a survey of actual conditions and studies on how the choice situation is perceived by different categories of women under present conditions, and how satisfied they are with the choice made from certain vantage points. We can then compare how the choice situation would be perceived under certain other given conditions, and determine how satisfying it would be from the same vantage points.

The demand for 'freedom for the family' is a reasonable enough principle, though somewhat vague and ill defined. We must specify what type or degree of outside influence would be acceptable. On this point there is in fact a certain consensus of opinion in the debate. Legislation that would require married women to pursue a given career would be unreasonable and unacceptable. On the other hand, objective instruction of the young in the functions of the home and the labour market is acceptable, even though such information actually involves pressure of a kind, owing to the prejudices currently acting in the opposite direction.

A necessary condition for surveying and co-ordinating the measures that affect the position of women in society is that we adopt an attitude on the question of the sex roles as a whole, i.e. on the ideological position. What are we attempting to achieve? We cannot hope to increase the freedom of men and women in all respects, i.e. with regard to all the advantages and rewards that are sought—or should be sought— by both sexes. We cannot simultaneously promote the progress of women on the labour market and their opportunity to be permanently supported as housewives. When we take our position we must balance the virtues of different solutions from the standpoints of women, men, the family and our overall economy.

REFERENCES

1. Quist, G., *Kvinnofrågan i Sverige 1909–1846*, Gothenberg, 1960, pp. 14–37.

2. Mill, John Stuart, *The Subjection of Women*, London, 1869.

3. Quist, G., *op. cit.*, Chs. 1 and 2.

4. Engels, F., *The Origin of the Family, Private Property and the State*, pp. 91–94.

5. Timasheff, N. S., *The Attempt to Abolish the Family in Russia*, and Spiro, M. E., *Is the Family Universal?—The Israeli Case*, in Bell, N. W., and Vogel, E. F., *A Modern Introduction to the Family*, Illinois, 1960; see also Yang, C. H., *The Chinese Family in the Communist Revolution*, Cambridge, Mass., 1959, Chs. VII and VIII.

6. See, e.g., *The Family in the U.S.S.R.; Changing Attitudes in Soviet Russia*, London, 1949; *Equality of Women in the U.S.S.R.*, Moscow, 1957; Inkeles, A. and Bauer, R., *The Soviet Citizen*, Cambridge, Mass., 1959, Ch. 8.

7. Merton, R. N., *Social Theory and Social Structure*, Glencoe, Ill., 1957, Ch. 9.

8. Dahlström, E., Mödrar i hem och förvarvsarbete, Gothenberg, 1959. (Mimeo.)

INDEX OF AUTHORS

Sears, R. R., 98
Siegel, A. E., 92, 94–5
Spiro, M. E., 175
Spitz, R., 88, 89
Strindberg, A., 12, 13

Thorsell, S., 18, V
Thyberg, S., 17, 49, 137–50

Tiller, P. O., 17, 37, III
Timasheff, N. S., 175

Weil, M. W., 36
Whiting, J., 99–100
Wolfe, D. H., 41

Zweig, F., 49

APPENDIX

THE STATUS OF WOMEN IN SWEDEN
Report to the United Nations 1968

This Report has, under the sanction of the Swedish Government August 25, 1967, been drawn up by Maj-Britt Sandlund, Head of Section at the Halland County Administration.

Contents   **Page**

The Government of Sweden has noted with satisfaction resolution No. 1133 (XLI) of the Economic and Social Council concerning a long-term programme within the framework of the United Nations aimed at raising the status of women and the suggestions put forward by the Secretary-General in conjunction with this resolution. In a world where human rights in various areas of society are still largely limited with respect to women either by law or in practice, the Swedish Government feels that any effort likely to promote greater equality between men and women should be accorded high priority. Continued and intensified efforts on the part of the UNO to make member countries conscious of the need for active measures to achieve better utilisation of the talent and labour potential represented by women are an important phase of the work of realising human rights. A long-term programme adopted by the UNO and containing both a definition of policy and proposals to concrete measures in this respect would undoubtedly represent a major contribution to the emancipation of women all over the world.

Before proceeding to a more detailed account of the activity which has taken place and is taking place in Sweden with a view to achieving greater equality between the sexes, the Government wishes to give its general views on what it considers to be important aspects of the aim of such an international programme.

The measures to raise the status of women recommended in resolution No. 1133 as well as in certain of the suggestions included in the Secretary-General's "Annex II" are felt to be relatively isolated from the general policy in various fields aimed at economic and social progress for the population as a whole. However, experience from both Sweden and other industrial countries suggests that the question of women's rights must be viewed as a function of the whole complex of roles and the division of labour imposed on both women and men by upbringing, tradition and practice (and to a lesser extent by legislation). A decisive and ultimately durable improvement in the status of women cannot be attained by special measures aimed at women alone; it is equally necessary to abolish the conditions which tend to assign certain privileges, obligations or rights to men. No decisive change in the distribution of functions and status as between the sexes can be achieved if the duties of the male in society are assumed a priori to be unaltered. The aim of reform work in this area must be to change the traditional division of labour which tends to deprive women of the possibility of exercising their legal rights on equal terms. The division of functions as between the sexes must be changed in such a way that both the man and the woman in a family are afforded the same practical opportunities of participating in both active parenthood and gainful employment. If women are to attain a position in society outside the home which corresponds to their proportional membership of the citizen body, it follows that men must assume a greater share of responsibility for the upbringing of children and the care of the home. A policy which attempts to give women an equal place with men in economic life while at the same time confirming woman's traditional responsibility for the care of home and children has no prospect of fulfilling the first of these aims. This aim can be realised only if the man is also educated and encouraged to take an active part in parenthood and is given the same rights and duties as the woman in his parental capacity. This will probably imply that the demands for performance at work on the man's part must be reduced: a continued shortening of working hours will therefore be of great importance. In this context it would be advisable to study how reductions in working hours could best be distributed over the working week with a view to making it easier for husbands to do their share of work in the home.

In this connection the Swedish Government would refer to the Memorandum of 23 October 1963 delivered to the Secretary-General in connection with General Assembly Resolution No. 1777 (XVII) concerning UN aid to improve the status of women in the developing countries. With reference to the proposal to draft a long-term programme for women in these countries, the following comment, among others, was made:

"The aim of such a programme must be to establish a situation where community efforts are directed as a matter of course towards all citizens within the respective countries, without any discrimination as to race, religion or sex. This implies that women must be integrated completely into the work of developing the community. . . . It is therefore necessary to emphasise that, in the long run, specific 'programmes for women' and specific 'efforts for women' should be abolished—as obviously the whole community shares the benefits."

The same principle applies, in the opinion of the Swedish Government, now that the question has been raised of a long-term programme within the United Nations framework covering all its member states. The aim of a long-term "programme for women" must be that every individual, irrespective of sex, shall have the same practical opportunities, not only for education and employment, but also in principle the same responsibility for his or her own maintenance as well as a shared responsibility for the upbringing of children and the upkeep of the home. Eventually to achieve complete equality in these rights and obligations, a radical change in deep-rooted traditions and attitudes must be brought about among both women and men, and active steps must be taken by the community to encourage a change in the roles played by both. The view that women ought to be economically supported by marriage must be effectively refuted—also in the legislative field—as this view is a direct obstacle to the economic independence of women and their ability to compete on equal terms in the labour market. Similarly, the husband's traditional obligation to support his wife must be modified to constitute a responsibility, shared with her, for the support of the children. This concern for the children should also be manifested in a greater degree of participation in the supervision and care of the children on the husband's part.

The Government is well aware that this view appears revolutionary and unrealistic in the eyes of the representatives of many other countries. A growing opinion in Sweden has however rallied to its support. In Sweden, as in the other Scandinavian countries, a lively debate has been going on for the past six or seven years in mass media, in organisations and in public bodies concerning the tasks of men and women in society and the home. This debate has brought forth a new approach which involves a departure from the traditional habit of regarding these problems as "women's questions."

The debate has received great support from scientific research concerning the roles of the sexes; the research has been conducted mainly by sociologists, although economists are now also beginning to make a contribution. The analyses hitherto available show that no rapid advancement of women in employment and the professions, politics, trade union activity, etc., is possible as long as men fail to assume that share of the work of the home which falls to them as husbands and fathers. The expression "male emancipation" has therefore been coined in Sweden to denote the right of a husband to remain at home while the children are small where it is found more appropriate for the mother to devote herself to gainful employment. The demand for male "emancipation" in family life is also supported by the results of recent psychological research, which have proved that the identification of growing boys may become uncertain· in a one-sided, mother-dominated home environment.[1] This lack of certainty in identification (of what is "manly" behaviour) may lead to overcompensation expressed in exaggerated aggressiveness and may be one explanation of the higher crime rate as compared to girls. In recent years demands have been made for a change in legislation whereby the father, like the mother (when she interrupts her career) would be entitled to a certain leave of absence with pay while the children are small. The need for male staff in child care institutions, day nurseries, nursery schools and the lower schools has been emphasized in many quarters.

In the discussion of woman's role which has been going on in Sweden, it has been particularly pointed out that the mothers—or fathers—of small children ought to be afforded a free and open choice between working inside or outside the home. This emphasis on the married woman's right to continue in gainful employment during the years when the family has small children has done a great deal to break down the negative attitude to mothers going out to work which was formerly common. It is another matter that society has not as yet been able to provide the facilities, e.g. for looking after children, that would be needed to guarantee full freedom of choice to all parents of small children. According to a survey made in 1967, there were over 200,000 mothers with children below the age of 10 who would like to go out to work if they could arrange to have their children looked after.

The great majority of married women in Sweden, however, do not have young children. The period of active motherhood now occupies only a comparatively small portion of a woman's adult life owing to the tendency to marry younger, have fewer children than in former times, and concentrate the bearing of children to an early age. A married woman can therefore devote the greater part of her adult life to gainful work. It is important in the discussion of gainful employment for married women to distinguish, on the one hand, between women with children at an age when they demand supervision and, on the other, women who no longer have children who require their mother's presence in the home (the latter group

1. Tiller, Per Olav, "Parental role division and the child's personality development," *The Changing Roles of Men and Women.* Ed. by Edmund Dahlström. PP. 79-104. (London: Gerald Duckworth and Co. Ltd., 1967; Boston: Beacon Press, 1971).

forms the great majority in Sweden). It can therefore hardly be argued that married women without young children should be regarded differently in any essential way to unmarried women as far as the labour market is concerned; on the contrary, the professional ambitions of women must be encouraged. The old idea that women bear the main responsibility for work in the home must be countered, as gainful work by married women is otherwise liable to be regarded as a mere supplement to housework.

It is further clear that the possibility of remaining at home which is open to many married women, even though their children no longer require their presence, cannot by any means always be taken as a manifestation of true freedom of choice. A woman's decision to remain at home often means in reality that she has limited the choices open to her on the labour market if she should wish to go out to work later. It may prove to be a great handicap if a woman is absent from the labour market for an extended period of time, for she finds, when she later wishes to return to work—or is compelled to do so for economic reasons—that she is at a considerable disadvantage as compared to someone who has been in continuous employment.

However, it would be unreasonable to presume that married women should devote themselves to gainful employment to the same extent as men and at the same time do all the work of the home. Surveys in both western and eastern Europe show that working married women today have less leisure time than any other group in society. Nor can one expect that women who devote themselves to permanent gainful employment will have access to the same opportunities for promotion as men under the present system of sex roles, as the individual employer considers the risk of women's leaving his service on marriage too high to justify the investment of training and promoting them. The character of matrimony as an institution for the support of women according to the occidental tradition has thus come to be an indirect obstacle to her emancipation in modern industrial society.

Swedish opinion, therefore, has made a great point of stressing the economic independence of every individual both inside and outside marriage. Instead of a one-sided emphasis on the function of motherhood, the importance of greater contact between father and children has been stressed. At the same time, the care and upbringing of children have come to be increasingly regarded as essential services to the community, which in principle ought to be paid for in cash in the same way as services to an employer. It has been felt that the social security of the parent who stays at home to look after the children should be equivalent to that of the one who goes out to work. This view is also reflected in the directives issued to the Committee currently reviewing our family policy.

The new view set forth here represents a sharp break with older tradition. Young married couples with children have been among the keenest supporters of the new equality. Incidentally, it is interesting to note that men have taken an active part in the debate on future sex roles. This new opinion, which is in practically all organisations, will undoubtedly exert a strong influence on future reform policies in Sweden.

Through a comprehensive social insurance system, the State in Sweden has assumed the main responsibility for the individual in case of sickness, disability and unemployment. Thus women are no longer so economically dependent on their husbands for their personal security.

It is however most important that social welfare legislation should be applied to the married woman as an individual and not indirectly via her husband. Studies now in progress in Sweden are aimed at putting men and women on an equal footing with regard to social security insurance.

Notwithstanding its basic attitude—that community measures and reforms must be clearly directed towards all citizens irrespective of sex—the Swedish Government fully appreciates the additional necessity of special action on behalf of women in the present situation and, in many countries, during a lengthy period of transition. Special efforts on the part of the community to strengthen the position of women will be necessary until the gap between men and women as regards the practical exercise of human rights has narrowed appreciably. The need for special action to stimulate female emancipation is certainly present in other countries besides those which have traditionally assigned a subordinate role to women. Steps must also be taken to ensure that women can maintain the strong or economically independent position which they have traditionally held in certain countries now embarking upon industrial development. It is most important that the UNO and its various special bodies should be conscious of the risk that women may be forced into greater economic dependence upon their menfolk when their country abandons a barter economy in favour of an industrial monetary economy. This happened in Sweden and a number of other European countries at the end of the nineteenth century and the beginning of the twentieth. It is so much more difficult to put right the defects afterwards.

Special efforts are clearly also called for to overcome prejudices against certain groups of women, e.g. unmarried mothers. This group undoubtedly has to face a difficult situation in many countries owing to prejudices against women who become mothers without benefit of matrimony. Experience from Sweden indicates that such prejudices can be broken down, partly through a series of measures on society's part to improve the economic and social status of unmarried mothers.

The special reforms affecting women must however be so designed as to encourage the full integration of women into all the facets of society. It is essential to keep this aim clearly in mind, as the risk otherwise arises that special action on behalf of women may serve to entrench a traditional division of labour which in the long view will hinder the achievement of practical equality between the sexes. A further complication attendant upon a division of various types of community effort according to sex is that it is all too easy to give the impression that public reform policy is mainly directed towards satisfying the needs of the male population, while questions affecting women must needs be resolved by special arrangements or supplementary regulations. At the same time as special provisions are made for giving women equality of opportunity with men, it is necessary to induce women to move into areas traditionally regarded as male preserves.

It is also important to the realisation of the programme to stress that the object of the action taken is to achieve parity not only in the matter of rights, but also of the duties of women. Women, just as much as men, have an obligation to take an active part in, for example, trade union and political work and to share the economic responsibility for the support of children. They should not be able to acquire social status and privileges automatically by virtue of their husbands' contributions to public life. On the contrary, women must be made aware of their personal responsibility as citizens. They must be encouraged to exercise the franchise and the opportunity of being elected to positions of trust in political life. Women should further be conscious of their obligations to give some return on the capital which society has invested in their education and training, as society has a right to expect this capital to pay dividends. This aspect is becoming all the more important now that education is rapidly becoming more widespread among young people and courses of training are becoming longer and longer.

The grounds for initiating a long-term programme for women should preferably also be given a broader content than the simple objective of creating equality in respect of rights and obligations. The economic profit and the more rapid economic progress that both the community as a whole and the individual business stand to gain through greater equality between the sexes must be emphasized. It should further be stressed that increased efficiency and more rapid economic progress are dependent on the abandonment of scales of evaluation based on physical characteristics such as sex and race instead of individual aptitude and ability. A Swedish economist and labour market researcher has calculated that the Swedish national income could be increased by some 25 per cent if the unused labour potential of women were to be fully utilised and by some 50 per cent if sex discrimination and other barriers were to be totally abolished. According to a calculation made in France, the standard of living of that country would rise by 35 per cent if women were professionally active to the same extent as men. Experience from Sweden shows, moreover, that many private employers are little inclined to show interest in the recruitment of female labour for what are traditionally regarded as "male" jobs simply in response to appeals for "fair play between the sexes." One must in the first instance be able to show proof of the economic gains a company can effect by increasing its recruitment of women. A number of Swedish industrial firms took a greater interest in part-time employment of women after it had been demonstrated that the average productivity of two women employed part-time to fill one full-time vacancy was higher than that achieved by one male worker employed full-time. In an area where there is a shortage of labour, it is possible to arouse interest in the employment of women if one can show that the company gains in productivity by broadening its field of recruitment to include women also. Unfortunately, however, the female skill that could be turned to profit is still an unknown quantity in many occupations where it has never been given a chance to prove itself.

Provided that the special programme for women is so formulated that it directly encourages the full integration of women into the work of the community outside the home, a programme designed to improve the status of women over the period 1968-1978 will be of great value. In view of what was said earlier about the need to modify the traditional division of roles between the sexes, it would, however, be advantageous if a long-term programme adopted by the UNO were to be formulated as a programme of equality between women and men. There can be no doubt that even the title of such a programme would be significant, and it would be valuable if the designation of the programme were such as to avoid giving the impression of being concerned with questions relating to women that could be dealt with and solved by women. It may be mentioned that the term "woman question" as applied to these problems is now being largely abandoned in Sweden in favour of the sociological term "sex role question."

With reference to the international conventions listed in "Annex II Suggestions, etc." to the Secretary-General's note, Sweden subscribed to all of these. Swedish law contains no formal obstacles to the exercise of civil, social or economic rights by women. Of some significance, however, are the limitations placed upon the entry of women into certain special spheres of activity with a particularly great aura of "male prestige" which tend to preserve the philosophy of segregation. In Sweden nowadays this applies only to the profession of arms; formerly it also applied to holy orders. The ultimate reason why women have been unable to achieve a status in society equal to that of men is to be sought in the traditional division of functions whereby women are by upbringing, habit and tradition assigned the prime responsibility for the care of home and children. It is this so-called primary female role which deprives women of equality in vocational training and employment and of equal representation in political and trade organisations.

To promote greater equality, one must always determine which political instruments will directly or indirectly encourage a more equal division of labour between the sexes, for every act on the part of the community affects the status of men and women—in a favourable or unfavourable direction. The question of the roles of the sexes must therefore be regarded as one of the chief problems in the continual work of reforming educational, employment, social, family and taxation policies.

As explained in the following, studies are now in progress in a number of fields which will make a direct contribution to greater equality. These studies are not being conducted by any special organisation for women, but by commissions charged with the task of making a general review of legislation within their respective fields.

Point A) General in the Secretary-General's Annex II raises the question of the "establishment of machinery to assist in the development of measures and techniques for the advancement of women, including national planning." Examples of such machinery quoted in the Annex include special sections within a department, a central unit of government, a national commission on the status of women, a joint committee or a group of liaison officers. The Swedish Government on its part, however, would question the appropriateness of setting up a special body for women's questions in the present situation, since so many of these questions have been integrated into the general policy of reform. Had such a body been established in Sweden four years ago, it would presumably have been charged with the task of resolving important questions relating to policies of employment, social welfare, taxation, family matters and education, which are now being dealt with by the committees working on the general reform of large areas of these policies. The problem of women's wages, which is an important component of the low-wage problem as a whole, is thus being dealt with by the Government commission set up to study the matter of low incomes. If these questions insofar as they affect women had been divorced from their context and handed over to a commission on women, there would have been a risk that the proposals might have been delayed owing to the many and widely varied aspects with which such a commission would have had to deal.

The fact that Sweden for its part feels best able to solve the problems of women's status in this "integrated" manner does not of course prevent the UNO from issuing a general recommendation to member states to set up a body of the type envisaged. Such a body may prove necessary to point out deficiencies and problems in this area and thus provide a stimulus to further reform in various special bodies, a work that might not otherwise have been undertaken.

I. PREVIOUS MEASURES FOR THE ADVANCEMENT OF WOMEN

A. Developments up to the 1930s

About a hundred years ago, Sweden was a poor agrarian society based on barter economy. Two-thirds of the population derived their livelihood from agriculture and associated occupations. Industrialisation had not yet begun. At the same time, the country was threatened by overpopulation; between 1830 and 1890 the population rose by nearly two millions, or 65 per cent.

The social environment of the overpopulated rural community was typified by the large family consisting of several generations living together. In this agricultural society, the patriarchal view of the family still predominated. The legal code of 1734 still regulated the legal relationship between the sexes; it decreed that both married and unmarried women must have guardians. A husband was his wife's guardian and managed all property. This law, it is true, gave a woman the right to conclude a marriage agreement with her future husband, but the agreement had to be approved by her sponsor, normally her father. The minimum legal age at marriage was as low as 15 for women; this was however raised to 17 in 1892 and is now 18.

In the barter economy, however, women fulfilled an important economic function as producers of food, clothing and other necessities. Despite this, women were long denied the right to earn money of their own. It was only in the Parliamentary Session of 1809-1810 that women were given almost complete freedom to engage in commerce and crafts. Equal inheritance rights for men and women did not come until 1845, however; before that, a woman inherited only half a man's share.

Women were still wards of their menfolk, which meant that a woman was not entitled personally to manage any property she might acquire through her newly-won freedom to earn money. After strong resistance, however, the Parliament of 1856-58 decided that a married woman over 25 could become legally competent if she personally applied to a court for this privilege. It was only in 1872 that unmarried women automatically came of age at 25, and a few years later married women, too, were given clear title to property derived from their own earnings. Married women, however, remained the wards of their husbands until 1921, when a new Marriage Act came into force.

These first steps toward equality in law had been preceded by a lively debate, sparked off by two eminent Swedish authors who advocated complete equality between man and woman. It may also be of interest to note that the above-mentioned reforms had been carried through in several other European countries earlier than in Sweden.

Industrialisation brought about great changes in the social and economic circumstances of women. Migration to the towns began, and women sought employment in industry, especially the textile industry. Need and poverty prevailed. Legislation forbidding child labour had not yet been introduced. Eventually the first laws giving some protection to employees were passed. At the beginning of the century employers were forbidden to employ women on industrial work for two weeks after childbirth. No compensation for loss of wages was provided for.

Consumer goods such as bread, beverages and textiles began to be manufactured to an increasing extent outside the home. Only women in the wealthier social groups had access to education beyond the compulsory elementary school. In 1859, however, teaching posts in the compulsory elementary school were opened to women. In 1870 women were given the right to enter for the university matriculation examination, and three years later they were allowed to proceed to all university degrees except theological degrees and the higher degrees in law.

The first women's organisations were formed at the end of the 19th century and the beginning of the 20th. At the same time a struggle was going on between the property-owning classes, who still held the reins of political power, and representatives of the majority of the citizens who demanded full democratic freedom. Only men enjoying a certain income or capital had the vote. The struggle for equality as it concerned women received a strong impetus from the demands for universal and equal suffrage for all citizens. A nation-wide organisation devoted to the cause of women's suffrage was formed in 1902. The democratic breakthrough came finally in 1918-19 with the Act that gave universal and equal suffrage to both women and men (this was exercised for the first time in the elections of 1921).

One of the most important reforms came in the 1920s: this was the establishment of legal and economic equality between husband and wife within the family by the Marriage Act of 1920. The married woman came of age at 21 and now had the right to plead her own case before the courts. Other discriminatory obstacles to the advancement of women were removed in the years that followed.

The Competence Act passed in 1925 gave women equal entitlement in principle to hold posts in the Government service. During the 1920s girls were also admitted to the public (i.e. State-maintained) grammar schools to which boys transferred after some years at the elementary school. It was not until 1927 that girls were enabled to sit for the matriculation examination on the same conditions as boys; at the same time, the higher schools began to be converted into co-educational establishments.

B. Developments up to the present day

A reaction against the strivings for equality occurred as a result of the economic crisis at the beginning of the 1930s. The rising unemployment among men prompted demands from various quarters that women married to men with a "reasonable income" should be dismissed from their jobs. These demands were however rejected by both Parliament and the Government. Instead, an expansive economic programme was launched in 1933 with a comprehensive programme of public works.

These public works, financed by loans, were an expression of the modern type of economic policy. Their object was not just to create work for the unemployed but also to increase purchasing power and reverse the economic depression.

The mid-1930s saw the beginning of a series of social reforms which lead to greater equality between the sexes. A National Pensions Act passed in 1935 provided equal pensions for men and women. An important principle was established by the Act of 1936 concerning pregnancy and confinement leave, which gave Government employees the right to the same pay as for sickness. This right is also enjoyed by unmarried women. In 1939 the principle was embodied in the law that an employee should not be dismissed from employment on the grounds of betrothal, marriage, pregnancy or confinement. Since 1945 this law has covered all forms of employment including domestic service.

In conjunction with the economic crisis the national birth rate fell sharply. Families with children were particularly hard hit by unemployment. The marriage rate was also low. Fears for the development of the population of the country stimulated a programme of family policy reform; this formed the basis of the purposeful family policies which have been pursued in Sweden ever since, even though the population problem from which it originated ceased to be acute after the 1930s. Public assistance to families with children took the form partly of collective measures of various kinds and partly of grants tied to certain types of consumption. These grants were later supplemented by a direct flat-rate cash allowance for each child irrespective of the parents' financial circumstances. The new family policy was concerned, among other things, with the health of mothers and children. Preventive medical care for mothers and children with free maternity nursing was introduced by a decision of 1937. Mother-and-child clinics were established at which medical examinations were conducted by doctors and midwives. At the same time it was decided to supply free medicines to expectant mothers.

Certain reforms of the educational system were also of great importance to families with children. Elementary education has long been provided free of charge in Sweden. A further major step was taken in 1946 when all elementary-school children were provided with free textbooks and free school materials. The reason for this reform was that if the State required children to attend school, it was felt that the State should also supply the necessary materials. This reform was a particularly welcome one for families with many children. An important form of service to families with children received a notable impetus in 1937, when State grants were first made to local authorities who provided meals for children attending the compulsory schools. The object of the scheme was partly to ease the burden of work in the home on women and to release female labour, and partly to provide the children with a nourishing and vitamin-rich meal. Nowadays nearly all local authorities operate free meal schemes for pupils in the compulsory schools.

Another benefit to families with children was the introduction in 1926 of State subsidies for school buses, which were provided in the first instance for children in rural areas living a long way from the nearest school.

An important principle was established in 1938 when a law was passed to permit the termination of pregnancy on medical, humanitarian and eugenic grounds.

In the 1940s, society assumed responsibility for the provision of more kindergartens, i.e. day nurseries, leisure-time homes and nursery schools. The two first-named types of establishment are intended to provide supervision for the children of parents in full-time employment. A Domestic Service Act was also passed to regulate certain conditions of employment and work for this occupational category. State subsidies were also provided for the training and payment of visiting home helpers, who assisted families in the difficult circumstances that may arise when a housewife for one reason or another is unable to manage the home.

These forms of family service were also supplemented by grants of various kinds. Direct cash allowances had been introduced in the 1930s for the children of widows and for orphans. Entitlement to advances from public funds was also introduced for children born out of wedlock and children of divorced parents. The object was to safeguard the maintenance of children in those cases where the father neglected to pay contributions. These contributions were then advanced by the authorities, who in return took steps to recover the money from the father.

New grants were created with a view to relieving the mother and family of expense in connection with pregnancy and confinement. From 1938 onwards, maternity benefit was paid to those covered by the then voluntary health insurance schemes, and a maternity allowance, subject to a means test, to others. These two forms of assistance were further supplemented by direct grants to specially needy mothers (maternity relief).

To improve the housing standards of families with several children, State aid for the building of "large-family" houses was introduced in 1935 as well as rent rebates for low-income families with three or more children. Since 1948, family dwelling allowances have been payable to families with at least two children, subject to a means test. Allowances are now also paid to single fathers or mothers with at least one child.

Housing policy measures during this period were largely concerned with improving the housing situation of certain groups—families with children, the aged, and the rural population. Since housework, and the care of children and the aged were the responsibility of women to an even greater extent during the 1930s than at present, these housing policy measures helped to ease the burden of women's work in the home.

An important family policy reform was the decision in 1947 to introduce general family allowances, i.e. a flat-rate allowance for every child in all families irrespective of income (the earlier income tax reliefs for children were abolished at the same time). Several other forms of allowance which had been introduced earlier were also revised and expanded.

Later, too, came the decision that the wife should be joint custodian with her husband of their children. Swedish women now also have the right to retain their Swedish citizenship upon marriage to an alien.

Quite early on, the question of family planning was regarded as an important matter affecting women. There were early and repeated demands from feminine quarters for the abolition of the law which prohibited the sale of contraceptives, and this law was repealed in 1938. The State nowadays supports sex education and prophylactic medical counselling by making grants to adult education organisations. The largest organisation is Riksförbundet för sexuell upplysning (the Swedish National Association for Sex Education). Advice on birth control is also provided by the maternity clinics. Since 1946, licensed dispensing chemists have been required by law to sell contraceptives, which are now also available from vending machines and shops. Sex education is also included in the curriculum of the compulsory school. According to a poll taken in 1963, the majority (92%) of Swedish women of child-bearing age plan the number of their children. Seventy-five per cent of the childless women stated that they practised birth control as against 93 per cent of those with one child and 97 per cent of those with three children.

In 1955 a national health insurance scheme came into force which guaranteed a basic benefit to married women and single mothers in the event of sickness, even to those with no earned income. The National Supplementary Pensions Act, which came into force in 1960, introduced new rules which made it easier—especially for women—to obtain a full retirement pension related to the number of years worked and annual income. At the same time the right to widows' pensions was introduced. Children's pensions are also payable to surviving children under 19 years of age upon the death of a gainfully employed father or mother.

The equal-pay principle in Government service—equal pay for men and women in the same kind of employment—was established in 1947. The year before, women had become eligible to apply for certain posts in the Government service which had previously been barred to women. An exception was made, however, in the case of the priesthood of the established church. It was not until 1961 that women were allowed to be ordained to the priesthood.

The year 1960 brought the next major step forward in the progress of equality when the largest trade union organisation, LO, and the Swedish Employers' Confederation agreed upon the introduction of equal pay for men and women doing the same work in industry. During the following five years the special pay scales for women in the collective wage agreements were abolished. It was only after this agreement had been reached, in 1962, that Sweden ratified the ILO convention on equal pay.

A law passed back in 1909 had prohibited women from working at night in certain industries, despite strong opposition on the part of the women workers. Later came the prohibition of night-time work by women in any industry or craft. This special ban on night work by women was abolished in 1962 in conjunction with a change in the law. Nowadays, the consent of the National Board of Industrial Safety is required if work is to be done by male or female employees between the hours of midnight and 5 a.m. It is still forbidden, however, to employ women for underground work in mines or quarries. Other provisions relating to women in the Industrial Welfare

Act concerns safeguards in connection with maternity.

Other important reforms which have led to a great increase in the recruitment of girls to education have been the gradual expansion of study grants during the post-war years.

II. REVIEW OF CURRENT EFFORTS TO PROMOTE EQUALITY BETWEEN THE SEXES

As will appear from the systematic account given later, Swedish legislation, with some few exceptions, makes no distinction between men and women with regard to rights or obligations. The few points on which the law still contains such distinctions, e.g. marriageable age in family law, surviving dependents' benefits in the national pensions scheme (currently payable only to widows but not to widowers) and the taxation system are now under review. It should be noted in this connection that the revision of the discriminatory rules in question is not dictated solely by a desire to extend the rights of women, but also in some cases to extend to men the same legal protection that is currently enjoyed by women. This applies for example to the basic benefit to which men working in the home are not at present entitled, although women are.

The educational system, labour market policy and institutions for the care of children of working parents in Sweden are at present undergoing vigorous expansion. The future of family taxation is being studied by a special committee which is expected shortly to present proposals for a changeover to individual taxation of married couples, in which the present more lenient taxation of married men with non-working wives will be reviewed. The establishment of this committee was prompted in the first instance by a desire to achieve a system of taxation which would not discourage married women from seeking gainful employment. The question of how direct financial assistance to families with children should be provided in future is also being considered at present by a family policy committee. One of its chief tasks is to consider whether the community should contribute to the cost of caring for children when they are small.

In all this reform work, the equality aspects are being given due consideration right from the study stage. If these aspects were to be neglected in proposals for new legislation, Swedish opinion as embodied in political parties, trade unions, the press, young people's and women's organisations, etc. would react most strongly.

There are probably few countries in which the roles of men and women in the family and in society have been so thoroughly analysed and discussed as in Sweden during the 1960s. All political parties in Sweden, or their women's and young people's organisations, have also produced programmes or manifestoes on the same subject. In 1964, for example, a political programme entitled "Kvinnans jämlikhet" (The Equality of Woman) was published; the contributors included members of the Government. The three biggest employees' associations in Sweden—LO (the Swedish Trade Union Confederation), TCO (the Central Organisation of Salaried Employees) and SACO (the Central Organisation of Swedish Professional Workers) have permanent bodies which also have drafted publications and programmes aiming at an equalisation of sex roles, primarily on the labour market. A special joint committee, the Swedish Women's Labour Market Committee, has been set up by SAF (the Swedish Employers' Confederation), LO and TCO for continuous study of questions affecting sex equality at work. Most of the women's organisations are also active in studying and disseminating information on sex role questions. A few examples of this widespread activity can be given.

The largest of the Swedish employees' organisations, LO, has for several years past made significant contributions in areas of great importance to equality. Particular mention may be made here of the interest shown by LO in increased support for the building of kindergartens to provide the children of working parents with proper supervision. During 1967, LO launched a campaign for better service on housing estates. In the field of labour market policy too, LO has shown awareness of the equality aspects. In a labour market policy programme adopted in 1967, LO stresses that the aim of such policy "must be increasingly directed towards the creation of employment opportunities for all the family . . . Full employment shall apply to everybody irrespective of sex, age or education." LO has recently replaced its former Women's Council by a Family Council, four of whose nine members are men. This step was a result of the resolution by the 1966 Congress that the task of the Council would in future be to promote the achievement of equality between the sexes and that the trade union movement now realised that social and employment equality questions are a matter of concern to both men and women.

In the autumn of 1967 a conference, "Facts and the Future" was organised in Stockholm by the National Labour Market Board and the Swedish Women's Labour Market Committee. This conference was attended by the leaders of the three major employees' organisations,

the Employers' Confederation and the Director-General of the
National Labour Market Board (the central governmental authority
for the implementation of labour market policies). All the delegates
supported the principle of equal conditions for men and women on
the labour market. A revision of the income tax system that would
discourage married women from working was also demanded, as well
as changes in the social insurance system to make the rules neutral
with respect to sex.

The Fredrika Bremer Association, an organisation named after the
famous Swedish authoress Fredrika Bremer, who was a prominent
advocate of full female emancipation in the mid-19th Century, staged
a radio debate during the autumn of 1967 in which the leaders of all
five political parties were asked to state what their respective parties
were doing to solve the sex role question and what measures had been
taken to increase female representation in the Riksdag at the 1968
elections.

Research concerning the effects of the sex roles is being conducted
by Swedish scientists in collaboration with colleagues in the other
Scandinavian countries. Finnish, Danish, Swedish and Norwegian
sociologists and social psychologists regularly exchange research
results. A first result of this collaboration was a major Swedish-Nor-
wegian scientific work entitled "Kvinnors Liv och Arbete" (Women's
Life and Work," 1962, 550 pp.), which was published and financed by
Studieförbundet Näringsliv och Samhälle, S.N.S. (an independent
research institute financed by Swedish private industry). A supplemented summary of this work was later published in English under
the title The Changing Roles of Men and Women.[1] A further paper,
"Kynne och Kön" (Temperament and Sex), has been published as a
result of a conference on sex role problems organised under
Scandinavian auspices. In addition to these and other activities there
are the surveys being conducted by various Government bodies and
commissions. Thus the following subjects relevant to the questions of
sex equality are currently being studied.

1. The syllabus of the compulsory comprehensive school is being
reviewed by the Department of Education: proposals include compulsory tuition for all pupils in domestic science, child care, needlework,
woodwork and metalwork.

---

1. *The Changing Roles of Men and Women.* Ed. by Edmund Dahlström. 205 pp.
(London: Gerald Duckworth and Co. Ltd., 1967; Boston: Beacon Press,
1971).

2. The question of child maintenance allowance to supplement the general family allowances for families with small children is being considered by the Family Policy Committee.

3. The Family Policy Committee is also reviewing the rules of the Health Insurance Scheme with special reference to the consequences of women's increasingly equal position with men as family breadwinners.

4. The Pensions Insurance Committee is reviewing those provisions of the National Pensions Scheme which at present make a distinction between men and women.

5. Proposals for a gradual transition to separate taxation of the incomes of husbands and wives are expected to be presented by the Family Taxation Commission before the end of 1968.

6. The Department of Justice is preparing the draft of a new Marriage Law.

7. A special commission has been set up to survey low-income groups and investigate the causes of low incomes; the relationship between sex discrimination and low income will be one of the points studied.

8. Another commission is studying the possible introduction of a compulsory unemployment insurance scheme; consideration will be given here to the special problems associated with the provision of unemployment security for those groups of employment-seekers, mainly women, who have been absent from the labour market for long periods. The Government has recently stated that it intends to propose such a scheme of compulsory national basic unemployment insurance which may be supplemented by voluntary forms of insurance.

9. The 1965 Abortion Committee is engaged in a general review of the abortion laws and is also considering the question of the right to free abortion.

10. It was decided in March 1968 that State grants will be paid, beginning in 1969, to local authorities who arrange for the supervision of children of working parents in family day nurseries (private homes which by agreement with the local authority undertake to look after children while their parents are at work). These grants have been constructed in such a way that they will also encourage the local authorities to build more kindergartens (day nurseries and leisure-time homes).

11. A Government Service Committee is investigating the question of improved tenants' services. It has been found that the existing

supplementary housing loans and grants have not been sufficiently generous to encourage more widespread building of service facilities in residential areas or of apartment houses with collective services. It is felt that improved tenants' services will be of special value to working parents and thereby help to promote equality between the sexes on the labour market. This committee will shortly submit proposals containing recommendations for financing, planning of service facilities, etc.

The National Labour Market Board has embarked upon a special programme to tap the resources of female labour and has carried out a great many investigations, e.g. into the results of the refresher courses which the Board provides for women wishing to return to employment. A poll has also been taken among Swedish industrial firms concerning their experience of female labour in occupations for which recruitment was previously confined to men.

Finally, the Swedish press has also devoted considerable space to sex role problems in both news and leader columns. The Swedish Broadcasting Corporation has recently decided to produce a series of ten programmes (with accompanying textbook) on the subject of "Conditions for Equality—Men and Women in the World of Today." The programmes will be broadcast during the autumn of 1968 to celebrate International Human Rights Year.

Men have also taken an active part in the widespread discussion of sex role problems. As the women's organisations have been especially active in this respect, the result has been that some of them have now opened their membership to men also.

The powerful growth of opinion in support of a revision of sex roles in recent years has thus brought with it the consequence that political proposals must be thoroughly scrutinised with respect to their equality aspects.

The efforts made up to now are still inadequate to offer any hope of practical equality between men and women for a long time to come. A great deal of work remains to be done in the form of both practical measures on the part of the authorities and a programme of education to alter the traditional attitudes of both men and women.

III. REFORMS IN DIFFERENT SPHERES –
   A DETAILED ACCOUNT

1. Education

The majority of the present population of Sweden grew up in a society in which only a small proportion of parents could afford to give their children any more than the elementary education prescribed by law. Those who were better off considered it a perfectly natural thing to give their sons priority as regards higher education. This attitude was so deeply rooted among the older generation that girls were actually excluded from certain schools, as we have already shown in a preceding section (Section I:A). The boys were to be given as good an education as possible, since they were the breadwinners of the next generation, whereas the task of the girls was traditionally seen to consist in getting married, being provided for by their husbands, and bearing children. The injurious consequences of this traditional, discriminatory attitude are still perceptible even in modern Sweden.

Nonetheless, great progress has been made in the emancipation of women. Most married women nowadays go out to work either full-time or part-time, even though they still bear the brunt of the housework. As a result, married women with outside employment generally have less leisure than other social groups. In spite of their commitments in the home, married women have answered for the major part of the increase in the labour force in recent years.

The difficulties confronting adult women on the labour market today are largely attributable to their inferior education compared to that of the men. They were not given the same chances in their youth.

The sheltered, "provided for" position of the married woman deprived her of the chance of attaining equality with the men as regards vocational and higher education. Although the formal qualifications for education are the same for men and women alike, women and young girls are still bound to be the victims of "indirect discrimination" in this field as long as marriage is considered their primary and "natural" source of income.

(a) Elementary Education

The first prerequisite of educational parity is of course that boys and girls be given the same elementary education free of charge. Pupils ought not to be hived off according to sex into different classes or schools. Another prerequisite is that children should not in the course of their education be given the idea that certain jobs and professions are suitable for men and others for women. On the contrary, schools should aim at making it clear to pupils that the differences between individuals of the same sex, are greater than any average differences between the sexes as a whole. Their lessons in domestic science and civics should leave pupils in no doubt as to the equal responsibilities of husband and wife in the home. Textbooks and other teaching aids ought not to further entrench traditional ideas concerning the separate roles of the sexes but on the contrary provide information designed actively to combat them.

The objective of equality between the sexes should be incorporated in the directives laid down for elementary education. When the nine-year comprehensive school was founded in Sweden in 1962, its objective was described as the right of every individual to the free development of his or her aptitudes and interests. The Government bill in the Riksdag underlined the role of the school in meeting "the needs and requirements of society for such qualities among men and women as will inspire and promote the democratic principles of co-operation and tolerance between the sexes and between different races and countries."

The aim of equality is clearly indicated in the syllabus containing the more detailed instructions for the work of the comprehensive school. The school is to work for the democratic principle of "the equal rights of the sexes," as well as helping pupils "to assess their suitability for different studies and professions as objectively as possible." It is further recommended that girls with a leaning towards technical and scientific subjects "be encouraged therein" and that "the conventional attitude towards these matters" be discouraged.

One distinctive feature of the comprehensive school is that all pupils are supposed to be given the chance of studying the same subject for as long as possible. This principle is also significant from the point of view of equality, since premature specialisation could easily result in boys and girls choosing different courses. Only in the senior classes school, i.e. grades 7–9, is it possible for pupils to opt for certain streams (5 periods out of 35 in grade 7). Pupils in grade 9 are divided up into a maximum of 9 different streams, and it is the pupils who, with the support of their parents, select their own streams. This selection of streams will ultimately be abolished, and instead pupils in grades 7–9 will be able to choose options for 4–5 periods a week.

During their eighth year at school, all pupils are given vocational guidance, a subject which has been accorded considerable prominence in the new school system. This guidance is designed to facilitate the pupil's choice of studies. The subject also includes practical vocational experience for a total of three weeks, during which pupils are enabled to try their hands at at least two different jobs chosen by themselves.

Surveys of the occupations chosen by boys and girls during the practical vocational experience period serve to show, unfortunately, that choice of occupation is still subject to considerable degree of demarcation between the sexes. In other words, the boys select typical "men's" jobs, and the girls those traditionally regarded as most suitable for women.

Table 1 covers the ten most popular occupations among boys and girls participating in practical vocational experience during the school years 1965/66 and 1966/67.

The health and medical services were the most popular field among the girls during both years. Everything seems to point to a continuing swift expansion of this sector in Sweden, and—given the strict demarcation between the sexes evidenced by the pupils' choice of occupations—the medical services can be expected to recruit an increasing proportion of the female labour force. The need for a correction of the balance in recruiting to the health services is strikingly illustrated by a calculation showing that one out of every three Swedish girls would be needed for the health services unless a larger proportion of men can be recruited.

The profoundly traditional nature of pupils' choices of occupations is further illustrated by the results of a survey carried out in Västerås, an average-sized Swedish city. Table 2 gives the ten most popular occupations among boys and girls in that city during the school year 1965/66.

	Boys		Girls	
	1965/66	1966/67	1965/66	1966/67
1.	Engineering, building and metal industries		Health and medical services	
2.	Electrical trades		Teaching	
3.	Technical trades		Domestic work	Commercial office work
4.	Commerical office work		Restaurant work	Domestic work
5.	Armed Forces		Commercial office work	Restaurant work
6.	Woodworking	Accounting and technical office work	Hygiene and cosmetics	Accounting and technical office work
7.	Accounting and technical clerical work	Civil security, protective work	Accounting and technical clerical work	Hygiene and cosmetics
8.	Food manufacturing	Woodworking	Artistic and literary work	
9.	Civil security, protective work	Artistic and literary work	Other occupations in health and medical services	
10.	Artistic and literary work	Food manufacturing	Sales work	
			Shorthand and typing	

Table 2. "Top ten" trades in practical vocational experience
for pupils in Västerås during the school year 1965/66

Boys, total:	Girls, total:
1. Motor mechanic (34)	1. Lower school teacher (53)
2. Aviation trades (24)	2. Kindergarten teacher (43)
	3. Child nurse (43)
3. Electrician (23)	4. Shop assistant (39)
4. Baker (23)	
5. Laboratory assistant (21)	5. Ladies' hairdresser (35)
	6. Clerical worker (35)
6. Serving with a regiment of	7. Medical service (25)
the armed forces in the city (19)	
7. Photographer (16)	8. Veterinary assistant (19)
8. Punched card operator	9. Window dresser (16)
computer operator (15)	Travel agency assistant (16)
9. Draughtsman (14)	
Shop assistant (14)	
Working for Swedish State	
Railways (14)	
Total jobs found = 469	Total jobs found = 473

These discouraging figures have aroused considerable attention through their striking illustration of the sex demarcation attending the pupils' choices of occupation. Although it is one of the tasks of the vocational advisers specially appointed in all schools to point out to the pupils that they should choose their occupations on the basis of their abilities and interests and not according to their sex, the pressure of their environment is obviously so strong as to make it impossible for the pupils to choose without prejudice.

This problem is at present being studied by the Ministry of Education in connection with the thoroughgoing revision of the syllabus proposed by the central school authorities. The new instructions for the practical vocational experience scheme must make it quite clear that vocational interest among girls ought particularly to be stimulated and pupils should choose their occupations with less regard to convention. Detailed information should be given concerning conditions of pay within different sectors so as to make the girls aware of the fact that these conditions are often worse in a large number of traditional women's occupations than in men's occupations. The lack of this kind of information is tantamount to evasion of the demand for objective occupational guidance. It should also be made quite clear, in instructions for future vocational advisers, that this objectivity of approach should involve not only the description of existing occupations but also a presentation of new occupations likely to come into being in the future. The pupils should also be given concrete examples of boys and girls who have ventured to contravene the hidebound traditions surrounding choice of occupation. Teaching should include visits to actual places of work for the purpose of studying such examples.

The girls should be made aware of the difficulties which can confront them on the labour market in the future as a result of their choosing to finish their education early. Nor should the girls' education be referred to as a kind of insurance policy which may come in useful after they marry if their husbands should die or fall ill or in the event of a divorce. This kind of argument can result in the girls' forming inferior occupational ambitions to the boys'.

In one important respect the comprehensive school makes a direct contribution towards the transformation of the traditional roles of the sexes, and that is obligatory instruction of boys as well as girls in domestic science, cooking and child care. It is to be hoped that this instruction will result in domestic work and child care being looked upon as the task of both partners in the family of the future. Instruction in domestic science is to be regarded as a kind of training in citizenship, something that everybody needs to be familiar with, whether they have a family or not.

The current syllabus offers pupils in grade three and upwards a free choice as regards handicraft between woodwork and metalwork, on the one hand, and needlework, on the other. Unfortunately this freedom of choice has in most schools resulted in a division into "boys' handicraft"—meaning woodwork and metalwork—and "girls' handicraft," or needlework. (On the other hand, pupils have been made to change over for 20 periods.) In certain schools, however, the authorities have experimented with the same amount of instruction in both kinds of handicraft for boys and girls alike. And now the Parliament of 1968 has decided to make the instruction in both kinds of handicraft obligatory for all pupils up to and including grade 6. This is a step in the right direction. The instruction of girls in woodwork and metalwork is of great importance, since it may result in more girls opting for technical and mechanical training in the future.

Textbooks and teaching material must also be cleared of all notions of male and female occupations. Instead, both text and illustrations should be designed to counteract prejudices of this kind, e.g. by showing men employed in nursing and women in technical jobs. The Swedish Women's Labour Market Board is at present conducting a survey of textbooks in civics. The National School-Book Board had instructions to continually look out for books tending to give pupils a traditional picture of male and female occupations.

(b) Education after the Comprehensive School

As can be seen in more detail from Tables 1 and 2, there are at present about as many male as female pupils in the various institutions to which pupils can go after comprehensive school in Sweden, namely schools of general studies, vocational schools, teacher training establishments, and so on. There are still fewer women university graduates than men but the number of women enrolling at universities and colleges is increasing rapidly. Out of a total of 22,300 newly enrolled students in the autumn of 1965, 9,300 were women.

Thus the problem of inequality is no longer due to women being heavily under-represented in education. The difficulties now consist rather in the considerable differences between the sexes as regards distribution between different kinds of education. Girls on the whole go in for vocational education on a far smaller scale than boys, and they choose shorter courses of further education. For instance, girls are now just as numerous as boys in the general, non-vocational streams in the high schools, whereas the technical high-school streams offering vocational education are dominated by the boys. In the continuation school, a new type of school offering two years' education after comprehensive school, over 95 per cent of the pupils in the technical stream are men, while 75 per cent of those in the social stream are women. The technical stream is the more vocationally oriented of the two, the social stream providing no more than preparatory instruction concerning vocational education.

All pupils who have completed the comprehensive school are at liberty to apply to vocational school, where they can be given basic or specialised vocational training. Female pupils make up a mere five per cent of those receiving vocational training for industry and handicraft, even though it is known that a far larger proportion of young women will later come to be employed in industry. According to the census figures for 1965, almost a quarter of the industrial labour force consisted of women. About 98 per cent of the youngsters who study health and welfare services are women.

Teacher training for kindergartens and the lowest grade of the comprehensive school is entirely dominated by women. By contrast, a quota system has been introduced for the training of teachers in the middle grades (4—6) of the comprehensive school, so that the places available are divided evenly between male and female applicants. A law has been passed by the Riksdag abolishing this quota system as from the 1968 intake in connection with a complete reform of the teacher-training system in Sweden. The consequences of the new regulations will be a matter of some interest. In the event of either sex attaining an overwhelming predominance, the question of reintroducing the quota system will have to be considered in a wider context, with a view to shaping the conditions of admission so as to govern the ratio between the sexes throughout the whole of the teaching profession. So far experience has shown that it is hard to achieve a swift redistribution between the sexes within a given branch of education when only a few isolated students of the opposite sex manage to gain admittance.

School organisation can also be of considerable consequence to parity within education. The high school ("gymnasium") was formerly divided into girls' and boys' schools. This division has now been almost completely abolished. Instead, the tendency in Sweden today is towards increasing integration in all respects. As a result of a law passed by Parliament in 1964, the general, commercial and technical high schools have been amalgamated to form one single type of establishment, known as the New High School ("Nya gymnasium"), and this in turn has been brought into line with the new continuation school now being developed.

With the development of the new continuation school, the special municipal girls' schools are now gradually being closed down. There are now no more than thirty or so girls' schools left in the country. Girls seeking a short high-school education can now apply to continuation schools, which are run on a co-educational basis.

One practical difficulty previously confronting girls attending industrial and handicraft technical schools was that there were no changing rooms for them on the premises. Male students wishing to apply to training centres for kindergarten teachers are faced by similar problems. All plans for new schools are now being checked to see to it that they are designed for students of both sexes.

The following tables provide a summary of certain data concerning male and female students in the education system. The first is a sketch of the total extent of education in percentages of the age groups around 1945 and 1970 respectively. The diagram reflects primarily the extension of the obligatory period of school attendance as well as the rapidly rising number of students receiving high school and further education. The total admission of new students in the first classes of high schools and vocational schools is now more than 40 per cent of the age group, but it is expected to rise to 90 per cent during the 1970s.

The extent of education by percentage of age group in 1945 and in 1970 approximately (see next page)

Extent of compulsory school attendance	1945	▬
	1970	▬
High school education after compulsory school	1945	▪▪▪▪▪
	1970	▪▪▪▪▪
Further education after high school	1945	·——·-
	1970	▰▰▰
Expansion	1945–1970	▨

Table 3 gives a summary of young persons' education and career plans. The survey was concerned with pupils in comprehensive and girls' schools. The lower section of the table concerning plans for further studies reflects the same demarcation of the sexes as has already been described.

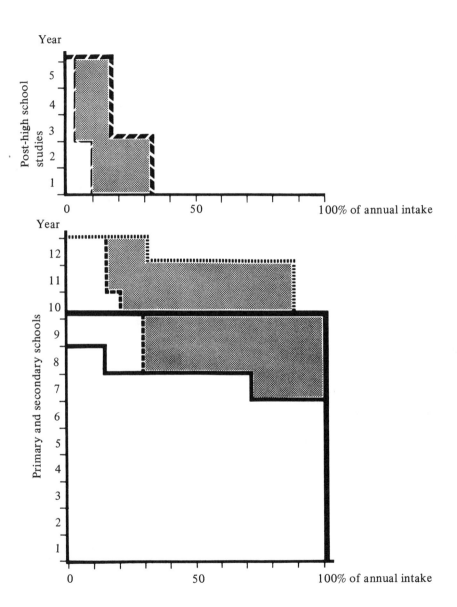

Table 3. Young persons' educational and career plans, autumn 1966

	Boys	Girls	Total
Further studies	40,700	38,021	78,721
Employment, etc.	6,620	8,256	14,876
No fixed educational or career plans	4,936	6,415	11,351
Not known	2,811	4,125	6,936
Total (compensated)	55,067	56,817	111,884

Educational plans:

	Boys	Girls	Total
General education	25,679	22,192	47,871
Teacher training	177	682	859
Technical training	1,102	523	1,625
Industrial and handicraft training	10,227	564	10,791
Clerical and commercial training	1,098	4,689	5,787
Training for domestic and restaurant work	264	5,919	6,183
Training for medical and welfare work	22	1,369	1,391
Agricultural, forestry and fishery work	494	101	595
Other vocational training	1,637	1,982	3,619
Total	40,700	38,021	78,721

Table 4 is concerned with the ratio between the sexes among pupils at general high schools in the autumn of 1966.

Table 4. Secondary education, higher stage: pupils in the old and new "gymnasium"

"Old" gymnasium[1]			"New" gymnasium		
Side	All pupils	Of which women	Side	All pupils	Of which women
General side	19,075	11,688	Liberal arts and social	12,919	9,599
Latin "	8,323	6,554			
Modern "	23,038	7,066	Economics	4,791	2,660
Total	50,436	25,308	Natural sciences	10,145	3,755
			Technology	7,189	417
			Total	35,044	16,431

1. This type of school is gradually being abolished.

Table 5 deals with pupils in certain vocational schools of high-school status.

Table 5. Pupils in vocational secondary schools and teacher-training colleges, autumn term 1966

	All pupils	Female pupils
Technical secondary schools[1]	14,229	834
Commercial secondary schools[1]	10,657	5,959
Continuation schools	16,796	6,936
Teacher-training colleges		
middle stage	2,817	1,638
junior stage	2,701	2,701

1. These schools are gradually being abolished following the introduction of the "New" High School.

As has already been pointed out, a more or less equal number of boys and girls receive the kind of high-school education that can lead to higher academic studies. However, women are still underrepresented among university and college graduates, as can be seen from Table 6, which provides a summary of data for 1958 and 1965 respectively.

Table 6. Numbers of female as compared to male graduates

Swedish degree	Rough equivalent	1958 Women	Men	1965 Women	Men
Teol.kand.	B.D.	9	71	12	66
Jur.kand.	Ll.B.	26	171	50	223
Statsvet.jur.	B.A. (law and political science)	3	10	-	3
Med.lic.	2nd degree in medicine	52	244	87	255
Med.dr.	M.D.	3	61	-	79
Fil.kand.hum.	B.A.	195	282	265	217
Fil.mag.hum.	B.A. (teaching qualification)	313	297	566	369
Fil.lic.hum.	M.A. (2nd degree)	18	91	30	66
Fil.dr.hum.	Ph.D. (arts)	1	30	1	27
Fil.kand.nat.	B.Sc.	33	144	133	360
Fil.mag.nat.	B.Sc. (teaching qualification)	63	167	191	334
Fil.lic.nat.	M.Sc.	9	72	30	149
Fil.dr.nat.	Ph.D. (science)	1	37	3	42
Civilingenjör	B.Sc. (Eng.)	7	525	49	914
Civilekonom	B.Sc. (Econ.)	11	193	44	367
		744	2,395	1,461	3,471

(c) Aid to Student

The principle of equal rights for everybody to education regardless of sex, race and economic and social circumstances cannot be realised in a society where the opportunities for children to study are governed by their parents' resources. Direct economic support has to be given to interested children with parents of limited means.

Previously in Sweden it was only well-situated families that could afford to let their children study, and the great majority of children had to start work immediately after elementary school. Higher academic studies were with a very few exceptions reserved for a privileged minority. The first steps towards State education aid to young people were taken in 1918. The aim was to make further education more readily available to children from poor homes and so dispel the fear and suspicion of such studies which for economic and other reasons was found to exist among large sections of the population. Another aim was that of improving the economic circumstances of those who were pursuing or had pursued advanced studies by means of student aid. Since then State aid to students has continually expanded and improved. The past five years have witnessed a particularly swift expansion. Current expenditure on student aid has risen since the financial year 1962/63 from 180 million to 500 million kronor.

Student aid has been of particular consequence to educational opportunities for women. If a family with several children could afford to educate just one of them, it was mostly the sons who were sent to school, since it was the traditional view that the husbands would provide for the wives. Accordingly, the education of girls was regarded as a matter of secondary importance since "they would go and get married anyway." This attitude still makes itself felt to a certain extent, with the result that girls tend to go in for shorter vocational courses than boys.

All schoolchildren in Sweden over sixteen years of age receive a grant of 75 kronor for every month at school; no means test is imposed. Pupils studying away from home can receive an extra grant to cover accommodation and travel expenses. One of the most important results of recent student aid measures has been to give all young people the same opportunities for study regardless of where they live. Apart from these universal benefits, supplements based on a means and need test can be paid to children with less well-situated parents.

Students continuing from high school to university, teacher-training colleges, nursing colleges and a number of other institutions for further education are entitled to State student assistance, a new system of student finance introduced in 1965 and consisting partly of a grant, which does not have to be repaid, and partly of a payable loan. (However, the obligation to repay the loan is reconsidered in the light of the income earned by the person concerned two years after qualifying, and the payments are spread out over a long period so as not to make them a burden.)

One important principle is that State student assistance is awarded on the basis of a means test applied exclusively to the income earned by the student and—if the student is married—by the student's husband or wife. Thus the student is regarded as independent of his or her parents. Considerable regard was given in the design of the State assistance system to the question of the equality of the sexes. Thus the spouse of the student can earn a normal income without any deduction being made from the student assistance received by the other spouse. The intention behind this was to emphasise that student assistance should not be applied to provide for husbands or wives not studying: the economic independence of the other spouse was to be encouraged through separate earning. (However, a demand has recently been made for the payment of student assistance to married students regardless of whatever income is earned by the other spouse.) If both partners in a marriage study, they both receive student assistance as if they were two single persons. Special child allowances are paid to students with children (or with obligations to support children).

The rapid expansion of student aid has considerably broadened the social range of recruitment to higher academic studies. Admissions to high schools have increased four times in the last 20 years and the proportion of children coming from working-class homes has doubled. All the same, working-class and agricultural families are still under-represented, and this must be corrected. The new comprehensive school will make it possible to make recruitment to higher academic studies independent of economic and social circumstances. This broader social basis ought further to contribute towards more even recruitment as between the sexes, since less well-situated families have often been unable to afford to let their daughters pursue the same studies as their sons.

(d) Adult Education

In the account presented above it has been shown that the education of young people has expanded with considerable rapidity.

In about 1940, ten per cent of all Swedish children between the ages of 16 and 18 were receiving education as compared to more than 30 per cent in 1960. At present 65 per cent of this age group are studying full-time.

This considerable expansion of educational facilities has reduced what was previously a formidable difference between the sexes as regards the general education on which vocational training can be based. On the other hand, the differences between various generations have increased. Eighty per cent of the young people of the 1930s left school after no more than the six years at elementary school then prescribed by law. The 1960 census showed that only 0.5 per cent of women aged between 50 and 54 had received any further education, the proportion being three times as great (1.5%) among those aged between 25 and 29. The corresponding figures for the male population in the same age groups were 2.5 per cent and 3 per cent respectively.

In a period when the educational system is changing as swiftly as it is doing in present-day Sweden, adult education must be expanded so as to give adults a real chance to acquire the same education as younger persons. Study and educational opportunities for adults have therefore aroused increasing attention in recent years. The main emphasis in the expansion of adult education has up to now been placed on instruction geared to labour market policy. The purpose of this kind of education has been to combat unemployment, facilitate structural changes in the economy and promote increased levelling-out of incomes.

In 1967, the Riksdag passed a law providing for the comprehensive expansion of general educational facilities for adults designed to bring them up to the same standard as the education of young people.

Adult education is, in terms of sheer numbers, of greater importance to women than to men. The marriage age has steadily fallen in Sweden. In 1966, the average age at marriage was 23 as against 26 in the 1940s. This tendency, together with the increased period of education, results in a great many women starting families before they have completed their education. Childbirth also resulted in prolonged studies for women, while for the fathers it had the opposite effect of making them complete their studies more quickly than they would otherwise have done. The incidence of dropouts from university studies is also greatest among female undergraduates. When their children are older and their commitments at home have decreased, women wish to resume their studies or even commence studies that they have not previously had any opportunity of pursuing. It is therefore of the utmost importance for society to provide educational opportunities with the same scope and conditions as the education of younger people.

The most important forms of adult education at present existing are as follows. There are a number of evening institutions. High-school education and courses leading to high-school admission are available at over thirty evening secondary schools throughout the country. Evening instruction is of great importance to women who have to stay at home during the day because they cannot arrange for their children to be taken care of. Another form of adult education is provided by what is known as part-time courses held at municipal vocational colleges. More than 90,000 students, about 60 per cent of them women, took part in these courses in 1966. Some 75,000 students took part in full-time courses, but little more than a third of them were women. This reflects the demarcation of the sexes in education; extensive part-time and evening instruction is called for if women are to catch up. It is to be expected that the number of schools offering high-school courses in the evening will be increased considerably during the next few years thanks to a law passed by the Riksdag in 1967.

There are two special adult high schools in Sweden drawing pupils from all over the country. The courses do not require the pupils to be present for more than short periods, during which they are given intensified standard school tuition. The rest of their studies take the form of correspondence courses. Since it is not necessary for pupils to attend throughout the school year, adult high schools are of vital importance to housewives. Correspondence colleges also make it possible to study during leisure time and in between chores at home.

The second important main type of adult education is that provided in connection with labour market policy, consisting of retraining courses providing basic vocational training for people who are either already unemployed or likely to be so within the immediate future. People who have been put out of the labour market altogether and lack employment are put on the same level as unemployed persons. Consequently, housewives can be given vocational training on the same conditions as unemployed men. Unmarried parents whose occupations make it difficult for them to take care of their children can also be retrained for other occupations (e.g. jobs with more convenient hours of work). The minimum age for participation in labour market courses is generally 21. This kind of training is very extensive and it does a great deal to explain the relatively low level of unemployment in Sweden during the 1960s. The Labour Market Board has taken a great interest in meeting and stimulating women's educational requirements and has set up a special organisation to deal with these questions. About 100,000 people had been offered labour market training of various kinds in the period ending 1966. It is expected that retraining will be available for 80,000 pupils during the school year 1968/69.

The proportion of women among the pupils has risen. During the academic year 1959/60, when the expansion of labour market training was begun, the proportion of women was 17 per cent. This figure rose later to almost 50 per cent. In October 1967 there were 8,500 women, i.e. 34 per cent of the total number of pupils, undergoing training. One great advantage of labour market training has been to give a number of women instruction in occupations previously regarded as exclusively male. Thus it is now far more common than previously for women to be employed as crane operators, instrument makers and taxi and bus drivers.

The Folk University, which is mainly concerned with the general education of people of all age groups, has long played a prominent part in adult education—not least where women are concerned. Throughout the postwar period the number of women attending this kind of institution has somewhat exceeded the number of men (52% of the pupils in 1966). The Folk Universities give adults the same education as young people receive in the comprehensive school, making it possible for them to gain admission to the institutions that come after the comprehensive school.

Another form of spare-time study is that offered by study organisations in their study circles (120,000 circles with about 1.2 million members in 1965/66). Also included in the category of adult education is the training offered by authorities, firms and organisations. The courses organised by the trade unions form an important part. The largest organisation, LO, has experimented with a new form of residential course designed to increase the recruitment of female pupils to courses. Parents attending courses could take their children with them and supervision was provided at the school. These courses proved popular among young families and more such courses were held in 1968. It was decided in 1967 to expand general adult education. In future, high-school courses are to be held in ordinary schools. The two special adult high schools are to be expanded. Also, the subsidies paid by the State to county colleges have been increased.

The mass media—radio and television—will play an important part in the adult education of the future. Since 1 July 1967 the State has been using a special television study for the production of educational programmes. The educational programmes already being broadcast on the radio have been augmented with high-school courses in English, business management and psychology. Use of the mass media makes it possible to reach a large element of the population consisting of women obliged to stay at home to look after their children, women who would not otherwise have the chance to study. The radio courses have been found to meet an enormous need. A university course in political science broadcast over the radio was followed by 60,000 persons, i.e. about the same number of people as were studying at universities and colleges in 1964.

2. Family Law

(a) Current Regulations

The present marriage law of Sweden, which came into force on 1 January 1921, is based on the principle of equality of man and woman. Marriages can be contracted by men who have attained the age of 21 and by women of at least 18. However, permission can be granted for marriage under these age limits. There are few impediments to marriage. The real impediments, apart from affinity, are certain diseases. The marriage can be solemnised by either religious or civil ceremony.

The spouses are invested with identical rights and obligations. Both of them are bound by their work within or outside the home to contribute to the best of their ability towards the maintenance of the family. In the event of the husband being the only party earning a cash income, he is under an obligation to contribute not only towards the expenses of the household but also towards the individual requirements of his wife. If the wife does not have any outside employment she is deemed to contribute towards the maintenance of the family by her work in the home.

The two spouses have separate finances, administer their own incomes and assets and are liable for their own debts. In the event of the marriage being dissolved through death or divorce, the so-called law of joint property comes into play. This implies the amalgamation of the assets and liabilities of both spouses. Each of them—or the estate of the deceased, whichever the case may be—is assigned half the net residue. It should be added, that the consent of one spouse is required for required for the sale or mortgaging even of real property owned by the other.

It is possible however for the property of one spouse to be converted into separate property so that the other spouse has no title to it. This can be accomplished by means of marriage settlement, i.e. a contract concluded between the partners before or after their marriage and registered with a court of law. In this case both spouses retain their property at the dissolution of the marriage. Marriages are dissolved by courts of law; in practice, divorce petitions are seldom rejected.

A marriage is generally dissolved by decree nisi following either a joint petition by both spouses or the suing of one of them by the other. A decree absolute is granted one year after the decree nisi at the earliest, and on condition that the spouses have not resumed cohabitation in the meantime. A decree absolute can be granted immediately on certain grounds such as adultery.

When issuing a decree nisi or absolute, the court rules which of the spouses is to have custody of any children. The court can also be requested to fix the amount of maintenance contributions payable to the other spouse and any children as well as the right to continuing occupation of the common home. The spouse not given custody of any children is generally required to contribute to their maintenance during the period of judicial separation and thereafter—in most cases until the children reach the age of 18.

The spouse earning the larger income—generally the husband—is as a rule liable to support the other spouse during the judicial separation period. After this, maintenance is payable only in cases of hardship, such as advanced age or illness.

(b) Revision of Legislation now in Progress

A proposal put forward in 1964 by a committee on family law provides for certain amendments to the current marriage legislation. The proposal has later been submitted to various organisations and authorities for their comments. The most important amendments proposed are as follows.

The committee proposes that the marriageable age for men be reduced to 20. Most of the considering bodies have supported this proposal—several of them even recommending a further reduction to 18, i.e. the same age as for women.

Concerning the economic relationship between the spouses, the committee proposes that the mutual obligation of the spouses to keep one another informed about their respective financial positions be extended to include matters of significance to their economic standing, maintenance commitments and claims under the law of joint property. Each of the spouses would also be required to inform the other concerning insurance policies, etc. providing mainly risk protection. It is proposed further to extend the duty of each spouse to pay regard to the interests of the other.

It is proposed by the committee that the rule at present in force whereby either spouse must secure the consent of the other before transferring, mortgaging or pledging real property coming under the law of joint property be extended to cover other joint property such as site leasehold, or a building on a leasehold site intended exclusively to provide the partners with a common home, tenancy or rights in tenant-owner property with the same end in view, household goods for common use, implements, pension or annuity assurance, and so on. The committee also proposes that the same restrictions be imposed on the right of disposition concerning private property of the kind mentioned here. Limitations of the right of disposition of site leasehold and real property would only apply to property exclusively or principally designed to provide the spouses with a common home.

In case it can be suspected that the other spouse is unduly reducing his or her share of their joint property, it is proposed to extend the possibilities for either spouse of obtaining judicial division of the joint property.

The committee proposes that the basic regulations concerning joint property be retained in all important respects. One interesting point of principle is provided however by a proposal that so-called reversionary partition be made possible in connection with judicial division of joint property, decree nisi or divorce. This would have the effect of limiting joint property to property acquired by the spouses during the marriage in other ways than by inheritance, deed of gift or legacy. Other property would not be included in the division of joint property. Reversionary partition is proposed primarily for cases where the marriage has lasted for less than five years prior to the filing of a petition for judicial separation or divorce. The proposal is designed to deprive either spouse of the possibility of "divorcing into money" after a short-lived marriage. This proposal too has been favourably viewed by the considering bodies; some of them have even proposed that it be extended still further.

Another highly interesting proposal by the committee in this connection would make it possible for spouses applying for judicial separation of their joint property to submit a declaration waiving their rights to each other's share of the joint property. This would mean that each spouse would be left with distrainable property of the same value after judicial separation as previously. This recommendation has also met with a favourable reception from the considering bodies to which it has been referred.

In connection with the division of property, any goods and chattels for the personal use of the children shall be set aside for them. The committee's proposal provides for the award of the common home to the spouse most in need of it.

The Ministry of Justice is at present preparing a bill for the revision of the rules governing the contracting and dissolution of marriage. It is hoped that the new bill will be submitted during the autumn session of the Riksdag in 1968. At the same time, a motion will be tabled for the reduction of the marriageable age for men.

Another bill is to be presented later based on the other proposals made by the committee concerning the economic effects of marriage, etc. In this connection, the Minister of Justice is to propose amendments to the law of inheritance giving illegitimate children the same testamentary rights as children born in wedlock.

(c) The Rights of the Children

The code concerning parenthood and guardianship contains regulations dealing with the position of legitimate and illegitimate children in family law. Special regulations are provided to safeguard the right of the illegitimate child to security and to support from the father; this in turn has been of great importance to the social and economic status of unmarried mothers. When a child is born out of wedlock, the father may acknowledge his parenthood. If he does not do so, paternity can be established by the court. The determination of paternity is in no way dependent on whether the father himself is married or not. The main rule is that the man is taken to be the father of the child if it is established that he had sexual intercourse with the mother at such a time that the child could have been conceived as a result of this and that it is not improbable that the child was conceived on the occasion in question. The importance attached to establishing the paternity of illegitimate children is due to their right to support from the father. If on the other hand it is the father who is given custody of the child, then, clearly, it is the mother who becomes liable to give financial assistance.

A special child welfare officer is appointed to assist unmarried mothers and their children until the children reach the age of 18. The child welfare officer is a man or woman appointed by the local child welfare committee (cf. Section 3) to assist mother and child and safeguard the rights and interests of the child. A child welfare officer is always appointed for illegitimate children and sometimes also for the children of parents living apart.

Children living with an unmarried or divorced mother or father are entitled by law to maintenance allowances. The amount of the allowance depends on the needs of the child and the financial circumstances of the parent liable to maintain the child. The allowance is fixed either through agreement between the parents or by the court. If the allowance is not paid and the child is under 16 years of age an advance can be made out of public funds.

It may also be mentioned that adopted children have essentially the same rights as children born in wedlock.

When a marriage is dissolved, the court decides which of the parents is better suited to have custody of the children. As the main thing is for the child to be given the best possible care, it is immaterial which of the parents has caused the marriage to be dissolved.

3. Family Policy

Out of Sweden's 7,843,000 inhabitants on 1 January 1967, 1,752,000 or about 22 per cent were children under 16 years of age. Sweden is probably one of the few countries in the world with such a low proportion of children. In 1966, the birth rate (i.e. the number of live births per 1,000 of the mean population) was 15.8.

According to the 1960 census, half the families in Sweden with children under 16 living at home had only one child. Only 16 per cent of families with children had three or more children. However, the children included in this last group amounted to a third of all the children in the country. This means that 7 per cent of the population between the ages of 18 and 66 were responsible for rearing a third of the next generation. Families with children are naturally taken to include families with only one parent, and these amounted to a tenth of the total.

Sweden has for a long time provided extensive protection for the safeguarding of the right of children to good care and upbringing. Each of the 900 municipalities in the country has a child welfare committee charged with the task of working for improved child and youth welfare.

(a) Important Points of Modern Family Policy

A basic child allowance of 900 kronor p.a. is paid to every child under 16 resident in Sweden, regardless of the parents' incomes. The allowance is intended to provide for the maintenance and upbringing of the child. Another objective is to reduce the difference in the standards of living of families with and without young children. The allowance is paid quarterly to the mother or to whomever has custody of the child instead of the mother. An extended allowance is paid to pupils over 16 years of age attending comprehensive school or similar institutions (vide supra, Section 1c).

Kindergartens, where children can be taken care of during the daytime while their parents are at work (cf. Section 4, Services to Families) are at present undergoing considerable expansion. Great importance has been attached to measures designed to safeguard the health of mother and child in connection with pregnancy and childbirth. All expectant mothers and mothers with newborn children are entitled to free examination and advice at maternity and pediatric clinics providing regular services; pregnancy can be established here and treatment given for illnesses caused by pregnancy or childbirth. These clinics also provide instruction in child care and birth control. Prophylactic medicines such as vitamin preparations and certain other medicaments are supplied free of charge.

The actual confinement is also free of charge at maternity hospitals as is the care given by midwives. Most deliveries nowadays take place in maternity hospitals or the maternity wards of general hospitals. When confinement takes place at home and the help of a doctor is required, three-quarters of the expenditure incurred by the parents in connection with treatment by a doctor are refunded. The cost of travelling to the nearest hospital in connection with confinement is refunded in full.

During pregnancy and for 270 days after childbirth, the mother can receive dental treatment on very favourable terms, up to three-quarters of the cost of such treatment being refunded. Every mother receives a special maternity benefit or 1,080 kronor when her child is born (even if it is stillborn). If she gives birth to twins, the sum is increased by 540 kronor for every additional child. Three hundred kronor of this benefit can be drawn prior to confinement.

In addition to the maternity benefit an employed mother receives supplementary sickness benefit if immediately before childbirth she has been insured for sickness benefit at her place of work for at least 270 days in succession. This supplementary sickness benefit is graduated according to income (though the income must exceed a certain minimum) and is payable for a maximum of 180 days.

In order to facilitate the formation of families, the State also grants homemaking loans for the purchase of furniture and other items for the home. Loans of this kind are granted, subject to a means test, to newly married couples and couples wishing to get married, and are also available to unmarried mothers or fathers with children under 16.

Special family housing allowances are also available, subject to a means test, to families with two or more children. The Swedish Riksdag has recently approved a Government proposal providing for an increase in the amount paid in allowances of this kind (vide inf. Section c).

A special treatment allowance of 3,420 kronor is paid to people with handicapped children at home in need of special care and attention.

(b) Principles of Family Policy

The number of families in which both spouses are gainfully employed is continually increasing. The employment incidence of young married women without children is almost as high as that of the men. Also, an increasing number of mothers are going out to work. Thus Sweden is approaching a situation in which it is normal for a family to have two members earning incomes.

The increasing part played by married women in the labour market has resulted in entirely new demands being made on family policy. This policy must be adopted to the changed roles of the sexes and be designed in such a way as to promote equality on the labour market and in the division of labour at home. This means that increased prominence will be given to care of the children and the cost thereof.

Families with small children generally solve the problem of taking care of them by one of the following methods:
1. The father or mother stops going out to work and stays at home with the children full-time for a number of years.
2. The parents engage somebody to supervise the children in the home during the day or else make use of a kindergarten.
3. Both parents try to obtain part-time employment and cooperate in taking care of the children. However, this alternative is not generally feasible owing to the prejudices still surrounding the role of the father in taking care of the children.

In all these cases the care of the children costs money: in cases No. 1 and 3 by reason of reduced income and in case No. 2 through direct costs of supervision reducing retained income. As it becomes more common for women to acquire vocational training they will wish to an increasing extent to go on working outside the home. Consequently, it is to be expected that the demand for services from families in which both parents go out to work will increase considerably. The other category of families with small children will as previously prefer one of the parents to refrain from earning money so as to be able to devote a shorter or longer time to looking after the children. Nevertheless, it will be considered unjust for a family to have to reduce its living standards to any appreciable extent during these years of increased need.

Society has therefore every reason to maintain the living standards of families with children as far as its resources permit. After all, the result of the care devoted to the children is to bring up a new generation which eventually will guarantee the incomes of the present working population when that population retires and begins to draw its pension.

Up to now, the Swedish Government has adhered to the principle of evening out living standards, as far as possible, between the period when the family's needs are greatest and the period when its maintenance burdens are most lenient. Failing this kind of evening-out, living standards are bound to fall considerably during the years when the children need care and attention. There is call therefore for additional support over and above the basic child allowance during the period when the children are most in need of attention. The political programme for women, adopted in 1964, laid down the following three guiding principles for family policy:

Social insurance comparable to that available to the working population should be provided for the spouse looking after the children.

Payment should be made for such care.

The direct consumption costs incurred through the child should be provided for.

Since it is to be expected that women will continue to play a more active part than men in looking after the children for a long time ahead, a family policy based on these principles would be of considerable importance to them. Social insurance during the period when children require most attention would also encourage parents to resume working when the children are old enough to take care of themselves. In this way child-care and outside employment combined would give parents the same old-age pension as persons with full-time employment are guaranteed through the general supplementary pensions scheme alone.

(c) Reforms in Progress

There has been a considerable amount of discussion in recent years concerning the future structure of family policy. Particular emphasis has been placed on the connection between family policy and equality of status between men and women. Today there seems in general to be a high degree of unanimity that the costs of child care should rank on the same level as outside employment. It has also been found appropriate for the parent, whether father or mother, who stays at home to look after the children, to be able to include this period to his or her credit in connection with the calculation of pension rights.

There has also been a great deal of unanimity concerning the need for society to increase the general economic support given to families with children. One expression of this demand has taken the form of the introduction of a special child care allowance for families with small children. Attention has also been drawn to the need for a special supplementary payment for families with three or more children, in addition to the basic child allowance. As a rule, it is the mother who has to stay at home and look after the children; her absence from the labour market is considerably prolonged in families with several children, and with it the loss of her income from gainful employment.

A special drafting committee on family affairs was appointed by the Government in 1962 the main task of which was to investigate and analyse the various problems affecting social services to families with children and to submit proposals based on its findings. Since the committee submitted its report in 1964, the State has increased its grants to local authorities for the building of kindergartens. The committee's terms of reference also included a closer study of the question of a child care allowance. The committee considered that extra support for families with small children over and above the basic child allowance was particularly called for while the children were in their infancy. Extra support of this kind should be given to all families with children in the age group it is decided to help, regardless of whether both parents are gainfully employed or not. The committee proposed that an investigation be made into the question of gradually extending a system of child care allowances and the possibility of gearing such a system to social insurance through financing it with contributions.

The drafting committee also considered the question of special support for families with three or more children. The committee drew attention to the fact that the proportion of the costs incurred through the children and borne by the families becomes more and more noticeable as the number of children increases. It is unjust for children in large families to have to grow up in less favourable circumstances than other children. The drafting committee therefore found good cause for families with three or more children to receive a supplementary family allowance rising in proportion to the number of children in the family.

The memorandum of the drafting committee has since been submitted to a number of authorities and organisations, all of whom—in so far as they have expressed any opinion—have been in favour of the basic idea of increased support for large families.

In view of the favourable response encountered by these statements of principle concerning future family policy, the Government appointed a committee on family policy in 1965, and this committee is now engaged in investigating the question of economic support for families with children. One particular task of the committee is to test the effect of different types of support as well as their structure and demarcation. According to the committee's directives, family policy is to be differentiated so as to provide support when and where it is most needed.

As can be seen from the foregoing, housing policy has been regarded as an important part of family policy in Sweden. A law passed by the Riksdag in 1968 provides for a considerable increase in the housing allowance payable as from 1969 to families with children. This allowance has been reshaped in order to make it available to far more families than previously. The amount payable varies according to the number of children, the family income and the size of the house or flat. About 430,000 families with several children out of a total of approximately one million are expected to be eligible for allowances of this kind. It is important for families with several children to be guaranteed decent housing, not only from the point of view of the children but also with a view to reducing the work to be done in the home by the parents.

4. Service to Families

Good facilities for child supervision are of direct significance to the promotion of equality between men and women in the labour market. A survey carried out in 1967 showed that there were more than

300,000 children under 10 years of age in Sweden whose mothers went out to work for more than 15 hours a week. The same survey revealed that there were more than 200,000 mothers with children under 10 who would like to go out to work if they could arrange for the supervision of their 350,000 children. Thus there is a very great demand for supervision facilities for children of employed parents.

In Sweden there are two forms of State-subsidised institutions for the supervision of children, viz. kindergartens and family day nurseries (supervision in private homes). The main responsibility for the extension of kindergartens rests with the 900 municipalities in the country, who receive subsidies from the State, mainly towards investment costs. Kindergartens are establishments where children of gainfully employed parents can be looked after all day or for half the day by qualified staff (nursery-school teachers and children's nurses). Places providing supervision all day are called whole-day places. Some of these can also be used for the supervision of children under school age for three hours a day or for the looking after of schoolchildren outside school hours (known as leisure-time homes). There are at present 24,000 places for the part-time or full-time supervision of children whose parents are gainfully employed. About 20,000 of these places are in kindergartens and the remainder in leisure-time homes. However, these places are quite insufficient to meet the demand, and there are still a number of urban areas without kindergartens. In order to increase the rate of expansion, State subsidies for the building of kindergartens were raised considerably as from 1 July, 1966. During 1968, the Government is to put forward a bill for a further increase of State support by 40 per cent, which will make it possible to provide 10,000 new places during 1968 and 1969 respectively.

Over the past five years the number of places at training colleges for nursery-school teachers has been doubled in order to increase the supply of personnel. The number of places now available is 1,110, and this will be increased to 1,560 in 1970. Efforts are also being made to recruit male trainees.

In addition to kindergartens, day supervision is also available in a number of private homes. Some of these places are made available by local authorities, who refund a certain amount of the cost to the daytime mother. A resolution has recently been passed by the 1968 Riksdag providing for a State subsidy starting in 1969 and amounting to 35 per cent of the costs incurred by local authorities through payments for day supervision in private homes, though in the case of the larger municipalities this is made subject to the condition that at least an equal number of places are available (whole-day) in kindergartens. This rule has been proposed in order not to discourage the local authorities from extending the institutional form of child supervision.

It can be added that the question of reliable child supervision during the parents' working hours has attracted the attention of both trade unions and employers. Out of their joint bodies, the Women's Labour Market Committee has done a great deal to increase the interest of local authorities in expanding facilities.

Popular opinion used to regard kindergartens as a sort of poor relief for families where mothers were forced by economic necessity to go out to work. Today they are regarded as a service providing the most reliable supervision possible, under the direction of qualified staff, and teaching children the rudiments of social behaviour before school age. The popularity of the kindergartens among young parents is shown by the fact that 200,000 mothers of small children desire this form of supervision for their children. Previously it was possible for better-situated families to solve the problem of child supervision by engaging maids. Today, however, there are only 20,000 home helpers in Sweden as opposed to 205,000 in 1930.

Another facility is provided by nursery schools, where children can be left for three hours per day. These are less frequently used by parents who are gainfully employed, but they make the same contribution towards the social acclimatisation of children as do kindergartens providing supervision all day. Nursery schools have a total of about 32,000 places and can thus take care of about 64,000 children.

The Swedish Government wish in this connection to emphasise the significance of organised child supervision to the attainment of equality between the sexes. The Government consider the question of child supervision to be as important for fathers as for mothers. Responsibility for the supervision and care of their children rests with both parents in the same way as both of them are responsible for the children being provided for. However, the rapid expansion which the Government expect to result from the increased subsidies in practice make kindergartens of greatest consequence to mothers, since it will enable them to go out to work. The costs incurred by society in building and running these institutions can pay dividends in a number of ways. The social acclimatisation of the children is stimulated and their health is regularly checked through medical examinations. The mother is enabled to make use of her vocational qualifications or to acquire the qualifications she desires, and she retains her job longer. The rewards reaped by society take the form not only of increased taxation revenues through the income tax paid by the mother and through increased turnover in the consumer sector, but also of the filling of positions in the economy and social services, which might otherwise remain vacant through lack of personnel.

Another service available to all families with children of school age is that of free school meals, a service which has now been extended to certain other school forms even after the comprehensive school. This service probably has been and still is of the utmost importance to the parents' possibilities of going out to work. At the same time it has fulfilled a particularly important nutritive function since it was first introduced on a more general scale during the 1940s.

Free health checkups for children of school age by school doctors and nurses and free dental care for children are other important aspects of the development whereby the school has assumed a greater share of responsibility for children.

Yet another form of service to families with children is provided in the form of municipal domestic help. Domestic help employed by the local authorities are detailed to help families with children in the event of sudden crises, e.g. when a parent is taken ill and the children must be looked after and supervised by somebody else in the home. Similar problems arise when the mother must be away from her children for a short time because of childbirth.

Most of the larger municipalities also employ children's nurses to take care of sick children at home who cannot be admitted to kindergartens.

Organisations also contribute to services for families with children. The State give grants to a number of organisations which provide children's holiday camps in the country so that children can get out into the sun and bathe and play during the summer.

There are also holiday homes, i.e. private homes in rural districts which provide accommodation for children during the summer. The grants are paid to cover, among other things, the travel costs of the children. Children on holiday with their families can also travel more or less free of charge.

Service in housing areas has been the subject of lively discussions during the last few years. Demands have been voiced from many quarters for the creation of service facilities, e.g. in the form of service centres within convenient walking distance of housing areas. Part of the reason for the growing demand for collective service facilities in housing areas is of course to be found in the rising employment frequency of married women. But other population groups, too, such as pensioners and unmarried persons desire more such facilities. A service centre may for example have a reception desk where cleaning, child-minding and messenger services can be booked. It should also include a post office, dispensing chemists' shops, a shop open in the evenings, a restaurant and café, as well as a kindergarten and leisure-time centre for the children. Another alternative would be to build special service houses, i.e. large multi-dwelling houses with their own kindergarten, restaurant, cleaning staff, etc.

In 1967, the Government appointed a special service committee to investigate, among other things, the regulations applying to Government loans for the service facilities with which such houses need to be provided. Service blocks, centres or houses are at present being built in the Stockholm and Gothenburg areas.

5. Social Insurance

The Swedish system of social insurance is based on compulsory national insurance covering sickness, childbirth (cf. Section III, Family Policy), disablement, old age and loss of the breadwinner. There is also a compulsory insurance scheme covering industrial injury. Most of the rules governing these types of insurance are the same for men and women. The following will take into account such cases where the law prescribes separate rules for the sexes.

The year 1960 was a landmark in the history of social policy, since it was in that year that the Supplementary Pensions Act entered into force. This law entitles people who have been gainfully employed between the ages of 16 and 65 to additional pension benefits besides those received through the basic old-age pension scheme. A certain part of the annual income from employment is regarded as pensionable income, giving a certain number of pension points for every year. In order to qualify for such a pension, one must have acquired pension points for at least three years. Thirty years' pension points are required for a full pension in the case of people born in 1924 or later. During the 1980s, the basic and supplementary pensions together will correspond to two-thirds of the income earned by the pensioner during his or her 15 best years of income.

By fixing the age limits at 16 and 65 in the new law, one of the obstacles was removed which previously had prevented women from obtaining positions carrying a pension; formerly the pension rights attaching to such positions in private industry were dependent on the person concerned securing the position before reaching the age of thirty. This meant that women who had had to stay at home and look after children were more often than not deprived of the right to a pension because they resumed gainful employment after the age of thirty. The pensionable age for male and female workers employed by the State is now 65 or 67 for both sexes. The retiring age for female salaried staff in private industry was previously 60 years but has now been raised to 62, while for male salaried workers it is 65.

The pension system guarantees the security of the woman in the event of her husband's death. Both the basic old-age pension scheme and the supplementary pension scheme provide for the payment of widow's pension after the death of the husband. On the other hand, there is no corresponding benefit for widowers. Full widow's pension is paid from the basic old-age pension funds to widows who have attained the age of 50 at the time of the decease of their husbands. Full widow's pension is also payable—regardless of age—to a widow with a child or children under 16. Widows without children and aged between 36 and 50 receive a reduced pension benefit. Widow's pensions are paid from the supplementary pensions fund regardless of age.

The basic old-age pension and the supplementary pension also include children's pension. If one or both parents have died, children's pension is paid out of the basic pension funds to children under 16. Children's pension from the supplementary pensions fund is paid to children under the age of 19 if one or both parents are dead, provided that the deceased was in receipt of a pension or would have received a supplementary disablement pension if he or she had become an invalid. Illegitimate children have the same right to children's pension as children born in wedlock after the death of the mother and father.

The decision made in 1959 regarding the right to widow's pension was based upon knowledge of the difficulties experienced by a great many women when they lost their husband. Women who have reached the age of 50 and have not been gainfully employed during their married life find it difficult to return to the labour market.

Since the introduction of widow's pensions the position has however radically changed. Labour market policy has been greatly expanded and now offers retraining and introductory courses for housewives wishing to return to work. In 1960, 3,200 women attended courses of this kind. By 1967, the figures had risen to 25,800. The employment frequency among women has also risen rapidly since the 1950s, and most marriages now number two income earners, even if the wife generally earns less than the husband. Widows, too, have a high employment frequency; this is the highest in the age group between 40 and 44 years, 64 per cent of whom were employed full-time in 1965.

During recent years objections have been raised against widows' pensions on the grounds that they are a form of social protection based on sex and marital status. Bearing in mind the aim of achieving complete equality between the sexes it is—so many people claim—unfair to make social protection of the surviving spouse dependent on which spouse dies. Employee organisations have also voiced a demand for a change in the law to provide equal rights for men and women in this respect.

Sickness benefit insurance also contains a number of rules discriminating between men and women. A married man not gainfully employed but working at home receives no sickness benefit when he falls ill, but a woman in the same position does. There are other distinctions besides.

Following a motion put forward in the Riksdag in 1967, the Swedish Government has instructed the committee on family policy mentioned previously to review the rules governing sickness benefit which discriminate between men and women. Another committee has been given the task of considering whether there is any justification for the distinction made between men and women regarding pension rights on the death of the other spouse. This committee is also to investigate the possibilities of family pension benefits being more closely attached to the children in future.

General insurance benefits for the sick, disabled and aged have also been matched by an extension of institutional facilities. Previously it was the duty of the family to take care of the sick and aged, and it was generally the women who did most of the work in this respect.

Today the responsibility for the care of the sick and aged has to a great extent been assumed by the community. The majority of pensioners want to live in their own homes. There are also special pensioners' homes with comfortable flats or small houses specifically designed for elderly people. Old people's homes provide comprehensive services for elderly persons not in need of care. Old people continuing to live in their own homes but who need assistance with certain household chores or with personal hygiene are entitled to the services of domestic helps engaged by the local authorities. Relatives providing this kind of service themselves can be remunerated by the municipality at the same rates as the municipal domestic helps.

The institutional and medical service has expanded rapidly during the 1950s and 1960s. Since hospital treatment is free of charge, everybody can afford it. Nobody need be a burden to his relatives because he cannot afford medical treatment. If however it is considered more suitable for old and sick people to be looked after at home, relatives can be remunerated for the work involved.

The increasing resources brought to bear by society to deal with the problems of the sick and elderly have relieved women of a number of traditionally unpaid tasks at home. The assumption of responsibility by society has transformed these tasks into paid occupations. The enormous investments made by society in medical facilities have thus contributed a great deal towards the emancipation and economic independence of women.

6. Taxation of Families

(a) Current Regulations

The Swedish fiscal system is based on what is known as the principle of taxable capacity, meaning that the size of the tax imposed is governed by the ability of the individual concerned to pay it. It is for instance this principle that lies behind the rule that a certain minimum portion of income (the existence minimum) be exempted from tax. The same principle has resulted in a progressive taxation system, i.e. the imposition of a proportionally heavier tax on high incomes than on low ones.

Family taxation in Sweden has been based on the concept of marriage as an economic unity. The economic partnership between married people has been taken to imply that the taxable capacity of one spouse cannot be assessed without regard being paid to the income and resources of the other spouse. Joint taxation of married couples has also been considered justified by the provisions of family law for equal living standards as between the two spouses, regardless of who earns the family income. It has therefore been considered proper to make the tax-free income larger for two married persons than for one single person, even in cases where only one spouse is in receipt of an income.

If both spouses have incomes it is considered that the tax payable should be assessed on the basis of their combined income. No regard is paid to the distribution of this combined income between the spouses. The taxable capacities of two families with identical incomes have been regarded as more or less equal, irrespective of the proportion of this income earned by the husband or the wife in either case. One result of the joint taxation of married couples is thus that a married person who is gainfully employed is not necessarily liable to the same taxation as another married person with the same income.

The principle of taxable capacity has also been considered important in the construction of family taxation. It has been taken to imply that regard must be given to the mutual maintenance obligations of spouses and that marital status should therefore be taken into account by the taxation authorities.

Joint taxation of married couples means that national income tax for married couples is based on their combined taxable incomes, and not until this calculation has been made is the tax divided according to the share of either spouse in the total income earned.

According to the rules at present in force, the tax-free basic sum (the basic deduction from income) is twice as large for married persons as for single persons. If one spouse accounts for the whole income, he or she can still claim the same double allowance. After this, the national income tax payable is worked out as a fixed basic sum in relation to the taxable income. The basic sum is calculated by means of two scales, one (lower) scale for married persons and single parents, the other (more progressive) for single persons. In these scales the bisectional principle, as it is called, is employed up to a certain income level—in other words, the tax paid by a married couple corresponds to the tax payable by two unmarried persons each earning half the amount of the married couple's combined income.

If the family includes children under the age of 16, the wife is entitled to certain tax concessions for earned income. These concessions take the form of what is known as an earned income allowance to cover the cost of obtaining supervision for the children.

(b) Reforms in Progress

Joint taxation of married couples has been the subject of a far-ranging debate in Sweden during recent years. In the course of this debate, the principle of joint taxation has been criticised on the grounds that it constitutes an impediment to the general campaign for increased equality between men and women. As the critics see it, joint taxation of married couples is based on outmoded views of marriage as a means of providing for the wife, as witness the rules giving married men with wives living at home twice the basic allowance accorded to single persons and providing for the assessment of their tax liabilities after this deduction according to a more lenient scale than that applied to single persons.

A great deal of criticism has in recent years been levelled against the effect of joint taxation on a married woman wishing to go out to work—the so-called threshold effect. When a married woman returns to work, she will become entitled to her tax-free basic deduction, while that available to her husband is reduced by the same amount, thus resulting in an increase in the amount of tax that he has to pay. The amalgamation of the couple's incomes also results in a proportionally higher tax being levied on the wife's income than would have been the case if she had not been married. The rules governing the joint taxation of married couples have therefore been seen to have the effect of imposing tax on the wives' newly-acquired incomes "from the bottom upwards" without any reduction in the basic allowance and together with the progressive taxation rate applied to the top end of the husband's previous income. This so-called threshold-effect, the inevitable consequence of any form of joint taxation of married couples, has been said to deter a great many married persons from returning to the labour market after spending a number of years in the home. In other words, joint taxation is said to be a direct obstacle to the economic independence of women. It is also alleged that joint taxation is by no means the corollary of the provisions of family law concerning mutual maintenance obligations and that married women, who cannot obtain gainful employment, should be helped by the community through the same extensive measures of labour market policy as are available to unemployed men.

These considerations have resulted in a steadily growing demand for the abolition of the joint taxation of married couples, which it is suggested should be replaced by a system of individual taxation whereby everybody should be assessed according to the same rules regardless of sex and marital status. This would avoid the threshold effect deterring married women from returning to the labour market. Married men with wives working full-time at home would be liable to the same tax as single persons. The tax payable by the individual would not be affected by marriage.

More consistent taxation of private persons would entail the replacement of certain general concessions reserved for couples without children. However, assistance to couples with children has been planned to take the form of direct payments, not tax concessions, so that this would lead to further redistribution between couples with children and those without.

In presenting the budget for 1965, the Minister of Finance declared that an investigation was called for into the technical and distributional problems involved in a complete or modified form of individual taxation. A government commission was appointed to investigate the possibilities of going over to this new system. A proposal to this effect is to be submitted by the commission in 1968.

Pending a more permanent solution to the problem of family taxation, couples were accorded the possibility, in 1965, of voluntary individual taxation. This alternative is at present made use of by the minority of marriages in which both partners earn incomes but would if taxed together be liable to pay more than if they had been unmarried.

7. Labour Market Policy

(a) Objectives

Perhaps the most powerful factor behind the enhanced status of women in Swedish society has been the policy of full employment pursued in Sweden since the economic crisis of the 1930s. At first this policy was confined to the cushioning of unemployment during recession periods by means of state projects. Measures of this kind have played an important part in securing women's right to employment on the same terms as men. Experience shows that unemployment is a grave menace to the equality of the sexes. During periods of rising unemployment the right of the married woman to work is challenged on the grounds that she ought to be provided for by her husband. A good example of the misogamy that can arise out of unemployment was provided by a motion tabled in the Riksdag in 1932, when a committee of investigation was called for into the right of married women to employment on the grounds that such employment "is to be regarded as disloyalty to the men, who, after all, are the breadwinners." However, the motion was not carried.

Another widespread but essentially discriminatory way of thinking has it that married women constitute a reserve labour force which by all means should be mobilised in periods of high prosperity but which can perfectly well be sent home again when the demand for labour begins to fall. Prejudices of this kind should be combatted by both the community organs and the unions, whose business it is—or ought to be—to increase the self-awareness of their women members. One must enlighten the women of the principle that every citizen is entitled to work.

Efficient labour market policy is regarded in Sweden as a sine qua non of continuing economic progress. Only by guaranteeing the economic and social security of the individual can one expect technical and structural change within the economy to win acceptance: thanks to an active labour market policy, the Swedish trade union movement has come to adopt a basically favourable attitude towards structural changes within the economy. This attitude is based on the knowledge that economic growth requires the constant adaption of the economic structure to new technological advances.

The task of modern labour market policy is no longer confined to maintaining employment during downward trends in the international business cycle. Rather, it is to a great extent committed to the role of a stabilising factor in economic policy. When the demand for labour exceeds the supply, labour market policy creates additional stability through measures designed to encourage mobility, e.g. by encouraging the migration of labour from surplus to deficiency areas. Another means is that of giving training to women and other groups who have not previously been gainfully employed.

A new labour market programme was adopted in 1966. Greater aspirations are now entertained and the original objective of full employment has been expanded into full, productive and freely chosen employment. One of the most important tasks to be faced will be that of adapting to the rapid structural changes taking place in the economy.

Following the adoption of this new programme, the Government has provided in its budget for 1968-1969 for a considerable expansion of the capacity of labour market policy. It is proposed to augment the resources of the central authority, the National Labour Market Board, by 40 per cent. The Government further proposes an expansion of regional planning policy. These measures will increase state expenditure on labour market policy and regional planning to over 1.8 billion kronor. Sweden probably has the most extensive labour market policy in the world in relation to its labour force of 3.8 millions.

The principle of equality of men and women on the labour market is affirmed in the labour market policy programme, as witness the following:

> The objectives of labour market policy are to be the same for male and female labour. The resources of the authority are not to be applied to separate measures for men and women.

> The demand for female labour is to be assessed by the same criteria as the demand for male labour. Married women seeking

work are not to be subjected to any test concerning their need of employment.

The latent unemployment affecting above all married women is to be combatted.

Measures designed to safeguard the employment of women are not to be reduced in periods of reduced labour demand.

Special measures—especially as regards training—are called for on a short-term basis to accelerate the trend towards complete equality.

More kinds of special training should be available to women seeking work.

The employment service should canvass for part-time posts to meet the large female demand for this kind of work.

The employment service should actively contribute towards the eradication of sex barriers on the labour market and, accordingly, test the stipulations as to sex made by employers when registering vacancies and catalogue jobs where recruiting is confined to one sex. This is to be done in collaboration with the enterprises concerned. Conversely, male applicants can be offered training and employment within sectors generally regarded as exclusively "feminine," e.g. welfare and services.

As regards those employment service offices where there still exists a division into two separate sections for male and female applicants respectively, this division should be abolished as soon as possible.

As early as 1961 the National Labour Market Board adopted a so-called activation programme for female labour; this programme was last revised in 1966. Special officials, known as activation inspectors, have now been engaged for eighteen months at the 24 regional head offices. Their task is to co-ordinate activation work for non-employed women and middle-aged and elderly labour. During the same period, research has been conducted at a research establishment, the Institute for Labour Market Questions.

An important complement to labour market policy is provided by state regional development assistance, which takes the form primarily of loans but also of grants to industrial enterprises with a view to stimulating economic expansion—above all in the north of Sweden. One of the objectives laid down here is that of increasing female employment in areas where it is low and above all encouraging greater differentiation in areas with a one-sided labour market so as to increase employment possibilities for women and others.

According to the latest Swedish analyses of the expected economic development in Sweden in the 1970s, married women will hold a key position in the labour market. Pursuant to the forecast, the number of men at work will be lower in 1980 than in 1960.

(b) Labour Market Policy Means

Labour policy means include employment exchanges, pre-vocational practical orientation, vocational guidance, disablement resettlement, and a number of measures for the rehabilitation and employment of those without work, such as transfer grants, vocational training, relief work, as well as payments from recognised unemployment funds for persons insured against unemployment, or, in the case of unemployed persons not so insured, relief payments in cash from the local authority.

Sweden has official employment exchanges, the services of which are free and may be used by all. In 1966 these employment exchanges were approached by 337,000 women and 484,000 men seeking work. Thus there are fewer women than men looking for work, despite the fact that, according to a survey, women accounted for 61 per cent of the increase in the amount of labour available from May 1966 to April 1967 inclusive. The differences in the use made by women and men of the services of the employment exchange can be accounted for partly by the fact that vacancies in certain typical "female" fields of employment are less frequently dealt with by the employment exchanges. Furthermore, female workers are to a lesser extent than men insured by unemployment funds and thus are not required to report to the employment exchange when they lose their jobs. However, the contact of women with the employment exchange will probably increase with the introduction of compulsory unemployment insurance. Such a form of insurance is now being studied in Sweden. Moreover, female workers seem not to take such a serious view of being unemployed. Studies of the labour situation have revealed that married women in particular register with the employment exchange to a lesser extent, despite the fact that they say that they are willing to take up gainful employment. A further explanation of the fact that married women fail to register at the employment exchanges is that they know that local work is not available. Owing to their dual role they cannot undertake long journeys to work. Also they do not move as often as men who are seeking employment. Men's work is still regarded as being more important than women's work. Should a wife become unemployed, it is by no means certain that the family will consider moving to another place where there are chances of good jobs for both spouses. According to a study of labour available in August, women made up 90 per cent of the so-called latent applications for employment, i.e. persons who say that they would have looked for work if they thought that they could obtain suitable employment locally.

The concealed unemployment is also reflected in the low figures for female employment in certain places. Where there is an industry or a sector of the economy which employs mainly men, female employment will be low. On the other hand, where there is a typical female field of work, then the employment figures will be high. The latter is the case in towns where there are clothing and textile industries, food processing industries or—as in the case of the capital—in cities where considerable employment is provided by offices and the retail trade. Female employment is low in industrial centres devoted to the iron, steel and metal industries.

In the long run the only possibility of adjusting these large regional variations in female employment is to do away with the division of jobs according to sex. This is an important task for labour market policy.

The official employment exchanges, which were finally put on a national basis in 1948, come under the central body responsible for labour market policy, namely the National Labour Market Board. On 30 June 1967 the total number of employment exchanges was made up of 24 regional head offices (one in each county), 231 local offices, and about 320 local employment service agents. The last-mentioned are active in rural districts and villages, but they are kept continuously informed of vacancies in all parts of the country. For purposes of organisation, the employment service agents come under the local offices.

During the 1960s there have also been mobile employment exchanges in areas where unemployment was particularly serious or which had been hit by closures in industry. In the larger towns information about vacancies can be obtained by telephone from what is known as "Fröken Plats" (Miss Vacancy) Service.

In 1966 the official employment exchanges filled 877,000 vacancies, of which 325,000 went to female applicants. In a few counties the number of vacancies filled was equally divided between men and women, while elsewhere, twice as many vacancies were filled by men as by women. This distribution reflects the differences in the structure of the economy, which itself has influenced the possibilities of female employment.

Prevocational Practical Orientation is provided for all school-children of 13-14 years of age (Class 8 in the compulsory schools in Sweden) and is intended to give them an idea about various jobs. Places are obtained by the employment service and the vocational guidance teachers. This activity has been described in more detail in Section III:1 Education.

Vocational Guidance for adult workers has become more and more important because of the increased vocational training provided for the unemployed and for women who, before returning to gainful employment, wish to take one of the training courses which are now available.

Disablement Resettlement Measures aim at solving the employment problems of the handicapped. There has been a marked expansion of the efforts in this field. Measures include the provision of protected workshops, the arrangement of special places of work and rehabilitation measures in the form of detailed examinations of working ability, vocational training and learning a trade. With the development of technical aids more and more seriously handicapped persons can be placed in employment. In 1966 the disablement resettlement offices received applications for work from 18,500 women and 56,300 men.

Furthermore, handicapped persons working at home can receive State grants for the procurement of technical aids so that they can look after their homes, for example to help housewives to do their daily chores. Grants are also made to property owners who provide accommodation for invalids in blocks of flats or in private houses.

The modern labour market policy includes very extensive measures to facilitate the adaption of the individual to a new job, a new occupation and a new place of residence.

Even if, on the whole, there is a certain equilibrium in the labour market, variations can occur in the supply of jobs within the same vocational field between different places or parts of the country; for instance, there might be a lack of trained labour in certain occupations in one region, while a surplus exists elsewhere. Relief work is arranged for non-mobile labour and older workers. Such relief work generally takes the form of road construction and building work. Almost all those provided with relief work by the employment exchanges are men. On the other hand, that which is of greater importance for unemployed women is that a person who is or who faces the risk of being unemployed, and who in all probability cannot be given a fresh job locally or in a neighbouring area can receive full remuneration from the employment exchange for the cost of moving;

such grants are called transfer grants. If the other members of the family cannot move, a family allowance is paid; this covers the rent of the original residence and allowances for the spouse and children. The regulations are the same for men and women, but these benefits are utilised to a much greater extent by men than by women. However, there have been cases where the wife has received a family allowance for her husband and children when she moved to take up employment in another area. In addition, the financial grants to encourage the movement of labour are utilised by single women.

Special grants are made for the procurement of equipment; also there are starting allowances to tide people over until the first payment of salary. It is proposed in the current budget to increase this starting allowance to 1,000 Swedish kronor for families and to 750 Swedish kronor for single persons. In order to facilitate the moving of unemployed persons who are rooted to their place of residence because they own a house for which no buyer can be found owing to the situation on the labour market, the Swedish State is purchasing, on an experimental basis in the northernmost parts of Sweden for the present, the homes of such persons.

The training of unemployed and of persons who are liable to become unemployed, or who find it difficult to get work, is carried out on an extensive scale. This retraining gives the individual greater possibilities in the choice of jobs and at the same time it furthers productivity. Vocational training can pay good dividends in the long run and reduce the cost of other labour market policy measures. Also retraining is perhaps the foremost means of increasing wages of the low-income groups, of which women make up a large part. For 1968-1969 it is estimated that 80,000 persons will undergo such training, i.e. more than two per cent of the total labour force of the country.

Table 7 and the accompanying bar diagram indicate the scope of the labour market training programme.

**Table 7. Number of persons who participated in the labour
market training program in 1960-1967.**

	Total	No. of women
1960	17,827	3,239
1961	20,976	5,698
1962	29,456	11,327
1963	36,814	14,557
1964	39,923	16,168
1965	46,002	19,084
1966	53,729	21,449
1967	69,534	25,780

During the period of training a training allowance is paid; this includes both a basic allowance and supplementary allowances for spouse and children. The allowances are subject to a means test with regard to the own income or that of the spouse, except in the case of supplementary allowances for children where the minimum amount is always payable.

The supplementary allowance for children is always granted to women, who thus receive a supplement to cover the increased costs of the supervision of their children during the period of training. Also it may be mentioned that the labour market policy is being directed increasingly to the whole family. Certain retraining centres are already provided with day nurseries so that both husband and wife can receive training at the same time.

Women under training provided by the Labour Market Board made up 17 per cent of the total in 1959-1960 and 46 per cent in 1965-1966. In October 1967 women made up 34 per cent. It is regrettable, however, to note that women, by and large, choose shorter training courses than men.

Women made up no less than 41 per cent of the trainees who were 45 years of age and older. Intensified measures formed part of a special campaign which was undertaken during 1966 and directed at female labour. The following is a quotation from the report of the Labour Market Board:

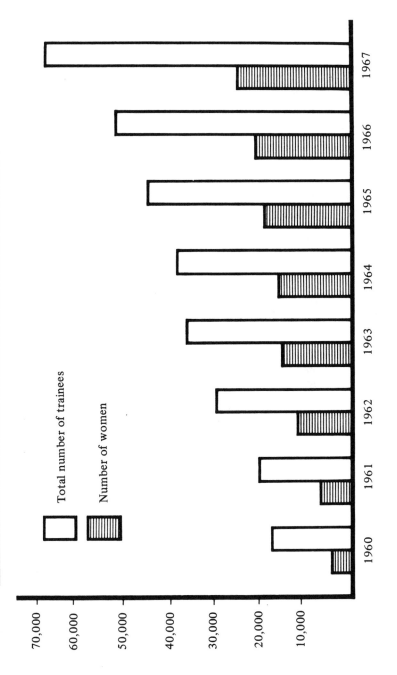

... market training programme in 1960-1967

During the period the campaign to inform the public of employment opportunities for women was intensified. One of the measures taken to interest women in a wider choice of occupations and to make them realize the need for longer and more qualified training was to repeat the radio series "Hemmafru byter yrke" (The Housewife Changes Her Occupation). In connection with these broadcasts comprehensive information on labour market and social matters was given at conferences arranged by the county labour boards in which women's organizations, educational associations, employer and employee organizations, public authorities, etc. participated. Study circles based on the radio series were organized in most counties under the auspices of various educational assocations.

A particularly favourable effect of the labour market training programme is that many women have undergone training for occupations which were previously regarded as being exclusively male work. It has even proved that women undergoing training provided by the Labour Market Board have, relatively speaking, made less conventional choices than the teenager girls in the vocational schools. The training for women in industrial work has been organised largely in the form of introductory courses and during the period of training the pupils have been given the opportunity for practice in a certain number of fields. However, most women still choose to train for office work and employment in the health and medical services.

During 1967 and early 1968 there was a marked decline in the demand for labour because of the downturn in the level of business activity, above all in western Europe. Efforts in the field of labour market policy must therefore be directed primarily towards providing new employment possibilities for those rendered unemployed. In mid-December 1967 the number of unemployed persons totalled 43,300, including some 8,000 women who had registered. The large part of the unemployed females came from the clothing, textile and metal industries, the distributive trades, and the hotel and restaurant trade. In its current budget the Swedish Government has provided increased assistance for older workers who become unemployed.

It has been seen that unemployment has hit the older workers harder than the younger ones, and at the same time the older workers have greater difficulties in adapting themselves to other jobs by retraining and moving. The Government now proposes to make a grant of 800 Swedish kronor a month to workers who are over 60 years of age and who cannot find new employment. Naturally, the regulations are the same for men and women. In such a situation it is most essential that the labour market policy has a capacity which is sufficiently great to provide powerful means for creating employment for both women and men. Despite the decline in the level of business activity, retraining and vocational training have proved to be very effective. During the second quarter of 1967 some 15,000 persons completed retraining courses and, despite the lack of buoyancy in the economy, 95.8 per cent of them had obtained new work by the beginning of October that year. In its current budget the Swedish Government has provided the means for a great expansion of labour market policy; this will help to ensure that there will be no discrimination in the labour market against women owing to a lack of resources in the labour market policy programme.

IV. ANSWERS TO ANNEX I: QUESTIONNAIRE ON THE ROLE OF WOMEN IN THE ECONOMIC AND SOCIAL DEVELOP-MENT OF THEIR COUNTRIES

1. What role do women currently play in the economic and social development of the country?

(a) The extent to which women participate in economic life:

The participation of women in the economic and social develop-ment of the country has increased considerably during the 1960s. The rapid increase in the employment rate among married women observed during the 1950s has continued to gain momentum. The increase becomes particularly apparent if one also includes married women in part-time employment in the sector of population directly concerned with production.

Unmarried women, like men, have tended to exhibit a reduced employment rate as regards the lower age groups, owing to the rising proportion of young people continuing their education up to the age of 25.

In order to give a complete picture of the direct contribution made by women on the Swedish labour market, the following results are given from an investigation made in 1966 into the structure of the Swedish labour force.

Table 1. Number of employed men and women by
number of weeks worked during 1966

Weeks worked	Men		Women		Both categories	
	1,000	%	1,000	%	1,000	%
1-13	208.3	8.0	277.3	15.9	485.6	11.2
14-26	139.9	5.4	189.5	10.9	329.4	7.5
27-49	324.7	12.5	309.1	17.7	633.8	14.6
50-52	1,933.6	74.1	968.4	55.5	2,902.1	66.7
Total	2,606.5	100.0	1,744.3	100.0	4,350.9	100.0

Out of a total labour force of 4,350,900 in 1966, 1,744,300 or 40 per cent were women. Seventy per cent of the total female population between the ages of 14 and 74 were gainfully employed during the year for periods of varying length. On the other hand, there is a considerable difference between men and women as regards the length of the period worked.

Two point six million men (87.7%) were employed during the year. Three out of every four men employed had worked throughout the year (i.e. 50-52 weeks), while a quarter of them were employed for shorter periods.

The number of women employed for various periods was 1.7 million, or 58.7 per cent of all women in the age groups concerned, but only just over half (55.5%) of the women employed had work throughout the year.

This implies that part-time employment, defined for the purpose of this survey as less than 35 hours a week is far more common among the female labour force. Thirty-six per cent of the women employed during the year had had part-time employment as against 3.8 per cent of the men.

The traditional division of labour as regards housework and child care has a considerable influence on the possibilities for women to earn their own incomes by going out to work. The following table shows that over three-quarters (77%) of the people in the age groups 14-74 years who had not been able to work during 1966 were women. The main reason for women not being gainfully employed are to be found in housework and child care (Table 2).

Table 2. Reasons for not working during 1966

Reason for	Men		Women	
not working	1,000	%	1,000	%
Studies	109.4	30.6	123.1	10.3
Illness	124.0	34.6	186.7	15.6
Child care			201.6	16.8
Housework	6.8	1.9	487.6	40.7
Could not get work			29.6	2.5
Of which part-time work			24.7	2.1
Other reason	117.3	32.9	166.1	14.1
Total	357.5	100.0	1,197.3	100.0

Although a large number of women were not able to work, professional activity among women with children in Sweden is to be regarded as high by international standards. The survey showed that 60 per cent of mothers with the youngest child under 17 had worked for at least a week or so during the year. What is more, every second professionally active woman with children at home under 17 worked throughout the year in 1966.

The age of the child is of great importance in determining the possibilities of going out to work, as is illustrated by Table 3.

Table 3. Frequency of employment among women with children in 1966

	Number of women with children			
	Youngest child aged 7		Youngest child aged 7−16	
	1,000	%	1,000	%
Employed part-time	136.0	23.9	189.3	39.4
Employed full-time	158.9	28.0	141.5	29.5
Not gainfully employed	273.1	48.1	149.1	31.1
Total	568.0	100.0	479.0	100.0

There is nonetheless a very strong tendency towards increased full-time employment among Swedish women. This is particularly true of married women. Table 4 illustrates the proportion of women in different age and marital status groups working at least half a normal working day at the time of the census in 1960 and 1965. It should be noted that farmers' wives helping their husbands are not included in the category of gainfully employed married women.

Table 4. Percentage of women employed[1] in Sweden in 1960 and 1965 by age and marital status

Age	Unmarried 1960	1965	Married[2] 1960	1965	Widows 1960	1965	Divorced 1960	1965	Total 1960	1965
-19	12.4	11.2	22.5	27.3	---	---	---	---	12.5	11.4
20-24	74.1	69.1	32.5	36.8	44.8	39.9	75.4	71.9	57.2	56.0
25-29	82.0	81.4	28.9	31.5	48.7	46.4	78.8	78.2	41.7	43.3
30-34	80.1	81.8	26.3	30.7	54.7	52.0	80.4	80.2	35.1	38.6
35-39	77.1	80.1	26.6	36.2	60.3	57.5	82.0	82.6	34.8	42.7
40-44	75.5	78.2	27.6	38.9	66.3	64.3	80.6	83.5	35.9	45.5
45-49	72.1	76.5	26.9	38.3	65.2	66.1	79.2	81.3	36.3	45.4
50-54	69.1	72.5	23.8	33.4	60.3	59.0	75.2	77.8	35.2	41.9
55-59	63.7	67.2	18.0	26.0	47.0	46.9	66.1	70.1	31.3	36.2
60-64	46.1	50.4	9.2	14.2	27.2	28.7	46.4	54.5	21.1	24.7
65-69	21.6	21.4	3.0	4.1	10.7	9.7	22.1	22.2	9.6	9.7
70-74	6.4	6.1	0.8	1.0	2.6	2.8	5.1	5.0	2.8	2.8
75-	1.9	1.6	0.2	0.3	0.8	0.7	2.2	1.2	1.0	0.8
Total	27.1	26.4	22.5	29.2	17.8	16.4	63.5	64.4	25.4	28.2

1. "Employed" is taken to mean persons gainfully employed for the equivalent of at least half a normal working day during the week in which the census was taken.

2. Excluding farmers' wives helping their husbands; these have been left out in order to facilitate comparison between the figures for 1960 and 1965.

One is struck above all by the increase in the full-time employment figures among married women of all age groups. Particularly noticeable is the increase in the age group 35–50, in which in 1965 just under four out of every ten women were putting in more than half a working day, i.e. (as a rule) working full-time. Nonetheless, comparison of married women to unmarried women reveals that marriage tends to a considerable extent to reduce married women's professional activity, which is normally more than twice as great among unmarried and divorced women over 25. This difference between married and unmarried women's professional activity is however largely attributable to the much lower degree of professional activity among married women with children. Moreover, Table 5 serves to show that unmarried mothers have the highest employment frequency of all marital status groups. Instead, children tend to have the effect of raising the employment frequency somewhat among this group, which suggests that provision for the children makes it a matter of economic necessity for them to go out to work.

Table 5. Employed women (= at least half a working day) as a percentage of all women in the group concerned according to the census figures for 1965

Age	Women without children under 16			Women with children under 16		
	Unmarried	Married	Other	Unmarried	Married	Other
20-24	68.7	77.0	66.5	73.1	20.0	54.9
25-29	81.6	79.4	74.9	80.0	23.0	66.8
30-34	81.8	74.1	80.5	81.8	29.1	71.7
35-39	79.4	68.2	82.3	84.0	35.2	73.0
40-44	78.0	58.0	82.6	80.7	36.8	71.6
45-49	76.4	49.5	78.5	79.4	36.0	66.6
50-	34.3	22.3	19.0	69.1	30.5	49.9
Total	54.1	34.5	25.7	73.4	30.5	66.1

In connection with the steep rise in employment frequency among married women, as described above, it is worth mentioning that women accounted for 61 per cent of the total increase in the labour force during the period 1.5.1966 to 30.4.1967. New male employers were drawn almost entirely from education and national service.

On the other hand, women coming onto the labour market have received less education than men: this presents a problem. Only 8.4 per cent of the women had taken the studentexamen[1] or more advanced examinations, as opposed to 23 per cent of the men. This is partly due to the fact that a higher proportion of the women were over 35 and had not received any high school education.

Employment frequency has been found to be subject to considerable regional variations, e.g. as between urban and rural areas. Of the total population of Sweden, 77.4 per cent lived in urban areas (including built-up areas with at least 200 inhabitants) in 1965. Employment frequency among women is generally lower in rural areas than in urban areas, as is shown by Table 6.

Table 6. Proportion of women employed by age and marital status in urban and rural areas according to the census figures for 1965 (employed = putting in at least half a working day)

Age	Unmarried		Married [2]		Other	
	Urban areas	Rural areas	Urban areas	Rural areas	Urban areas	Rural areas
20-24	71.0	58.8	40.2	26.0	68.6	64.3
25-29	83.9	67.5	35.0	27.1	75.4	63.7
30-34	85.8	65.6	34.8	31.1	76.9	65.0
35-39	85.1	60.9	41.4	35.3	78.7	61.4
40-44	84.1	57.6	45.3	37.1	79.3	63.0
45-49	83.0	55.5	40.7	37.2	77.4	57.8
50-54	78.6	54.0	40.8	33.3	70.4	49.5
55-59	73.2	49.6	32.4	27.4	57.6	36.2
60-64	54.0	40.1	18.5	18.4	36.2	22.8

1. University entrance qualifying examination.

2. Including farmers' wives helping their husbands, mainly in rural areas.

There are considerable regional differences, particularly as regards employment frequency among married women. According to the 1965 census, the city of Stockholm had the highest employment frequency (46.1%), while Västerbotten County in northern Sweden had the lowest (23.6%).

The significance of women in different branches of the economy is shown by Table 7 concerning the proportion of women in the labour force in 1960 and 1965.

Table 7. Women as percentage of the labour force in different sectors of the economy according to the census figures for 1960 and 1965 (employed = putting in at least half a working day)

	1960	1965
Agriculture, forestry, etc. (incl. members of the family helping on the farm, etc.)	--	22.7
Mining, manufacturing industry	21.6	22.9
Building and construction	3.3	4.0
Trade	47.7	48.1
of which:		
wholesale trade	23.7	26.6
retail trade	56.9	58.3
banking and insurance as well as real estate management	48.4	53.4
Communications	17.9	19.0
Services, etc.	63.1	62.4
of which:		
administration	31.8	35.1
education	63.3	63.1
medical service	80.5	85.7
domestic work	99.4	99.4
hotels and restaurants	76.3	72.6
other branches	59.9	54.5
Proportion of women of total labour force	29.8	33.6

In terms of sheer numbers, women play a predominant role in services: retail trade, banking and insurance, domestic work, hotels and restaurants, as well as such important branches of the public

sector as education and the medical service. But this predominance
has not resulted in women occupying the best paid and most
influential positions within the branches concerned.

Most of the female labour force—no less than 44 per cent—is
employed in public administration. Manufacturing industry and trade
are next in importance. Table 8 illustrates the distribution of the male
and female labour forces between different branches of the economy
according to the labour force survey carried out in November 1967.

Table 8. Labour force by sex, marital status and branch of the economy. Percentage employed in different branches in November 1967

Branch of economy (ISIC categories)	Men	Women un mar- ried	mar- ried	total	Both sexes	Proportion of women in each branch
Agriculture, forestry, etc.	11.8	8.3	2.6	6.1	9.7	23.6
Mining and manufacturing industry, etc.	39.5	22.2	20.3	21.5	32.7	24.6
Of which: engineering industry	17.0	5.8	5.7	5.8	12.8	17.0
Building	14.7	1.4	0.9	1.2	9.7	4.7
Trade, etc.	11.3	23.2	21.5	22.6	15.6	54.5
Communications, postal and telegraph services	8.7	4.4	3.7	4.1	7.0	22.2
Public administration, etc.	13.7	40.3	50.5	44.2	25.2	66.1
Total (incl. unspecified employment)	100.0	100.0	100.0	100.0	100.0	37.6

As can be seen from the table, men are far more evenly distributed between the different branches of economy than women. The division between the sexes in the labour market becomes even more apparent if one studies the distribution between different jobs. According to the 1960 census, 71 per cent of the women employed were concentrated within no more than 20 or so occupations containing a mere 12 per cent of the male labour force. By far the two most important female occupations are office work and serving in shops, which account for no less than 29 per cent of women employed (see further The Changing Roles of Men and Women, Table 6, p. 114). Thus most of the labour market is divided into a male and a female sector, the sectors with a more even distribution between the sexes being no more than a very modest residue. This segregation is one of the causes behind the difficulties experienced by women in trying to attain both real and formal economic parity in terms of salaries and wages. Experience seems to show that the typically "male" jobs are better paid than the typically "female" ones, regardless of whether the latter require the same degree of education. Not until men and women are employed on the same tasks within the same sectors does it become possible to give real weight to the demand for equal pay.

(b) The levels of responsibility at which women are participating in, and contributing to, each area of development.

The degree of responsibility for and influence in different sectors of society is to a very great extent reflected by wage and salary levels. Similarly, wage distribution between men and women is reflective of the extent to which society and the economy have elected to enlist women and, conversely, of the extent to which women have been encouraged to make use of the possibilities open to them. The following account is concerned with the relation between men's and women's wages in most important branches of the economy.

b.1 Women as entrepreneurs

Direct participation by women as entrepreneurs in the private sector of the economy (which employs over three-quarters of the Swedish labour force) is rather insignificant. Out of a total of just over 385,000 entrepreneurs, 39,600 were women according to the 1965 census, and as such were responsible for the management of the enterprises concerned and of their employees, if any. Forty-four per cent of the female entrepreneurs were married. Women entrepreneurs are commonest in services and trade, less common in agriculture and industry.

Table 9. Proportion of women among entrepreneurs in different branches of the economy according to the 1965 census.

Agriculture	4.3%
Manufacturing industry	10.5%
Building industry	0.4%
Trade	21.7%
Communications	1.3%
Other services	35.5%
All enterprises	10.3%

b.2 Women in public services

As was shown in Table 8, women constitute no less than 66 per cent of those employed in public administration, etc. This might well lead one to expect to find 66 per cent women and 34 per cent men in senior and highly paid national and local government administrative post. However, this is not the case, although the principle of equal pay has long since been stipulated within the public service. The majority of women employed in national and local government offices are placed in low salary grades, whereas male predominance becomes all the greater as one progresses upwards (cf. p. 120, Tables 8 and 9 in The Changing Roles of Men and Women). Further to these details Table 10 illustrates the distribution of civil government employees between different salary grades in October 1966. (Most positions in the public service are governed by Salary scheme A. The top positions are divided between schemes B and C. The lower of the two, scheme B, mainly includes heads of departments or their equivalent, while the higher of them, scheme C, includes divisional heads and their superiors.)

Table 10. Civil government employees in salary scheme A, B and C by salary grade and by sex on 1 October 1966. Total civil service.

Salary scheme A[1]			Salary scheme B[2] Number			Salary scheme C[3] Number		
Salary grade	Men %	Women %	Salary grade	Men	Women	Salary grade	Men	Women
1-9	10.7	58.2	1	--	--	1	2,138	42
10-14	52.6	31.6	2	1	--	2	459	4
15-19	21.2	6.6	3	105	12	3	148	2
20-24	9.8	2.9	4	2	--	4	99	--
25-29	5.7	0.7	5	2,467	94	5	71	1
Total	100.0	100.0	6	308	6	6	91	--
			7	7	--	7	2	--
						8	10	--
141,855	84,628			2,890	112		3,018	49

1. Monthly salary from approx. kr 1,000 in grade 1 to approx. kr 4,000 in grade 29.

2. Monthly salary from approx. kr 4,200 in grade 1 to approx. kr 5,700 in grade 7.

3. Monthly salary from approx. kr 5,800 in grade 1 to approx. kr 10,000 in grade 8.

The overwhelming under-representation of women in higher salary grades is often put down to their lower average age and shorter average period of service. There is quite a lot in this. Thus in October 1966, 53 per cent of the women in the general civil service and defence organisation were under 35 as opposed to 40 per cent of men. However, this difference seems mainly due to the concentration of recruiting to younger women, especially for office work.

On the other hand, when studying the distribution of very young salaried employees as to salary grades—the number of working hours does not play a decisive role in the setting of salaries for young people—it appears that to a large extent the young women are to be found in the lowest grades, Table 11.

Table 11. Government employees[1] under 19 years in salary scheme A by salary step and by age

Salary step	Men % under 19 years	Women % under 19 years
1-4	20.0	43.8
5-6	21.1	42.2
7-8	42.3	8.2
9	12.0	4.7
10-	4.6	1.1
Total	100.0	100.0
Number	1,577	5,214

1. General civil service and the defence organisation

Since men and women are to an overwhelming extent engaged for totally different tasks, the reason for the discrepancy must—even as regards younger civil servants—be largely due to the fact that the posts filled by women are generally more poorly paid.

b.3 Participation of women in the distributive trades

As we have already seen, the distributive trades are one of the most important branches of female professional activity. Trade is partly private and partly cooperative. Table 12 illustrates the proportion between the sexes in the most important occupational categories in this sector during 1966.

Table 12. Employees in various occupational categories in private and consumer cooperative wholesale and retail trade, October 1966

Categories	Private[1]		Cooperative	
	Men	Women	Men	Women
Clerical personnel	20,859	14,535	2,877	2,416
Sales people and shop assistants	14,664	26,489	4,366	8,438
Storekeepers and chauffeurs	14,719	1,530	1,149	313

1. Blown up numbers.

Both male and female employees are most commonly active as salespeople and shop assistants. Table 13 presents a comparison between men's and women's wages in this branch.

Table 13. Monthly earnings (arithmetic medium) in 1966 of salespeople and shop assistants in private and consumer cooperative trade by age. Women's earnings as a percentage of men's.

Age	Private	Cooperative
-17	86.3	97.9
18-19	90.7	96.9
20-24	81.5	86.9
25-29	78.0	84.1
30-39	73.8	79.4
40-49	76.1	80.7
50-59	80.0	86.2
60-	84.1	93.0

In none of the various age groups does the women's average wage come up to the men's. Relatively speaking, it is the youngest shop assistants who fare best among the women, particularly in the Cooperative Movement.

b.4 Women in Swedish Industry

The mining and manufacturing industries employed 33.5 per cent of the Swedish labour force in 1965, and 23 per cent of the total industrial labour force of 1,156,000 were women.

The different branches of manufacturing industry have long been marked by a rigid segregation of the sexes between certain branches. The proportion of women employed is highest in the textile and clothing branches and lowest in the timber and furniture branches. Table 14 illustrates the proportion of female and male labour in different industrial branches according to the census figures for 1960 and 1965 respectively. (Owing to certain discrepancies of classification, only major differences between the two periods should be taken into account.)

Table 14. Women as a percentage of the labour force within different branches of industry

	Proportion of women by per cent of labour force	
	1960	1965
Food, beverage and tobacco industries	38.3	41.7
Textiles and clothing	60.7	62.2
Timber and furniture	6.4	9.0
Paper industries	14.4	17.1
Printing and allied industries	29.7	31.6
Leather and rubber industries	28.9	27.8
Chemical industry	25.2	28.2
Quarrying industries	12.0	13.3
Metal, machinery and vehicle manufacturing industries	11.9	13.9

Women have between 1960 and 1965 further secured their position in the traditional "female" branch, i.e. textiles, clothing and food-stuffs. The proportion of women employed has also increased in all other branches except the leather and rubber industries.

As was shown on page 116 in The Changing Roles of Men and Women, women are still predominant in the lowest-paid tasks in industry.

The hold of traditional ideas concerning the separate roles of the sexes on the minds of employers, women themselves and their male colleagues, together with the various resultant attitudes towards and evaluations of male and female labour respectively, are reviewed in Chapter 5, Employer attitudes to female employers (pp. 135-169).

Although Sweden has been a signatory to the ILO Convention on Equal Pay for Men and Women since 1962, there are still considerable differences between the average industrial wage rates for men and women.

Further to the statistical material supplied in the above-mentioned book, the following section presents a review of the latest details for 1966.

Ever since the end of the last war, the average wage for female workers has been only about 70 per cent of the men's. It is only during the last five years that an improvement has taken place, with the result that the average woman's wage was 76.6 per cent of the average man's wage in 1966.

Table 15. Wage development 1946-1966 for adult workers in mining and manufacturing. Women's average hourly earnings[1] as percentage of men's.

1946	66.8	1951	70.0	1956	69.3	1961	69.0
1947	69.2	1952	69.6	1957	69.3	1962	70.5
1948	70.5	1953	69.1	1958	69.0	1963	72.2
1949	71.0	1954	69.0	1959	68.8	1964	73.6
1950	70.3	1955	69.2	1960	68.8	1965	74.9
						1966	76.5

[1]. Including overtime supplements and extra shift pay, public and annual holiday pay, lay-off pay and other supplements.

296

There are quite considerable variations from one branch to
another. Women's average wages in 1966 varied from 69.7 per cent of
the men's in the printing and allied industries to 87.2 per cent in the
beverage and tobacco industries. However, the latter branch is too
small to have any effect on the average wages of women in industry as
a whole.

Table 16. Average hourly earnings[1] in öre of adult workers in various industrial groups by sex. Year: 1966.

Industrial Group	Men	Women	Women's as a per-centage of men's
Mining	1,175	838	71.3
Metal and engineering ind.	1,051	869	82.7
Quarrying and manufacturing of stone, clay and glass, etc.	1,004	734	73.1
Wood ind. incl. furniture	938	790	84.2
Pulp and paper ind.	987	764	77.4
Printing and allied ind.	1,206	841	69.7
Food manufacturing ind.	991	789	79.6
Beverage and tobacco ind.	1,008	879	87.2
Textile and clothing ind.	898	724	80.6
Leather, fur and rubber product ind.	980	751	76.6
Chemical ind.	975	760	77.9
All industrial groups	1,026	785	76.5

1. See note 1, Table 15.

If we study the position of women among salaried employees in
industry, we find that women are overwhelmingly over-represented
among assistant personnel. In 1966, 71.4 per cent of female salaried
employees belonged to this category. Only a small minority of women
are to be found in higher-paid leading technical and administrative
positions or among foremen (cf. Table 17).

Table 17. Number of adult employees in various occupational groups in mining and manufacturing, September 1966

Occupational group	Men	Women	All	Women in % of all
Technical personnel in management, excl. top executives	5,453	16	5,469	0.3
Technical personnel in responsible positions	29,186	461	29,647	1.6
Other technical personnel, excl. technical assistants	16,446	575	17,021	3.4
Technical assistants	6,788	2,698	9,486	28.4
Head foremen	9,308	69	9,377	0.7
Foremen	25,217	680	25,897	2.6
Clerical personnel in management, excl. top executives	4,009	46	4,055	1.1
Clerical personnel in responsible positions	19,079	2,428	21,507	11.3
Other clerical personnel, excl. assistant salaried employees	11,066	6,454	17,520	36.8
Assistant salaried personnel	16,925	35,986	52,911	68.0
Sales representatives	11,719	122	11,841	1.0
Managers of exhibitions, spare part stocks, etc.	91	27	118	22.9
Other sales personnel (exhibitions, spare part stocks, etc.)	204	222	426	52.1
Attendants, receptionists, messengers, etc.	2,172	152	2,324	6.5
Teachers, social welfare workers, nurses, etc.	452	475	927	51.2
Forestry, farming and garden personnel	1,190	---	1,190	---
All groups	159,305	50,411	209,716	31.6

Just as in other sectors of the labour market, there is a considerable difference in the wages of men and women within the same occupational group, even allowing for the age factor. The wages of female assistant clerical personnel between the ages of 18 and 19 years were 93.8 per cent of those earned by the men, falling gradually to 80-81 per cent for those aged around 30.

The obvious conclusion to be drawn from the statistical material which has been presented here is that women have by no means attained real parity with men on the Swedish labour market. Employers—the State, municipalities and private entrepreneurs—all recruit women predominantly for the lowest-paid positions. The women themselves seem to a great extent to have adapted themselves to this segregated market. As was shown in Chapter III:1, they acquire education appropriate to these tasks; as a rule, few women apply for posts generally filled by men. The exceptions simply serve to prove the rule. It seems, too, as though women applying for traditionally "male" and better-paid posts have less chance of being accepted than the men, even if the men have inferior formal qualifications.

Active co-operation between the parties concerned—schools, parents, young people themselves and employers—will be needed to break down this kind of woolly stick-in-the-mud thinking, which has no connection whatsoever with the criterion of individual suitability. Thus the future position of women on the labour market is bound to figure as a crucial social question.

(c) The appointment and election of women to positions of responsibility in community and national affairs of Sweden

Women's participation in general elections is almost as high as men's. The participation of married women is admittedly somewhat less than that of married men in the top age groups, but this fact is counterbalanced by the higher participation of unmarried women compared to unmarried men. A survey on the 1964 elections to the Second Chamber resulted in the following voting frequencies:

Table 18. Election to the Second Chamber of the Riksdag in 1964: participation in different ages of population[1]

Age	Men			Women		
	Not married	Married	Total	Not married	Married	Total
21-24	75.6	83.9	77.9	73.6	83.5	77.8
25-29	78.4	87.9	84.7	72.4	87.6	84.3
30-34	74.8	89.7	86.5	77.5	89.1	87.6
35-39	72.1	92.1	88.4	78.2	89.9	88.3
40-44	75.2	93.0	89.7	77.0	92.2	89.9
45-49	79.6	92.4	90.0	83.1	90.3	89.0
50-54	78.4	91.9	89.3	83.6	92.4	90.4
55-59	78.2	93.5	90.7	79.2	92.9	88.4
60-64	80.2	91.7	89.3	82.1	91.8	88.4
65-69	83.7	92.0	89.5	78.4	85.9	82.1
70-74	71.3	89.1	83.4	73.4	88.5	79.0
75-79	74.4	81.5	78.5	64.2	78.9	68.0
80-84	66.7	83.9	75.5	52.0	55.2	52.6
85-	41.9	---	51.9	32.8	---	34.2
Total	75.8	91.1	86.9	74.1	89.7	84.8

1. Figures based on a sample amounting to approx. 0.3% of all those entitled to vote.

Although the election participation of women is virtually as high as the men's, only a small proportion of women are returned at national, regional and municipal elections.

National elective bodies

The Swedish Riksdag consists of two chambers. The First Chamber is indirectly elected by the County Assemblies, the Second Chamber is constituted by direct elections held every four years. Table 19 illustrates the number of women members in the two chambers of the Riksdag during the period 1929-1968.

Table 19. Members of the Riksdag, number of which are women 1929-1968

	First Chamber		Second Chamber	
	Total	of which women	Total	of which women
1929	150	1	230	3
1933	150	1	230	5
1937	150	–	230	10
1941	150	–	230	18
1945	150	2	230	18
1949	150	6	230	22
1953	150	6	230	28
1957	150	10	231	29
1959	151	11	231	31
1961	151	11	232	32
1965	151	13	233	31
1966	151	15	233	33
1967	151	16	233	34
1968	151	15	233	35

During this period the proportion of women in the directly elected Second Chamber has slowly risen to 15.0 per cent. Two out of the 18 present members of the Swedish Government are women: the Minister for Disarmament Questions, Alva Myrdal, and the Family Minister, Camilla Odhnoff.

Regional elective bodies

Sweden is divided into 24 administrative counties. Each county has a County Assembly responsible for health administration and a considerable proportion of vocational training. The County Assembly has a statutory right to impose taxation. Its members are directly elected every four years. The three largest cities constitute County Assembly areas in their own right. Although the principal activity of the County Assembly—health administration—ought to be connected with the traditional interest of women in such matters (they constitute the majority of the labour force in the health service), women are quite under-represented. Of 1,749 people elected in 1962, 218 (12.4%) were women, as compared to 212 out of 1,753 (12.1%) in 1966. Thus women are less well represented here than in the directly elected chamber of the Riksdag.

Municipal elective bodies

Each county is divided into primary municipalities: cities, small towns and rural districts. The municipalities are at present 900 in number but this figure is gradually going to be reduced by amalgamation to 282. The municipalities enjoy a considerable degree of autonomy together with the right to impose taxation. Questions of policy are decided in a council constituted through direct municipal elections, which in turn elects the municipal executive committees. Out of a total of 29,641 councillors elected in 1966, 3,548 (12%) were women.

The three largest cities have the largest proportion (19.6%) of women councillors, while the rural municipalities have the lowest.

The proportion of women is even lower in the most important executive organ—the board of municipal finance department. The proportion of women is relatively high in the bodies concerned with child care, social welfare and educational questions, low in bodies dealing with town planning, housing administration, roads, health administration, etc.

The reasons for the low proportion of women in national, regional and local Government authorities—in spite of the fact that women have had the vote for nearly fifty years—can be summed up as follows: traditional attitudes among both men and women to the effect that politics are more men's business than women's; the inferior participation of women in party politics which results from this attitude; and the still smaller proportion of women who stand for election. Further, the tendency of the political parties to place women on their voting tickets in such a way that they have only a small chance of being elected makes the proportion of women elected smaller again than the proportion standing for election. Thus, step by step the proportion of women is cut down from about 50 per cent of the electorate to a small minority in the policy-making bodies.

The possibilities of increasing the proportion of women in the municipalities have been estimated as minimal owing to the drastic reduction of council seats resulting from the new amalgamations. Only in a few exceptional cases have the temporary co-operative organs between the municipalities set up prior to amalgamations contained any women members.

Both political and other women's organisations are launching a campaign for better representation for women in connection with the 1968 elections. The leaders of the five largest political parties have all declared themselves in favour of increased representation for women in the Riksdag, at the same time professing not to have any possibility of directly influencing the nomination of candidates, which is conducted by the party organisations in the various constituencies.